Drones and
Targeted Killings

Drones and Targeted Killings

Ethics, Law, and Politics

Sarah Knuckey, editor

International Debate Education Association

New York, Brussels & Amsterdam

Published by
International Debate Education Association
P.O. Box 922
New York, NY 10009

This book is published with the generous support of the Open Society
Foundations.

Library of Congress Cataloging-in-Publication Data

Drones and targeted killings : ethics, law, politics / Sarah Knuckey,
editor.
      pages cm
  ISBN 978-1-61770-099-6
1. Drone aircraft--Government policy--United States. 2. Drone aircraft--
Moral and ethical aspects. 3. Drone aircraft--Law and legislation--United
States. 4. Targeted killing--Government policy--United States. 5.
Targeted killing--Moral and ethical aspects. 6. Targeted killing--Law and
legislation--United States. I. Knuckey, Sarah, editor of compilation.
  UG1242.D7D77 2014
  363.325'16--dc23

                                                    2014036086

Design by Kathleen Hayes
Printed in the USA

 **IDEBATE Press**

Contents

Acknowledgements

For excellent research assistance, I would like to thank Paula Iwanowska, Sebastian Bates, Bassam Khawaja, and Surya Gopalan.

The framing and focus adopted in this text are the result of many years of dialogue with and learning from individuals with an array of perspectives and views, including Pakistani and Yemeni civilians, government and military officials, academics from various fields, journalists, human rights and humanitarian law experts and advocates, UN officials, as well as students who have worked on these issues with me over the years.

I would like to thank those who gave permission for their work to be reproduced in this text; it is their work over many years that makes an edited text like this possible. I would also like to thank the Open Society Foundations for inviting me to edit this anthology.

Introduction

A 16-year-old American teenager, born in Denver, Colorado, was sharing a meal with his cousin at a restaurant in Yemen when U.S. officials ordered that a missile be fired from a drone flying overhead. The teenager, Abdulrahman Al-Aulaqi, and at least five others were killed in the October 14, 2011 strike. The teenager was not the intended target of the strike, which might have been intended to kill an al-Qaeda member, but the United States has not accounted for his death. His grandfather has spoken publicly about how painful the loss of Abdulrahman has been for the family, recalling that Abdulrahman was "a typical teenager" who enjoyed Harry Potter books, The Simpsons, *and Snoop Dogg.*

The teenager's father, Anwar Al-Aulaqi, also an American citizen, had been intentionally targeted by the United States and killed in a drone strike in Yemen just two weeks before Abdulrahman was killed. U.S. officials stated that Anwar Al-Aulaqi was an al-Qaeda terrorist and a threat to America.

* * *

An alleged senior al-Qaeda leader named Shawki Ali Ahmed al-Badani was reportedly killed in a U.S. drone strike in Yemen in November 2014. The U.S. government had designated him a "Global Terrorist," and said that he played key roles in a number of very serious attacks, and that he was involved in plots to attack the U.S. embassy in Yemen. The government of Yemen described him as one of "the most dangerous terrorists affiliated with al-Qaeda."

* * *

U.S. drone strikes are fiercely debated around the world. They have become—together with detentions at Guantánamo Bay, the use of torture, rendition, and expanded surveillance—one of the most contentious aspects of the U.S. response to the threat of terrorism.

Is it legal and ethical to kill, rather than arrest, a suspected terrorist? Is targeting with drones different from other methods used now and in the past? What impacts do the strikes have on civilians? Can drones be effectively used to target terrorists and minimize civilian harm? Do the strikes reduce the overall threat of terrorism?

The United States began deploying armed drones to track and kill suspected terrorists after the September 11, 2001 attacks, in which members of the al-Qaeda terrorist group killed almost 3,000 people. For years, U.S. drone strikes were only rarely discussed publicly and very little was known about them. But in the years 2008–2011, the United States dramatically increased the number of drone strikes carried out in Pakistan and Yemen. The United States has now conducted hundreds of strikes in those countries, killing and injuring thousands of individuals. The U.S. government has acknowledged only a handful of specific strikes, and many details about the drone strike program remain secret.

Debates about drone strikes and targeted killings reflect deep concerns and divisions about whether the strikes are effective, ethical, and legal, and about the levels of government transparency and accountability around the strikes. Many different views have been expressed about these issues by government and military officials, human rights organizations, academics, policy experts, and those most directly affected by U.S. strikes.

Reports of the kind of strikes that kill alleged terrorists like al-Badani help explain why some support U.S. drone strikes. The groups the United States is fighting are very dangerous, and have caused incredible harm to civilians in numerous countries. Armed drones have been effectively used to kill alleged leaders of dangerous terrorist groups and have done so without immediate risk to American soldiers' lives, and—many have argued—with less civilian harm than some other weapons or methods of attack. Strikes like the one on al-Badani have led some to call drones the "weapon of choice." Yet such strikes have also caused controversy; even where alleged terrorists are killed, many have challenged the legality and appropriateness of killing rather than arresting suspects. And, after more than a decade of drone strikes, many are asking whether the strikes are an effective tactic long term to reduce the threat of terrorism. And, what message do the strikes send to other governments?

Debates about U.S. drone strikes became particularly heated in the United States after the killing of American citizen and alleged al-Qaeda terrorist Anwar Al-Aulaqi and the subsequent killing of his 16-year-old son. Should a government be allowed to kill its own citizens in this way? Reports of civilian harm resulting from drone strikes, put forward by families of alleged victims and nongovernmental organizations (NGOs), have caused significant international criticism of U.S. strikes. They have also generated debates about the reliability of such allegations, and led to calls for the United States to explain its strikes. Are the strikes causing more harm than good to civilian populations? Or, are they a better option than other weapons or tactics (such as a large-scale military intervention)? How can we know?

The debates surrounding drone strikes and targeted killings involve many complex issues often knotted together, and the issues can be difficult to disentangle. This book focuses on some of the key issues of effectiveness, ethics, legality, transparency and accountability raised at the intersection of three areas: armed drones, targeted killings, and U.S. counterterrorism practices outside traditional battlefields. While focusing on where these issues overlap, the anthology also raises broader issues of profound importance, including the proper limits on government and presidential power, the risks and benefits of new technologies, and how best to promote security while respecting fundamental human rights and civil liberties.

This introduction provides an overview of what targeted killings and drones are, and also of the current U.S. drone strike and targeted killing program. It then outlines the views and arguments raised in each of the main areas of debate.

Background and Key Concepts

TARGETED KILLINGS

"Targeted killing" is a phrase that typically refers to an intentional, preplanned killing of a specifically identified individual.[1] The killings of alleged terrorists Anwar Al-Aulaqi and al-Badani described above, for example, are targeted killings because those two individuals were specifically identified by the U.S. government as suspects, their names were placed on U.S. "kill lists," and they were tracked and intentionally killed in targeted strikes on their known locations. The category *targeted killing* has been employed as a way to analyze and distinguish this type of killing from other forms—such as the death penalty (a killing that follows a trial); massacre (unlawful killings of a large number of individuals at once); deaths in custody (the death of a person while in police detention or prison); or cases in which soldiers come under attack and return fire at enemies without knowing their specific identities.

Designating a killing a "targeted killing" does not indicate whether or not the killing was legal. It is a form of killing rather than a legal category, and is thus different from legal terms like *extrajudicial execution* or *murder*, which are types of unlawful killings. During war, a targeted killing of an enemy fighter can be legal. In most other circumstances, targeted killings are illegal. The legal rules and debates are described further below.

Drone strike and *targeted killing* are sometimes used interchangeably in public debate. This is because, currently, nearly all targeted killings by the United States in Pakistan and Yemen are carried out with armed drones. But the terms are overlapping, rather than synonymous. For example, some commentators note that not all U.S. drone strikes kill people individually identified and targeted by the United States. In addition, while many current U.S. targeted killings use drones, a targeted killing could be committed with any form of weapon or by any means—a manned aircraft, a cruise missile, an improvised bomb, or a sniper. In recent years, targeted killings have often been associated with the United States, but a number of other countries are reported to have engaged in the practice, including Israel and Russia.

The use of targeted killings has often sparked debate about the circumstances in which such actions are or should be legal, the ethics of carrying out a preplanned killing, and whether killing individuals is an effective way to reduce future violence and tackle the threat of terrorism. These questions arise for any targeted killing, and not only those carried out with drones.

What Are Drones and How Are They Used?

The term *drone* can refer to a huge and growing range of remotely piloted or remotely controlled technologies. This book focuses specifically on *armed drones*—"unmanned" or "remotely piloted" aircraft that can be used for aerial surveillance as well as to fire missiles at enemy targets. But armed drones are just one of the many types of drone, and it is important to put debates about armed drones into the broader context of general drone developments and uses.[2]

Many other types of drones are not used for military purposes and do not raise the kinds of issues discussed in this book. Drone technologies are developing rapidly, and drones can take many shapes and sizes and be used to carry out an array of tasks. For example, drones equipped with cameras have been used to help fight wildfires in California, counter illegal poaching of protected animals like elephants and rhinos, and to deliver drinks at music festivals. Some commentators have proposed that drones could be used to document human rights violations, such as illegal shootings of peaceful protesters. Police have also become interested in how drones might be useful in detecting crimes. The public safety and privacy implications of drones equipped with cameras are now often discussed.[3]

Much current debate on armed drones focuses on how they have been used by the United States after the September 11 attacks. But remotely controlled aircraft and the unmanned delivery of weapons are not new.[4] During the Civil War (1861–1865), for example, both the Union and the Confederate forces attempted to use balloons loaded with explosive devices to attack the other side. In the 1930s, the United Kingdom and the United States developed remote-controlled aircraft for target practice,[5] and, after World War II, the United States developed the intelligence-gathering capabilities of these aircraft.[6] During the Vietnam War, the United States deployed drones equipped with cameras in reconnaissance flights over North Vietnam.[7] The United States also used surveillance drones during the First Gulf War (1990–1991) and the Kosovo War (1998–1999).

In 2000, the United States flew surveillance drones over Afghanistan, including as part of efforts to track Osama bin Laden.[8] The United States tested weaponized drones between May and June 2001, but results were reportedly mixed.[9] After September 11, the United States increased its efforts to use armed drones, and the first armed mission was reportedly in October 2001.

Armed drones now used by the United States, such as the MQ-1 Predator and the MQ-9 Reaper, are controlled remotely by human operators at ground control stations—such as Creech Air Force base near Las Vegas. At military bases, operators can watch real-time video of the areas over which drones are flying. At the command of human operators, missiles, like the AGM-114 Hellfire, can be launched from the drones at targets on the ground.

A number of other countries are known or reported to have armed drones, including China, Israel, and the United Kingdom. Additional countries have stated that they also intend to obtain armed drones, and scores of governments have already built or purchased surveillance drones. Many commentators predict that more and more countries will develop or obtain armed drones in the near future.

In addition to becoming more common, drones are also likely to become increasingly sophisticated. This book focuses on the kinds of armed drones in current use, but there is much investment and research in developing new kinds of drones. In the future, insect-sized drones may be deployed, while other drones will be able to carry more weapons than current versions, fly further and faster, and loiter for longer periods. Some will be able to fly coordinated with other drones, potentially in swarms. Drones are also likely to become more autonomous, able to perform tasks via sophisticated programming and without human control, including, potentially, having the ability to kill autonomously. Currently, governments around the world are discussing whether and how to regulate such weapons.

Some aspects of the current drone strike debates have been specifically about armed drones as a weapon, but much debate has centered on how the United States is actually *using* armed drones. As noted above, these issues can sometimes be hard to disentangle. Questions that relate specifically to drones include the extent to which the technology enables improved surveillance and more precise targeting, whether drones lower the threshold for the use of force (and the consequent pros and cons), and the potential effects of drone proliferation around the world. Much debate also concerns whether and how drones actually raise any new kinds of issues.

U.S. DRONE STRIKES AND TARGETED KILLINGS

Reliable information about many facets of U.S. drone strikes is hard to come by. Many of the government's records about strikes are classified, and officials rarely provide detailed information. A general picture of the drone program has been built up piecemeal over the years through a combination of officials' speeches, news reports, litigation, and freedom of information requests, as well as independent investigations of strikes, NGO and United Nations' work, academic studies, and witness and victim testimony. Yet much is unknown—and what has been reported should be treated with caution.

Drone strikes are carried out by both the Central Intelligence Agency (CIA) and the Department of Defense (DOD), including its Joint Special Operations Command (JSOC), a specialized counterterrorism unit. In particular cases, it can be difficult to determine exactly who or which agency was responsible for a strike because the United States does not generally officially confirm or deny its involvement in specific strikes. Other countries—such as Australia, Djibouti, Germany, and the United Kingdom—also reportedly assist U.S. strikes by sharing intelligence or hosting U.S. military bases on their territory.

The United States has used drones in countries where it has been involved in conventional war, such as Iraq and Afghanistan, where manned aircraft and ground troops have also been deployed, and where it is internationally accepted that an armed conflict exists. More controversially, the United States has also carried out drone strikes and targeted killings in Pakistan, Somalia, and Yemen. These areas are sometimes referred to as being outside "traditional" or "defined" battlefields or outside the "hot" battlefield. They are areas in which the existence of an armed conflict is contested, and where the United State undertakes strikes against individuals but is not engaged in the kind of large-scale military operations seen in Afghanistan and Iraq. Almost all of the killings by the United States in these places have been carried out with drones, and it is strikes in these countries on which this book focuses.

According to the *New York Times*,[10] the United States maintains "kill lists"—lists of individuals whom the United States considers to be lawful military targets. It is not publicly known how much evidence is required for an individual to be put on the kill list or how many names are on it. The *Times* reported that regular government meetings are held in which the lists are reviewed, and that the president personally approves many of the killings. Over the years, reports have also referred to various types of drone strikes—"personality strikes," which are strikes on individual, identified targets, and "signature strikes," which are reportedly against targets who are believed to exhibit certain "signatures" of militant or terrorist behavior.[11] Little public information is available on what kinds of "signatures" might lead to a U.S. strike, although critics have expressed concerns that civilians have been killed due to inaccurate U.S. assumptions that certain behavior indicated militancy.

In Yemen, the United States targets members of a group called Al-Qaeda in the Arabian Peninsula (AQAP), while in Pakistan, it has targeted al-Qaeda, the Pakistani Taliban, and other armed groups. These groups have committed gross human rights violations and war crimes against civilian populations, including by threatening, kidnapping, torturing, and killing many innocent people. Some drone strikes are carried out against alleged "high-level" military targets, but studies suggest that the majority of targets are lower-level members of armed groups.[12]

According to counterterrorism targeting policy guidance released by the government in 2013, when the United States targets outside areas of active hostilities, it will strike only individuals who pose a "continuing, imminent threat to U.S. persons."[13] However, some critics argue that it is not clear in which countries this guidance applies, or what the United States means by "imminent." Critics have also argued that the circumstances of some strikes suggest that the United States may use an overly broad definition of that term, thus killing a wider range of people than it should.

Based on currently available information, it is difficult to accurately determine the precise number and identity of all those killed. In 2012, President Obama stated that "drones have not caused a huge number of civilian casualties,"[14] and John Brennan, then assistant to the president for homeland security and counterterrorism, said that civilian deaths were "exceedingly rare."[15] However, the U.S. government has never released information about how many strikes it has carried out, the numbers of military targets, or the numbers of civilians killed or injured.

In the absence of government figures, various organizations have attempted to keep track of drone strikes. By one overall estimate, the United States has carried out more than 500 targeted killings in Pakistan, Yemen, and Somalia (98% of them with drones), killing 3,674 people, of whom 473 were reportedly civilians.[16] Pres. Barack Obama authorized the majority of those strikes (450); Pres. George Bush authorized 50. Those numbers were compiled by averaging the data of three separate organizations that keep track of drone strikes and reported deaths, each of which has somewhat different methods for doing so and, accordingly, has come to different results. For example, one organization, The Bureau of Investigative Journalism, estimates that 416–959 civilians were killed in Pakistan between 2004 and 2014, whereas the New America Foundation estimates 258–307 civilians have been killed there.[17] These numbers are arrived at through recording and compiling individual media reports of specific strikes. Some critics contest these numbers because their accuracy depends on the accuracy of the underlying media reports, which may not be reliable. News reports about particular strikes often rely on local government officials, quoted anonymously, and sometimes on the testimony of alleged witnesses and victims. Local militant groups, officials, and others could have cause to falsify reports—denying or making up militant or civilian deaths.

Although drones offer distinct advantages for surveillance and targeting, commentators have pointed to a number of limitations in their use that may lead to targeting mistakes or civilian harm. Analysts have noted that the government intelligence informing decisions about whom and when to target may be inaccurate or incomplete, leading to mistakes. The video footage drone operators view may offer a narrow view of the relevant area. Concerns have also been expressed that U.S. definitions of "lawful military target" may be too broad, including people who should instead be considered "civilian." Some have suggested that that factor, together with a lack of on-the-ground investigations following strikes, may in part explain the lower U.S. government estimates for civilian deaths. Others argue that the higher estimates by the tracking organizations are incorrect and inflated. Different views about these kinds of facts can affect how commentators understand and assess the strategic, moral, and legal issues around drone strikes.

The many and varied reports about specific strikes and their impacts have raised difficult questions of fact. To what extent is the testimony of alleged victims reliable? What about the reliability of claims made by government officials? Is it possible to investigate and assess the impacts of strikes? In any armed conflict or for any use of military or police force, it can be difficult to determine the facts, and this is also the case for drone strikes. Some have argued that terrorist groups have made up "civilian" casualties for propaganda purposes; others point to a history of incorrect statements about strikes by government officials. In some cases, even where it is clear that an individual was killed, it may not be clear whether the strike was, in fact, a U.S. drone strike or whether it might have been the result of an attack by another country's military (for example, Pakistan, which also uses military force in the areas where the United States carries out drone strikes).

Arguments about facts also raise questions about *who* bears the burden of proof. The U.S. government holds much of the information that would be necessary to determine the legality of strikes, but—at least so far—it will not make such information public. Should victims, their families, and independent investigators bear the burden of proving that civilians were killed? Or should the U.S. government need to prove that its strikes are appropriate and lawful, particularly when credible allegations have been brought forward?

Key Debates in Current U.S. Drone Strike and Targeted Killings Practice and Policy

"I watched a U.S. drone kill my grandmother," said 13-year-old Zubair, testifying before members of the U.S. Congress in October 2013. "I, myself, was injured in this strike," he added, referring to a shrapnel injury to his leg that has required many expensive surgeries. Zubair had traveled from his home in Pakistan to the United States with his younger sister, nine-year-old Nabila, and their father, schoolteacher Rafiq ur Rehman. The Rehman family came to the United States to testify about a drone strike they and NGO investigators say injured both Zubair and Nabila and killed Mamana Bibi, their 67-year-old grandmother.

The Rehman family traveled to the United States to explain how the alleged drone strike harmed them. And they came seeking answers and accountability. "Nobody has ever told me why my mother was targeted that day," said Rafiq ur Rehman. "I would just like to ask

the American public to treat us as equals. Make sure that your gov-
ernment gives us the same status of a human with basic rights."

*Some commentators have suggested that the strike may have
been carried out by Pakistan, rather than the United States, and
have queried the alleged victim testimony and the adequacy of NGO
investigations. The U.S. government has not publicly responded to
the Rehman family's allegations.*

The debates about U.S. drone strikes and targeted killings
can be structured around four key areas: effectiveness, ethics,
legality, and transparency and accountability. These topics inter-
relate and cannot always be neatly separated; some issues, such
as the alleged deaths of civilians like grandmother Mamana Bibi,
cross multiple areas and are relevant to arguments about strike
effectiveness, as well as ethics and legality. In each key area, it
is also important to understand the relationships and distinguish between the kinds of issues raised by armed drones as a
weapon, by targeted killings as a practice, and by current U.S.
drone strike methods and policies.

EFFECTIVENESS

The extent to which drone strikes and targeted killings are "effective" is often debated. What does it mean to claim that drone
strikes are, or are not, effective? The discussion includes various kinds of questions and issues. For example: Are drones an
effective weapon with which to kill suspected terrorists? Is the
practice of targeted killings—that is, targeting individual leaders or other key members of a group—an effective strategy to
disrupt terrorist groups and reduce terrorism? Are current U.S.
drone strike practices effective at promoting security? Do they
advance U.S. strategic interests?

When effectiveness is debated, it is important to clarify what kind of effectiveness is meant: Is *what* (a weapon? a tactic?) effective toward *what* end or goal?

Some argue that U.S. strikes have been effective at killing suspected terrorists or members of dangerous armed groups, including suspected high-level targets like al-Badani. Some also argue that the strikes have disrupted terrorist groups and made it harder for such groups to carry out attacks—and are thereby an important tactic to address serious security threats. U.S. officials state that new drone technologies have been crucial to this effectiveness. This is because armed drones like the Predator can remain in the air for 14 hours, enabling extensive and continuous surveillance of particular locations and potential targets for many days or weeks and also enabling targeting (firing missiles) at an opportune moment. For example, because the target can be tracked, an individual can be killed while traveling in a car on an empty road, rather than in a house where civilians may also be present.

Others contend that the strikes have been counterproductive. They may agree that strikes have been effective with respect to killing individual suspects and also agree that drones are an effective weapon to that end, but disagree that they are effective in the long term. Some argue that even as the strikes have killed suspected terrorists, those individuals are quickly replaced with new individuals joining the armed group's ranks and that the size of terrorist groups has not decreased despite many strikes. Some argue that drone strikes have been used as a recruitment tool by terrorist groups. In addition, some critics maintain that certain strikes, like the alleged strike on the Rehman family, have harmed civilians and alienated potential U.S. allies in other countries, causing anger at and resentment of the U.S. government.

Concern has also been expressed that U.S. practices may set precedents for other countries—which may then use armed drones in ways counter to U.S. strategic interests.

ETHICS

Is it ethical to kill at a distance via remotely piloted aircraft? Some argue that it is not, but others have responded that drones are not unique in their remote killing—many other weapons have steadily increased the distance between the attacker and the attacked. If we allow bombs to be dropped from manned aircraft or missiles to be fired from ships at great distances from targets, why should we object to drones? Some believe that drones may actually have ethical benefits because they can offer improved targeting accuracy and reduce civilian harm while also minimizing risks to the attacking side's soldiers.

On the other hand, there are concerns that the technological advantages of drones may make it too easy to kill and to do so secretly and without accountability, thus posing a serious moral hazard. And some critics argue that whatever ethical benefits drones might generally offer in the abstract, the *current* way that the United States uses drone strikes and targeted killings raises serious moral concerns because of their alleged effects on civilians and concerns that suspects are killed when they could, instead, be arrested and prosecuted for their alleged crimes.

LEGALITY

The legality of U.S. targeting practices and policies has been written about and debated in great detail. Do drones raise new legal issues? In what circumstances are targeted killings lawful?

To what extent do particular U.S. strikes, practices, or policies comply with the law?

Generally, drones themselves—simply as a weapon and considered separately from any specific use—do not raise novel legal concerns. Drones are not a prohibited or specifically regulated weapon, and their use is governed by the same laws that govern the use of any kind of force. However, the prospect of drone proliferation to numerous countries has led to debate about whether or how drones as a weapon should be the subject of new international regulation or arms control.

The majority of legal debate has been about current uses of armed drones for killing and the circumstances in which targeted or other killings by the United States are lawful. This is less a debate about drones than it is about the circumstances in which killings are permitted. U.S. officials argue that U.S. strikes comply with all relevant domestic and international laws. But numerous academics, other governments, NGOs, and UN officials have raised concerns, arguing that at least some strikes appear to violate international law, U.S. constitutional law, or declared U.S. policy.

The law guarantees to every individual the fundamental right to life. As a general rule, killings are thus prohibited. But drone strikes and targeted killings may be lawful in limited circumstances. Outside of war, intentional killing is only permitted in very narrow circumstances and when strictly necessary to protect life. But during war, special rules (the laws of war, or "international humanitarian law") come into play. Those rules govern how the warring sides may fight each other, and the rules are more permissive than peacetime law about when killings are permitted.

The United States is not in an armed conflict with Pakistan or Yemen, countries in which the United States has launched many strikes. But is the United States in a war with armed groups like al-Qaeda in these countries, such that the special rules of armed conflict would apply? The United States argues that it is in an armed conflict with al-Qaeda and affiliated groups, wherever those groups are—not just in the traditional battlefield of Afghanistan, and that it is authorized by international and U.S. domestic law to attack those groups. But others contest whether an armed conflict really exists, and argue that current U.S. laws do not permit the government to attack in all the countries where it currently uses drones. In addition, while Yemen has vocally consented to U.S. strikes on its territory, the validity or scope of any consent from Pakistan is unclear, raising questions about whether the United States has violated Pakistan's sovereignty by firing missiles there.

In addition, some argue that even if one accepts that the special rules of armed conflict apply, particular strikes and practices may breach those rules. For example, the laws of war require all parties to the conflict to distinguish between fighters and civilians and to not target civilians. Civilian casualties may be lawful in war, but they must be proportionate to an anticipated military advantage. It can be difficult to target terrorists because they often hide themselves among civilians (a violation of the rules of war). Still, a number of NGOs, after investigating drone strikes, have alleged that some strikes may not have complied with the rules—for example, because too many civilians were killed or injured. The alleged strike that killed Mamana Bibi and injured the Rehman children is an example, and numerous similar cases have been reported.

The killings of Anwar and Abdulrahman Al-Aulaqi described above also raise separate U.S. domestic law questions about whether the government upheld or violated fundamental constitutional protections owed to them as U.S. citizens.

Some scholars and other experts have argued that even if U.S. targeting practices comply with the law, they do not comply with fundamental rule of law principles such as legal certainty, access to courts, and government accountability.

TRANSPARENCY AND ACCOUNTABILITY

How much information about drone strikes should the U.S. government make public? What are the risks of transparency and also the costs of secrecy? If civilians are killed, what should the United States do?

In recent years, U.S. officials have noted their efforts to be more transparent about drone strikes and have also explained some of the risks of releasing too much information. Too much transparency, for example, might reveal to enemies the sources and methods involved in U.S. intelligence gathering and thus put operations and security at risk.

However, while some secrecy around a country's counterterrorism actions can be necessary, many have argued that U.S. drone strikes have been too secretive. For example, critics note that U.S. officials generally do not acknowledge the U.S. role in particular strikes and that the United States has released very little information about the facts of specific strikes, most of which remain shrouded in mystery. The secrecy of U.S. strikes has been an issue that numerous commentators—who otherwise disagree about the effectiveness, ethics, and legal issues—argue has been very troubling. They argue that such secrecy undermines important goals and values, such as deterring government wrongdoing, democratic accountability, and enabling informed public debate about important government practices and policies. Are these issues unique to drone strikes, or do they arise generally for CIA or DOD actions? Is too much transparency demanded specifically of drone strikes?

In response to U.S. drone strikes, alleged victims, family members, and numerous groups have mobilized. They have sought to understand U.S. legal positions and to investigate strikes, and they have worked to secure U.S. compliance with international law, greater transparency, accountability for past strikes, and redress for the deaths of civilians. Some organizations and alleged victims have filed lawsuits in U.S. courts. Others have filed suit in countries that may be assisting U.S. drone strikes. NGOs have also engaged directly with civilian and military government actors as well as UN bodies such as the Human Rights Council. Family members, like the Rehmans, have traveled to the United States to seek answers.

Yet accountability efforts have thus far largely been blocked. Relatives of those killed in drone strikes have tried to obtain answers from the U.S. government, but have been rebuffed, and their court cases have not been successful. While the numbers of civilians killed is contested, what is clear is that under current arrangements most of those civilians who have been injured, and the families of those killed, have virtually no way to have their harms acknowledged, explained, or compensated. In 2014, some news reports suggested that the United States might be secretly compensating the relatives of civilian victims, but the extent of any such practice is currently unclear.[18]

It has been over ten years since the United States began using armed drones to kill suspected terrorists. Drone strikes have been debated around the world, from the halls of U.S. Congress to the United Nations, and among citizens of many nations. As the strikes continue, debate has turned to whether the United States is in a "forever war," and the proper role of military force in addressing terrorism. What have these strikes achieved, overall? What are the long-term implications for rights, peace, and security?

About the Book

Drones and Targeted Killings was designed to stimulate debate among those who are new to the issues. It brings to the fore human rights, civil liberties, and civilian protection issues, while introducing readers to a range of diverse views from a variety of sources. In the past few years, an incredible amount of writing and analysis of drone strikes has been produced; this book includes just a tiny fraction of the many speeches, reports, news accounts, and opinion pieces addressing the issues. This book breaks down the issues into some of the key debates that have repeatedly arisen. Part 1 asks whether the United States' use of drone strikes is effective, and whether and how we can know if U.S. strikes have been effective. Part 2 asks what ethical risks or benefits the U.S. use of drone strikes might entail. Part 3 asks whether, or in what circumstances, U.S. strikes are legal in terms of both U.S. domestic and international law. Part 4 addresses issues related to the transparency around and accountability for drone strikes.

Each of the book's parts includes a short overview of the issue —with questions for readers to consider as they approach the articles—and a sample of readings providing different perspectives. In introducing key issues and arguments, this book aims to provide readers a base from which they can continue to question, research, and contribute to public debate.

Sarah Knuckey
Lieff Cabraser Associate Clinical Professor of Law
Director, Human Rights Clinic
Faculty Co-Director, Human Rights Institute
Columbia Law School

NOTES

1. The phrase does not have an entirely fixed definition or agreed denotation, however, and is occasionally used in a much broader sense to describe any use of force that is "targeted" as opposed to indiscriminate or random.

2. For an excellent history and analysis of robotic systems and war, see Peter W. Singer, *Wired for War* (New York: Penguin Books, 2009).

3. For more information on these privacy issues, see: American Civil Liberties Union, "Domestic Drones," Blog of Rights, https://www.aclu.org/blog/tag/domestic-drones

4. For a brief military history, see Jim Garamone, "From U.S. Civil War to Afghanistan: A Short History of UAVs," Department of Defense, April 16, 2002, http://www.defense.gov/news/newsarticle.aspx?id=44164; and "Aerial Surveillance & Reconnaissance: From Early Spy Balloons to Unmanned Drones," *IRReview*, April 26, 2013, http://irr.buiaa.org/2013/04/aerial-surveillance-reconnaissance-from-early-spy-balloons-to-unmanned-drones/

5. Chris Cole, "Raise the Reapers: A Brief History of Drones," Global Research, October 9, 2014, http://www.globalresearch.ca/rise-of-the-reapers-a-brief-history-of-drones/5407126?print=1

6. Ibid.

7. Garamone, "From U.S. Civil War to Afghanistan."

8. "Written Statement for the Record of the Director of Central Intelligence Before the National Commission on Terrorist Attacks Upon the United States," 9/11 Commission, March 24, 2004, 15, http://govinfo.library.unt.edu/911/hearings/hearing8/tenet_statement.pdf

9. Ibid., 16.

10. "Secret 'Kill List' Proves a Test of Obama's Principles and Will," *New York Times*, http://www.nytimes.com/2012/05/29/world/obamas-leadership-in-war-on-al-qaeda.html?pagewanted=all

11. Cora Currier, "Everything We Know So Far About Drone Strikes," ProPublica, February 5, 2013, https://www.propublica.org/article/everything-we-know-so-far-about-drone-strikes

12. Adam Entous, "Drones Kill Low-Level Militants, Few Civilians: U.S.," Reuters, May 3, 2010, http://www.reuters.com/article/2010/05/03/us-pakistan-usa-drones-idUSTRE6424WI20100503; Greg Miller, "Increased U.S. Drone Strikes in Pakistan Killing Few High-Value Militants,"

Washington Post, February 21, 2011, http://www.washingtonpost.com/wp-dyn/content/article/2011/02/20/AR2011022002975.html

13. "U.S. Policy Standards and Procedures for the Use of Force in Counter-terrorism Operations Outside the United States and Areas of Active Hostilities," The White House, May 23, 2013, http://www.whitehouse.gov/sites/default/files/uploads/2013.05.23_fact_sheet_on_ppg.pdf

14. BBC, "Obama Defends US Drone Strikes in Pakistan," BBC News, January 31, 2012, http://www.bbc.com/news/world-us-canada-16804247

15. John O. Brennan, "The Efficacy and Ethics of U.S. Counter-terrorism Strategy" (speech delivered at the Wilson Center, Washington, D.C., April 30, 2012), http://www.wilsoncenter.org/event/the-efficacy-and-ethics-us-counterterrorism-strategy#field_speakers

16. Micah Zenko, "America's 500th Drone Strike," Council on Foreign Relations, November 21, 2014, http://blogs.cfr.org/zenko/2014/11/21/americas-500th-drone-strike/

17. "Get the Data: Drone Wars," Bureau of Investigative Journalism, http://www.thebureauinvestigates.com/category/projects/drones/drones-graphs/; "Drone Wars Pakistan: Analysis," New America, http://securitydata.newamerica.net/drones/pakistan/analysis

18. Mohammed Ghobari and Mark Hosenball, "U.S. Funds Used to Compensate Drone Victims—Yemen Presidency Source," Reuters, November 13, 2014, http://uk.reuters.com/article/2014/11/13/uk-yemen-drones-payments-idUKKCN0IX21I20141113

PART 1:

Are They Effective?

Is the United States' use of drone strikes effective? This is a crucial question that is difficult to answer. Obtaining reliable data about the short- and long-term impacts of strikes has proved challenging. In addition, opinion differs about what *effective* means. Effective toward what ends? A wide range of effects have been debated. Clearly, U.S. strikes have killed some senior terrorist group leaders and many "low-level" members. But analysts disagree about how much the strikes have reduced the threat of terrorism overall or the extent of countervailing negative effects, such as civilian casualties or the loss of civilian allies' support for the United States.

U.S. officials and some commentators argue that, overall, U.S. strikes have been effective. Part 1 begins with a speech by the director of the CIA, John Brennan, "The Efficacy and Ethics of U.S. Counterterrorism Strategy," in which he maintains that al-Qaeda in Pakistan has "suffered heavy losses" and that it is now harder for the group to carry out attacks. He also states that drones enable strikes to be carried out with "surgical precision." This section also includes pieces by two U.S. scholars. In "Why Drones Work," Daniel Byman, whose work focuses on terrorism, security, and the Middle East, argues that drone strikes have been a better option and cause less harm to civilians than other weapons or tactics. Kenneth Anderson, a law professor, argues in "The Case for Drones" that the U.S. use of drones is strategically effective and that the strikes are not simply a "whack-a-mole" tactic; rather, he contends that killing terrorist leaders has real, positive security effects.

In contrast, others have argued that U.S. strikes have been counterproductive and have caused significant harm, undermining the U.S. government's long-term goal of reducing terrorism. Yemeni democracy and human rights activist Farea Al-Muslimi testified before members of the U.S. Congress that drone strikes have caused anger and a backlash toward the United States, fear among Yemeni civilians, civilian injuries and deaths, and that they can help to empower militant groups. Yemeni democracy activist Ibrahim Mothana maintains in "How Drones Help Al Qaeda" that drone strikes alienate Yemeni civilians and, in the long term, harm both Yemeni and U.S. security interests. Yemen's minister for human rights, Hooria Mashour, penned an op-ed, "The United States' Bloody Messes in Yemen," for the *Washington Post* in which she argues that drone strikes are deeply unpopular in Yemen and undercut Yemenis' democratic will.

Pakistani journalist Pir Zubair Shah offers a different perspective. In "My Drone War," he argues that Pakistanis have divergent views about drones, but that anti-Americanism in Pakistan is caused more by how the press covers drones, rather than drone strikes themselves. He also explains why obtaining clear information about drone strikes is so difficult and calls into question the reliability of reports about strikes.

A number of U.S. think tanks have issued detailed reports on drone strikes, often noting the complex ways in which the strikes may have both negative and positive aspects. "Recommendations and Report of the Task Force on US Drone Policy," a bipartisan study of drone strikes by the Stimson Center, argues that drones should be "neither glorified nor demonized." The report explains why the United States has seen drones as an important weapon, but also addresses the weapons' vulnerabilities and strategic concerns about their use for targeted killings outside traditional battlefields. In "Limiting Armed Drone Proliferation," Micah Zenko and Sarah Kreps of the Council on Foreign Relations assess the strategic impacts of the proliferation of armed drones to other countries, argue that drones may destabilize the international order, and stress the importance of U.S. leadership on shared, clear standards for use.

As you read the articles in this section, consider the following questions:

- What does it mean to ask about the effectiveness of U.S. practices? What kinds of outcomes and impacts do you think are relevant to considering the "effectiveness" of U.S. strikes?

- Taking these outcomes and impacts together, to what extent do you think U.S. strikes are effective, overall? In what ways might U.S. practices be effective in some respects, but ineffective or counterproductive in others? Which specific aspects of U.S. strike practices may lead to positive or negative outcomes?

- How can we know whether U.S. practices are effective? Is existing data reliable? What kinds of additional information would we need to assess effectiveness?

The Efficacy and Ethics of U.S. Counterterrorism Strategy

*by John O. Brennan**

[…]

I very much appreciate the opportunity to discuss President Obama's counterterrorism strategy, in particular its ethics and its efficacy.

[…]

[President Obama] said that we would carry on this fight while upholding the laws and our values, and that we would work with allies and partners whenever possible. But he also made it clear that he would not hesitate to use military force against terrorists who pose a direct threat to America. And he said that if he had actionable intelligence about high-value terrorist targets, including in Pakistan, he would act to protect the American people.

[…]

[…] We've always been clear that the end of bin Laden would neither mark the end of al-Qaida, nor our resolve to destroy it. So along with allies and partners, we have been unrelenting. And when we assess that al-Qaida of 2012, I think it is fair to say that, as a result of our efforts, the United States is more secure and the American people are safer. Here's why.

In Pakistan, al-Qaida's leadership ranks have continued to suffer heavy losses. This includes Ilyas Kashmiri, one of al-Qaida's top operational planners, killed a month after bin Laden. It includes Atiyah Abd al-Rahman, killed when he succeeded Ayman al-Zawahiri, al-Qaida's deputy leader. It includes Younis al-Mauritani, a planner of attacks against the United States and Europe, until he was captured by Pakistani forces.

With its most skilled and experienced commanders being lost so quickly, al-Qaida has had trouble replacing them. This is one of the many conclusions we have been able to draw from documents seized at bin Laden's compound. [...] For example, bin Laden worried about, and I quote, "The rise of lower leaders who are not as experienced and this would lead to the repeat of mistakes."

Al-Qaida leaders continue to struggle to communicate with subordinates and affiliates. Under intense pressure in the tribal regions of Pakistan, they have fewer places to train and groom the next generation of operatives. They're struggling to attract new recruits. Morale is low, with intelligence indicating that some members are giving up and returning home, no doubt aware that this is a fight they will never win. In short, al-Qaida is losing badly. And bin Laden knew it at the time of his death. In documents we seized, he confessed to "disaster after disaster." He even urged his leaders to flee the tribal regions, and go to places, "away from aircraft photography and bombardment."

For all these reasons, it is harder than ever for al-Qaida core in Pakistan to plan and execute large-scale, potentially catastrophic attacks against our homeland. Today, it is increasingly clear that compared to 9/11, the core al-Qaida leadership is a shadow of its former self. Al-Qaida has been left with just a handful of capable leaders and operatives, and with continued pressure is on the path to its destruction. And for the first time since this fight began, we can look ahead and envision a world in which the al-Qaida core is simply no longer relevant.

Nevertheless, the dangerous threat from al-Qaida has not disappeared. As the al-Qaida core falters, it continues to look to affiliates and adherents to carry on its murderous cause. Yet these affiliates continue to lose key commanders and capabilities as well. In Somalia, it is indeed worrying to witness al-Qaida's merger with al-Shabaab, whose ranks include foreign fighters, some with U.S. passports. At the same time, al-Shabaab continues to focus primarily on launching regional attacks, and ultimately, this is a merger between two organizations in decline.

In Yemen, al-Qaida in the Arabian Peninsula, or AQAP, continues to feel the effects of the death last year of Anwar al-Awlaki, its leader of external operations who was responsible for planning and directing terrorist attacks against the United States. Nevertheless, AQAP continues to be al-Qaida's most active affiliate, and it continues to seek the opportunity to strike our homeland. We therefore continue to support the government of Yemen in its efforts against AQAP, which is being forced to fight for the territory it needs to plan attacks beyond Yemen. In north and west Africa, another al-Qaida affiliate, al-Qaida in the Islamic Maghreb, or AQIM, continues its efforts to destabilize regional governments and engages in kidnapping of Western citizens for ransom activities designed to fund its terrorist agenda. And in Nigeria, we are monitoring closely the emergence of Boko Haram, a group that appears to be aligning itself with al-Qaida's violent agenda and is increasingly looking to attack Western interests in Nigeria, in addition to Nigerian government targets.

More broadly, al-Qaida's killing of innocents, mostly Muslim men, women and children, has badly tarnished its image and appeal in the eyes of Muslims around the world.

[...]

Despite the great progress we've made against al-Qaida, it would be a mistake to believe this threat has passed. Al-Qaida and its associated forces still have the intent to attack the United States. And we have seen lone individuals, including American citizens, often inspired by al-Qaida's murderous ideology, kill innocent Americans and seek to do us harm.

Still, the damage that has been inflicted on the leadership core in Pakistan, combined with how al-Qaida has alienated itself from so much of the world, allows us to look forward. Indeed, if the decade before 9/11 was the time of al-Qaida's rise, and the decade after 9/11 was the time of its decline, then I believe this decade will be the one that sees its demise. This progress is no accident.

[...]

[...] I venture to say that the United States government has never been so open regarding its counterterrorism policies and their legal justification. Still, there continues to be considerable public and legal debate surrounding these technologies and how they are sometimes used in the fight against al-Qaida.

Now, I want to be very clear. In the course of the war in Afghanistan and the fight against al-Qaida, I think the American people expect us to use advanced technologies, for example, to prevent attacks on U.S. forces and to remove terrorists from the battlefield. We do, and it has saved the lives of our men and women in uniform. What has clearly captured the attention of many, however, is a different practice, beyond hot battlefields like Afghanistan, identifying specific members of al-Qaida and then targeting them with lethal force, often using aircraft remotely operated by pilots who can be hundreds, if not thousands, of miles away. [...]

[...]

I stand here as someone who has been involved with our nation's security for more than 30 years. I have a profound appreciation for the truly remarkable capabilities of our counter-terrorism professionals, and our relationships with other nations, and we must never compromise them. I will not discuss the sensitive details of any specific operation today. I will not, nor will I ever, publicly divulge sensitive intelligence sources and methods. For when that happens, our national security is endangered and lives can be lost. At the same time, we reject the notion that any discussion of these matters is to step onto a slippery slope that inevitably endangers our national security. Too often, that fear can become an excuse for saying nothing at all, which creates a void that is then filled with myths and falsehoods. That, in turn, can erode our credibility with the American people and with foreign partners, and it can undermine the public's understanding and support for our efforts. In contrast, President Obama believes that done carefully, deliberately and responsibly we can be more transparent and still ensure our nation's security.

So let me say it as simply as I can. Yes, in full accordance with the law, and in order to prevent terrorist attacks on the United States and to save American lives, the United States Government conducts targeted strikes against specific al-Qaida terrorists, sometimes using remotely piloted aircraft, often referred to publicly as drones. And I'm here today because President Obama has instructed us to be more open with the American people about these efforts.

[...]

[T]argeted strikes are ethical. Without question, the ability to target a specific individual, from hundreds or thousands of miles away, raises profound questions. Here, I think it's useful to consider such strikes against the basic principles of the law of war that govern the use of force.

Targeted strikes conform to the principle of necessity, the requirement that the target have definite military value. In this armed conflict, individuals who are part of al-Qaida or its associated forces are legitimate military targets. We have the authority to target them with lethal force just as we target enemy leaders in past conflicts, such as Germans and Japanese commanders during World War II.

Targeted strikes conform to the principles of distinction, the idea that only military objectives may be intentionally targeted and that civilians are protected from being intentionally targeted. With the unprecedented ability of remotely piloted aircraft to precisely target a military objective while minimizing collateral damage, one could argue that never before has there been a weapon that allows us to distinguish more effectively between an al-Qaida terrorist and innocent civilians.

Targeted strikes conform to the principle of proportionality, the notion that the anticipated collateral damage of an action cannot be excessive in relation to the anticipated military advantage. By targeting an individual terrorist or small numbers of terrorists with ordnance that can be adapted to avoid harming others in the immediate vicinity, it is hard to imagine a tool that can better minimize the risk to civilians than remotely piloted aircraft.

For the same reason, targeted strikes conform to the principle of humanity which requires us to use weapons that will not inflict unnecessary suffering. For all these reasons, I suggest to you that these targeted strikes against al-Qaida terrorists are indeed ethical and just.

Of course, even if a tool is legal and ethical, that doesn't necessarily make it appropriate or advisable in a given circumstance. This brings me to my next point.

Targeted strikes are wise. Remotely piloted aircraft in particular can be a wise choice because of geography, with their ability to fly hundreds of miles over the most treacherous terrain, strike their targets with astonishing precision, and then return to base. They can be a wise choice because of time, when windows of opportunity can close quickly and there just may be only minutes to act.

They can be a wise choice because they dramatically reduce the danger to U.S. personnel, even eliminating the danger altogether. Yet they are also a wise choice because they dramatically reduce the danger to innocent civilians, especially considered against massive ordnance that can cause injury and death far beyond their intended target.

In addition, compared against other options, a pilot operating this aircraft remotely, with the benefit of technology and with the safety of distance, might actually have a clearer picture of the target and its surroundings, including the presence of innocent civilians. It's this surgical precision, the ability, with laser-like focus, to eliminate the cancerous tumor called an al-Qaida terrorist while limiting damage to the tissue around it, that makes this counterterrorism tool so essential.

There's another reason that targeted strikes can be a wise choice, the strategic consequences that inevitably come with the use of force. As we've seen, deploying large armies abroad won't always be our best offense.

Countries typically don't want foreign soldiers in their cities and towns. In fact, large, intrusive military deployments risk playing into al-Qaida's strategy of trying to draw us into long, costly wars that drain us financially, inflame anti-American resentment, and inspire the next generation of terrorists. In comparison, there is the precision of targeted strikes.

[…] [There] is absolutely nothing casual about the extraordinary care we take in making the decision to pursue an al-Qaida terrorist, and the lengths to which we go to ensure precision and avoid the loss of innocent life.

Still, there is no more consequential a decision than deciding whether to use lethal force against another human being, even a terrorist dedicated to killing American citizens. So in order to ensure that our counterterrorism operations involving the use of lethal force are legal, ethical, and wise, President Obama has demanded that we hold ourselves to the highest possible standards and processes.

This reflects his approach to broader questions regarding the use of force. In his speech in Oslo accepting the Nobel Peace Prize, the president said that "all nations, strong and weak alike, must adhere to standards that govern the use of force." And he added:

"Where force is necessary, we have a moral and strategic interest in binding ourselves to certain rules of conduct. And even as we confront a vicious adversary that abides by no rules, I believe the United States of America must remain a standard bearer in the conduct of war. That is what makes us different from those whom we fight. That is a source of our strength."

The United States is the first nation to regularly conduct strikes using remotely piloted aircraft in an armed conflict. Other nations also possess this technology, and many more nations are seeking it, and more will succeed in acquiring it. President Obama and those of us on his national security team are very mindful that as our nation uses this technology, we are establishing precedents that other nations may follow, and not all of those nations may—and not all of them will be nations that share our interests or the premium we put on protecting human life, including innocent civilians.

If we want other nations to use these technologies responsibly, we must use them responsibly. If we want other nations to adhere to high and rigorous standards for their use, then we must do so as well. We cannot expect of others what we will not do ourselves. President Obama has therefore demanded that we hold ourselves to the highest possible standards, that, at every step, we be as thorough and as deliberate as possible.

This leads me to the final point I want to discuss today, the rigorous standards and process of review to which we hold ourselves today. [...]

Over time, we've worked to refine, clarify, and strengthen this process and our standards, and we continue to do so. If our counterterrorism professionals assess, for example, that a suspected member of al-Qaida poses such a threat to the United States to warrant lethal action, they may raise that individual's name for consideration. The proposal will go through a careful review and, as appropriate, will be evaluated by the very most senior officials in our government for a decision.

First and foremost, the individual must be a legitimate target under the law. [...] [The] use of force against members of al-Qaida is authorized under both international and U.S. law, including both the inherent right of national self-defense and the 2001 Authorization for Use of Military Force, which courts have held extends to those who are part of al-Qaida, the Taliban, and associated forces. If, after a legal review, we determine that the individual is not a lawful target, end of discussion. We are a nation of laws, and we will always act within the bounds of the law.

Of course, the law only establishes the outer limits of the authority in which counterterrorism professionals can operate. Even if we determine that it is lawful to pursue the terrorist in question with lethal force, it doesn't necessarily mean we should. There are, after all, literally thousands of individuals who are part of al-Qaida, the Taliban, or associated forces, thousands upon thousands. Even if it were possible, going after every single one of these individuals with lethal force would neither be wise nor an effective use of our intelligence and counterterrorism resources.

As a result, we have to be strategic. Even if it is lawful to pursue a specific member of al-Qaida, we ask ourselves whether that individual's activities rise to a certain threshold for action, and whether taking action will, in fact, enhance our security.

For example, when considering lethal force we ask ourselves whether the individual poses a significant threat to U.S. interests. [...] We do not engage in legal action—in lethal action in order to eliminate every single member of al-Qaida in the world. Most times, and as we have done for more than a decade, we rely on cooperation with other countries that are also interested in removing these terrorists with their own capabilities and within their own laws. Nor is lethal action about punishing terrorists for past crimes; we are not seeking vengeance. Rather, we conduct targeted strikes because they are necessary to mitigate an actual ongoing threat, to stop plots, prevent future attacks, and to save American lives.

And what do we mean when we say significant threat? I am not referring to some hypothetical threat, the mere possibility that a member of al-Qaida might try to attack us at some point in the future. A significant threat might be posed by an individual who is an operational leader of al-Qaida or one of its associated forces. Or perhaps the individual is himself an operative, in the midst of actually training for or planning to carry out attacks against U.S. persons and interests. Or perhaps the individual possesses unique operational skills that are being leveraged in a planned attack. The purpose of a strike against a particular individual is to stop him before he can carry out his attack and kill innocents. The purpose is to disrupt his plans and his plots before they come to fruition.

In addition, our unqualified preference is to only undertake lethal force when we believe that capturing the individual is not feasible. I have heard it suggested that the Obama Administration somehow prefers killing al-Qaida members rather than capturing them. Nothing could be further from the truth. It is our preference to capture suspected terrorists whenever and wherever feasible.

For one reason, this allows us to gather valuable intelligence that we might not be able to obtain any other way. In fact, the members of al-Qaida that we or other nations have captured have been one of our greatest sources of information about al-Qaida, its plans, and its intentions. And once in U.S. custody, we often can prosecute them in our federal courts or reformed military commissions, both of which are used for gathering intelligence and preventing future terrorist attacks.

[...]

The reality, however, is that since 2001 such unilateral captures by U.S. forces outside of hot battlefields, like Afghanistan, have been exceedingly rare. This is due in part to the fact that in many parts of the world our counterterrorism partners have been able to capture or kill dangerous individuals themselves.

Moreover, after being subjected to more than a decade of relentless pressure, al-Qaida's ranks have dwindled and scattered. These terrorists are skilled at seeking remote, inhospitable terrain, places where the United States and our partners simply do not have the ability to arrest or capture them. At other times, our forces might have the ability to attempt capture, but only by putting the lives of our personnel at too great a risk. Oftentimes, attempting capture could subject civilians to unacceptable risks. There are many reasons why capture might not be feasible, in which case lethal force might be the only remaining option to address the threat, prevent an attack, and save lives.

Finally, when considering lethal force we are of course mindful that there are important checks on our ability to act unilaterally in foreign territories. We do not use force whenever we want, wherever we want. International legal principles, including respect for a state's sovereignty and the laws of war, impose constraints. The United States of America respects national sovereignty and international law.

[...]

We review the most up-to-date intelligence, drawing on the full range of our intelligence capabilities. [...]

We listen to departments and agencies across our national security team. We don't just hear out differing views, we ask for them and encourage them. We discuss. We debate. We disagree. We consider the advantages and disadvantages of taking action. We also carefully consider the costs of inaction and whether a decision not to carry out a strike could allow a terrorist attack to proceed and potentially kill scores of innocents.

Nor do we limit ourselves narrowly to counterterrorism considerations. We consider the broader strategic implications of any action, including what effect, if any, an action might have on our relationships with other countries. And we don't simply make a decision and never revisit it again. Quite the opposite. Over time, we refresh the intelligence and continue to consider whether lethal force is still warranted.

In some cases, such as senior al-Qaida leaders who are directing and planning attacks against the United States, the individual clearly meets our standards for taking action. In other cases, individuals have not met our standards. Indeed, there have been numerous occasions where, after careful review, we have, working on a consensus basis, concluded that lethal force was not justified in a given case.

As President Obama's counterterrorism advisor, I feel that it is important for the American people to know that these efforts are overseen with extraordinary care and thoughtfulness. The president expects us to address all of the tough questions I have discussed today. Is capture really not feasible? Is this individual a significant threat to U.S. interests? Is this really the best option? Have we thought through the consequences, especially any unintended ones? Is this really going to help protect our country from further attacks? Is this going to save lives?

Our commitment to upholding the ethics and efficacy of this counterterrorism tool continues even after we decide to pursue a specific terrorist in this way. For example, we only authorize a particular operation against a specific individual if we have a high degree of confidence that the individual being targeted is indeed the terrorist we are pursuing. This is a very high bar. Of course, how we identify an individual naturally involves intelligence sources and methods, which I will not discuss. Suffice it to say, our intelligence community has multiple ways to determine, with a high degree of confidence, that the individual being targeted is indeed the al-Qaida terrorist we are seeking.

In addition, we only authorize a strike if we have a high degree of confidence that innocent civilians will not be injured or killed, except in the rarest of circumstances. The unprecedented advances we have made in technology provide us greater proximity to target for a longer period of time, and as a result allow us to better understand what is happening in real time on the ground in ways that were previously impossible. We can be much more discriminating and we can make more informed judgments about factors that might contribute to collateral damage.

I can tell you today that there have indeed been occasions when we decided against conducting a strike in order to avoid the injury or death of innocent civilians. This reflects our commitment to doing everything in our power to avoid civilian casualties, even if it means having to come back another day to take out that terrorist, as we have done previously. And I would note that these standards, for identifying a target and avoiding the loss of innocent—the loss of lives of innocent civilians, exceed what is required as a matter of international law on a typical battlefield. That's another example of the high standards to which we hold ourselves.

Our commitment to ensuring accuracy and effectiveness continues even after a strike. In the wake of a strike, we harness the full range of our intelligence capabilities to assess whether the mission in fact achieved its objective. We try to determine whether there was any collateral damage, including civilian deaths. There is, of course, no such thing as a perfect weapon, and remotely piloted aircraft are no exception.

As the president and others have acknowledged, there have indeed been instances when, despite the extraordinary precautions we take, civilians have been accidently killed or worse—have been accidentally injured, or worse, killed in these strikes. It is exceedingly rare, but it has happened. When it does, it pains us, and we regret it deeply, as we do any time innocents are killed in war. And when it happens we take it very, very seriously. We go back and we review our actions. We examine our practices. And we constantly work to improve and refine our efforts so that we are doing everything in our power to prevent the loss of innocent life. This too is a reflection of our values as Americans.

Ensuring the ethics and efficacy of these strikes also includes regularly informing appropriate members of Congress and the committees who have oversight of our counterterrorism programs. Indeed, our counterterrorism programs, including the use of lethal force, have grown more effective over time because of congressional oversight and our ongoing dialogue with members and staff.

This is the seriousness, the extraordinary care, that President Obama and those of us on his national security team bring to this weightiest of questions: Whether to pursue lethal force against a terrorist who is plotting to attack our country.

[...]

To recap, the standards and processes I've described today, which we have refined and strengthened over time, reflect our commitment to: ensuring the individual is a legitimate target under the law; determining whether the individual poses a significant threat to U.S. interests; determining that capture is not feasible; being mindful of the important checks on our ability to act unilaterally in foreign territories; having that high degree of confidence, both in the identity of the target and that innocent civilians will not be harmed; and, of course, engaging in additional review if the al-Qaida terrorist is a U.S. citizen.

[...]

This includes our continuing commitment to greater transparency. With that in mind, I have made a sincere effort today to address some of the main questions that citizens and scholars have raised regarding the use of targeted lethal force against al-Qaida. I suspect there are those, perhaps some in this audience, who feel we have not been transparent enough. I suspect there are those, both inside and outside our government, who feel I have been perhaps too open. If both groups feel a little bit unsatisfied, then I probably struck the right balance today.

Again, there are some lines we simply will not and cannot cross because, at times, our national security demands secrecy. But we are a democracy. The people are sovereign. And our counterterrorism tools do not exist in a vacuum. They are stronger and more sustainable when the American people understand and support them. They are weaker and less sustainable when the American people do not. As a result of my remarks today, I hope the American people have a better understanding of this critical tool, why we use it, what we do, how carefully we use it, and why it is absolutely essential to protecting our country and our citizens.

I would just like to close on a personal note. I know that for many people in our government and across the country the issue of targeted strikes raised profound moral questions. It forces us to confront deeply held personal beliefs and our values as a nation. If anyone in government who works in this area tells you they haven't struggled with this, then they haven't spent much time thinking about it. I know I have, and I will continue to struggle with it as long as I remain in counterterrorism.

But I am certain about one thing. We are at war. We are at war against a terrorist organization called al-Qaida that has brutally murdered thousands of Americans, men, women and children, as well as thousands of other innocent people around the world. In recent years, with the help of targeted strikes, we have turned al-Qaida into a shadow of what it once was. They are on the road to destruction.

Until that finally happens, however, there are still terrorists in hard-to-reach places who are actively planning attacks against us. If given the chance, they will gladly strike again and kill more of our citizens. And the president has a Constitutional and solemn obligation to do everything in his power to protect the safety and security of the American people.

Yes, war is hell. It is awful. It involves human beings killing other human beings, sometimes innocent civilians. That is why we despise war. That is why we want this war against al-Qaida to be over as soon as possible, and not a moment longer. And over time, as al-Qaida fades into history and as our partners grow stronger, I'd ho pe that the United States would have to rely less on lethal force to keep our country safe.

[…]

*John O. Brennan served as chief counterterrorism advisor to Pres. Barack Obama. He is currently director of the Central Intelligence Agency.

Brennan, John O. "The Efficacy and Ethics of U.S. Counterterrorism Strategy." Speech delivered at the Wilson Center, Washington, D.C., April 30, 2012. http:// www.wilsoncenter.org/event/the-efficacy-and-ethics-us-counterterrorism-strategy#field_speakers.

Why Drones Work: The Case for Washington's Weapon of Choice

by Daniel Byman*

[...]

The Obama administration relies on drones for one simple reason: they work. According to data compiled by the New America Foundation, since Obama has been in the White House, U.S. drones have killed an estimated 3,300 al Qaeda, Taliban, and other jihadist operatives in Pakistan and Yemen. That number includes over 50 senior leaders of al Qaeda and the Taliban—top figures who are not easily replaced. In 2010, Osama bin Laden warned his chief aide, Atiyah Abd al-Rahman, who was later killed by a drone strike in the Waziristan region of Pakistan in 2011, that when experienced leaders are eliminated, the result is "the rise of lower leaders who are not as experienced as the former leaders" and who are prone to errors and miscalculations. And drones also hurt terrorist organizations when they eliminate operatives who are lower down on the food chain but who boast special skills: passport forgers, bomb makers, recruiters, and fundraisers.

Drones have also undercut terrorists' ability to communicate and to train new recruits. In order to avoid attracting drones, al Qaeda and Taliban operatives try to avoid using electronic devices or gathering in large numbers. A tip sheet found among jihadists in Mali advised militants to "maintain complete silence of all wireless contacts" and "avoid gathering in open areas." Leaders, however, cannot give orders when they are incommunicado, and training on a large scale is nearly impossible when a drone strike could wipe out an entire group of new recruits. Drones have turned al Qaeda's command and training structures into a liability, forcing the group to choose between having no leaders and risking dead leaders.

Critics of drone strikes often fail to take into account the fact that the alternatives are either too risky or unrealistic. To be sure, in an ideal world, militants would be captured alive, allowing authorities to question them and search their compounds for useful information. Raids, arrests, and interrogations can produce vital intelligence and can be less controversial than lethal operations. That is why they should be, and indeed already are, used in stable countries where the United States enjoys the support of the host government. But in war zones or unstable countries, such as Pakistan, Yemen, and Somalia, arresting militants is highly dangerous and, even if successful, often inefficient. In those three countries, the government exerts little or no control over remote areas, which means that it is highly dangerous to go after militants hiding out there. Worse yet, in Pakistan and Yemen, the governments have at times cooperated with militants. If the United States regularly sent in special operations forces to hunt down terrorists there, sympathetic officials could easily tip off the jihadists, likely leading to firefights, U.S. casualties, and possibly the deaths of the suspects and innocent civilians.

Of course, it was a Navy SEAL team and not a drone strike that finally got bin Laden, but in many cases in which the United States needs to capture or eliminate an enemy, raids are too risky and costly. And even if a raid results in a successful capture, it begets another problem: what to do with the detainee.

Prosecuting detainees in a federal or military court is difficult because often the intelligence against terrorists is inadmissible or using it risks jeopardizing sources and methods. And given the fact that the United States is trying to close, rather than expand, the detention facility at Guantánamo Bay, Cuba, it has become much harder to justify holding suspects indefinitely. It has become more politically palatable for the United States to kill rather than detain suspected terrorists.

Furthermore, although a drone strike may violate the local state's sovereignty, it does so to a lesser degree than would putting U.S. boots on the ground or conducting a large-scale air campaign. And compared with a 500-pound bomb dropped from an F-16, the grenadelike warheads carried by most drones create smaller, more precise blast zones that decrease the risk of unexpected structural damage and casualties. Even more important, drones, unlike traditional airplanes, can loiter above a target for hours, waiting for the ideal moment to strike and thus reducing the odds that civilians will be caught in the kill zone.

Finally, using drones is also far less bloody than asking allies to hunt down terrorists on the United States' behalf. The Pakistani and Yemeni militaries, for example, are known to regularly torture and execute detainees, and they often indiscriminately bomb civilian areas or use scorched-earth tactics against militant groups.

Some critics of the drone program, such as Ben Emmerson, the UN's special rapporteur on the promotion and protection of human rights and fundamental freedoms while countering terrorism, have questioned the lethal approach, arguing for more focus on the factors that might contribute to extremism and terrorism, such as poverty, unemployment, and authoritarianism. Such a strategy is appealing in principle, but it is far from clear how Washington could execute it. Individuals join anti-American terrorist groups for many reasons, ranging from outrage over U.S. support for Israel to anger at their own government's cooperation with the United States. Some people simply join up because their neighbors are doing so. Slashing unemployment in Yemen, bringing democracy to Saudi Arabia, and building a functioning government in Somalia are laudable goals, but they are not politically or financially possible for the United States, and even if achieved, they still might not reduce the allure of jihad.

In some cases, the most sensible alternative to carrying out drone strikes is to do nothing at all. At times, that is the right option: if militants abroad pose little threat or if the risk of killing civilians, delegitimizing allies, or establishing the wrong precedent is too high. But sometimes imminent and intolerable threats do arise and drone strikes are the best way to eliminate them.

The Numbers Game

Despite the obvious benefits of using drones and the problems associated with the alternatives, numerous critics argue that drones still have too many disadvantages. First among them is an unacceptably high level of civilian casualties. Admittedly, drones have killed innocents. But the real debate is over how many and whether alternative approaches are any better. The Bureau of Investigative Journalism reports that in 2011, U.S. drone strikes killed as many as 146 noncombatants, including as many as 9 children. Columbia Law School's Human Rights Clinic also cites high numbers of civilian deaths, as does the Pakistani organization Pakistan Body Count. Peter Bergen of the New America Foundation oversees a database of drone casualties culled from U.S. sources and international media reports. He estimates that between 150 and 500 civilians have been killed by drones during Obama's administration. U.S. officials, meanwhile, maintain that drone strikes have killed almost no civilians. In June 2011, John Brennan, then Obama's top counterterrorism adviser, even contended that U.S. drone strikes had killed no civilians in the previous year. But these claims are based on the fact that the U.S. government assumes that all military-age males in the blast area of a drone strike are combatants—unless it can determine after the fact that they were innocent (and such intelligence gathering is not a priority).

The United States has recently taken to launching "signature strikes," which target not specific individuals but instead groups engaged in suspicious activities. This approach makes it even more difficult to distinguish between combatants and civilians and verify body counts of each. Still, as one U.S. official told *The New York Times* last year, "Al Qaeda is an insular, paranoid organization—innocent neighbors don't hitchhike rides in the back of trucks headed for the border with guns and bombs." Of course, not everyone accepts this reasoning. Zeeshan-ul-hassan Usmani, who runs Pakistan Body Count, says that "neither [the United States] nor Pakistan releases any detailed information about the victims . . . so [although the United States] likes to call everybody Taliban, I call everybody civilians."

The truth is that all the public numbers are unreliable. Who constitutes a civilian is often unclear; when trying to kill the Pakistani Taliban leader Baitullah Mehsud, for example, the United States also killed his doctor. The doctor was not targeting U.S. or allied forces, but he was aiding a known terrorist leader. In addition, most strikes are carried out in such remote locations that it is nearly impossible for independent sources to verify who was killed. In Pakistan, for example, the overwhelming majority of drone killings occur in tribal areas that lie outside the government's control and are prohibitively dangerous for Westerners and independent local journalists to enter.

The Pakistani government and militant groups frequently doctor casualty numbers, often making reports from local Pakistani organizations, and the Western organizations that rely on them, unreliable. After a strike in Pakistan, militants often cordon off the area, remove their dead, and admit only local reporters sympathetic to their cause or decide on a body count themselves. The U.S. media often then draw on such faulty reporting to give the illusion of having used multiple sources. As a result, statistics on civilians killed by drones are often inflated. One of the few truly independent on-the-ground reporting efforts, conducted by the Associated Press last year, concluded that the strikes "are killing far fewer civilians than many in [Pakistan] are led to believe."

But even the most unfavorable estimates of drone casualties reveal that the ratio of civilian to militant deaths—about one to three, according to the Bureau of Investigative Journalism—is lower than it would be for other forms of strikes. Bombings by F-16s or Tomahawk cruise missile salvos, for example, pack a much more deadly payload. In December 2009, the United States fired Tomahawks at a suspected terrorist training camp in Yemen, and over 30 people were killed in the blast, most of them women and children. At the time, the Yemeni regime refused to allow the use of drones, but had this not been the case, a drone's real-time surveillance would probably have spotted the large number of women and children, and the attack would have been aborted. Even if the strike had gone forward for some reason, the drone's far smaller warhead would have killed fewer innocents. Civilian deaths are tragic and pose political problems.

But the data show that drones are more discriminate than other types of force.

Foreign Friends

It is also telling that drones have earned the backing, albeit secret, of foreign governments. In order to maintain popular support, politicians in Pakistan and Yemen routinely rail against the U.S. drone campaign. In reality, however, the governments of both countries have supported it. During the Bush and Obama administrations, Pakistan has even periodically hosted U.S. drone facilities and has been told about strikes in advance. Pervez Musharraf, president of Pakistan until 2008, was not worried about the drone program's negative publicity: "In Pakistan, things fall out of the sky all the time," he reportedly remarked. Yemen's former president, Ali Abdullah Saleh, also at times allowed drone strikes in his country and even covered for them by telling the public that they were conducted by the Yemeni air force. When the United States' involvement was leaked in 2002, however, relations between the two countries soured. Still, Saleh later let the drone program resume in Yemen, and his replacement, Abdu Rabbu Mansour Hadi, has publicly praised drones, saying that "they pinpoint the target and have zero margin of error, if you know what target you're aiming at."

As officials in both Pakistan and Yemen realize, U.S. drone strikes help their governments by targeting common enemies. A memo released by the antisecrecy website WikiLeaks revealed that Pakistan's army chief, Ashfaq Parvez Kayani, privately asked U.S. military leaders in 2008 for "continuous Predator coverage" over antigovernment militants, and the journalist Mark Mazzetti has reported that the United States has conducted "goodwill kills" against Pakistani militants who threatened Pakistan far more than the United States. Thus, in private, Pakistan supports the drone program. As then Prime Minister Yousaf Raza Gilani told Anne Patterson, then the U.S. ambassador to Pakistan, in 2008, "We'll protest [against the drone program] in the National Assembly and then ignore it."

Still, Pakistan is reluctant to make its approval public. First of all, the country's inability to fight terrorists on its own soil is a humiliation for Pakistan's politically powerful armed forces and intelligence service. In addition, although drones kill some of the government's enemies, they have also targeted pro-government groups that are hostile to the United States, such as the Haqqani network and the Taliban, which Pakistan has supported since its birth in the early 1990s. Even more important, the Pakistani public is vehemently opposed to U.S. drone strikes.

A 2012 poll found that 74 percent of Pakistanis viewed the United States as their enemy, likely in part because of the ongoing drone campaign. Similarly, in Yemen, as the scholar Gregory Johnsen has pointed out, drone strikes can win the enmity of entire tribes. This has led critics to argue that the drone program is shortsighted: that it kills today's enemies but creates tomorrow's in the process.

Such concerns are valid, but the level of local anger over drones is often lower than commonly portrayed. Many surveys of public opinion related to drones are conducted by anti-drone organizations, which results in biased samples. Other surveys exclude those who are unaware of the drone program and thus overstate the importance of those who are angered by it. In addition, many Pakistanis do not realize that the drones often target the very militants who are wreaking havoc on their country. And for most Pakistanis and Yemenis, the most important problems they struggle with are corruption, weak representative institutions, and poor economic growth; the drone program is only a small part of their overall anger, most of which is directed toward their own governments. A poll conducted in 2007, well before the drone campaign had expanded to its current scope, found that only 15 percent of Pakistanis had a favorable opinion of the United States. It is hard to imagine that alternatives to drone strikes, such as SEAL team raids or cruise missile strikes, would make the United States more popular.

[…]

Follow the Leader

The fact remains that by using drones so much, Washington risks setting a troublesome precedent with regard to extrajudicial and extraterritorial killings. Zeke Johnson of Amnesty International contends that "when the U.S. government violates international law, that sets a precedent and provides an excuse for the rest of the world to do the same." And it is alarming to think what leaders such as Syrian President Bashar al-Assad, who has used deadly force against peaceful pro-democracy demonstrators he has deemed terrorists, would do with drones of their own. Similarly, Iran could mockingly cite the U.S. precedent to justify sending drones after rebels in Syria. Even Brennan has conceded that the administration is "establishing precedents that other nations may follow."

Controlling the spread of drone technology will prove impossible; that horse left the barn years ago. Drones are highly capable weapons that are easy to produce, and so there is no chance that Washington can stop other militaries from acquiring and using them. [...]

The spread of drones cannot be stopped, but the United States can still influence how they are used. The coming proliferation means that Washington needs to set forth a clear policy now on extrajudicial and extraterritorial killings of terrorists—and stick to it. [...]

[...]

The U.S. government also needs to guard against another kind of danger: that the relative ease of using drones will make U.S. intervention abroad too common. The scholars Daniel Brunstetter and Megan Braun have argued that drones provide "a way to avoid deploying troops or conducting an intensive bombing campaign" and that this "may encourage countries to act on just cause with an ease that is potentially worrisome." Although al Qaeda remains a threat, it has been substantially defanged since 9/11, thanks to the destruction of its haven in Afghanistan and effective global police, intelligence, and drone campaigns against its cells. In addition, the U.S. government needs to remember that many of the world's jihadist organizations are focused first and foremost on local regimes and that although the United States has an interest in helping its allies fight extremists, Washington cannot and should not directly involve itself in every fight. The Obama administration should spell out those cases in which the AUMF does not apply and recognize the risks of carrying out so-called goodwill kills on behalf of foreign governments. Helping French and Malian forces defeat jihadists in Mali by providing logistical support, for example, is smart policy, but sending U.S. drones there is not.

In places where terrorists are actively plotting against the United States, however, drones give Washington the ability to limit its military commitments abroad while keeping Americans safe. Afghanistan, for example, could again become a Taliban-run haven for terrorists after U.S. forces depart next year. Drones can greatly reduce the risk of this happening. Hovering in the skies above, they can keep Taliban leaders on the run and hinder al Qaeda's ability to plot another 9/11.

***Daniel Byman** is a professor in the Security Studies Program at the Edmund A. Walsh School of Foreign Service with a concurrent appointment with the Georgetown Department of Government. He served as director of Georgetown's Security Studies Program and Center for Security Studies from 2005 until 2010.

Byman, Daniel. "Why Drones Work: The Case for Washington's Weapon of Choice." *Foreign Affairs* July/August 2013. http://www.foreignaffairs.com/articles/139453/daniel-byman/why-drones-work.

The Case for Drones (excerpt)

by Kenneth Anderson*

[...]

3. What Makes Drone Warfare Strategically Effective?

Are drone technology and targeted killing really so strategically valuable? The answer depends in great part not on drone technology, but on the quality of the intelligence that leads to a particular target in the first place. The drone strike is the final kinetic act in a process of intelligence-gathering and analysis. The success—and it is remarkable success—of the CIA in disrupting al-Qaeda in Pakistan has come about not because of drones alone, but because the CIA managed to establish, over years of effort, its own ground-level, human-intelligence networks that have allowed it to identify targets independent of information fed to it by Pakistan's intelligence services. The quality of drone-targeted killing depends fundamentally on that intelligence, for a drone is not much use unless pointed toward surveillance of a particular village, area, or person.

It can be used for a different kind of targeting altogether: against groups of fighters with their weapons on trucks headed toward the Afghan border. But these so-called signature strikes are not, as sometimes represented, a relaxed form of targeted killing in which groups are crudely blown up because nothing is known about individual members. Intelligence assessments are made, including behavioral signatures such as organized groups of men carrying weapons, suggesting strongly that they are "hostile forces" (in the legal meaning of that term in the U.S. military's Standing Rules of Engagement). That is the norm in conventional war.

Targeted killing of high-value terrorist targets, by contrast, is the end result of a long, independent intelligence process. What the drone adds to that intelligence might be considerable, through its surveillance capabilities—but much of the drone's contribution will be tactical, providing intelligence that assists in the planning and execution of the strike itself, in order to pick the moment when there might be the fewest civilian casualties.

Nonetheless, in conjunction with high-quality intelligence, drone warfare offers an unparalleled means to strike directly at terrorist organizations without needing a conventional or counterinsurgency approach to reach terrorist groups in their safe havens. It offers an offensive capability, rather than simply defensive measures, such as homeland security alone. Drone warfare offers a raiding strategy directly against the terrorists and their leadership.

If one believes, as many of the critics of drone warfare do, that the proper strategies of counterterrorism are essentially defensive—including those that eschew the paradigm of armed conflict in favor of law enforcement and criminal law—then the strategic virtue of an offensive capability against the terrorists themselves will seem small. But that has not been American policy since 9/11, not under the Bush administration, not under the Obama administration—and not by the Congress of the United States, which has authorized hundreds of billions of dollars to fight the war on terror aggressively. The United States has used many offensive methods in the past dozen years: Regime change of states offering safe havens, counterinsurgency war, special operations, military and intelligence assistance to regimes battling our common enemies are examples of the methods that are just of military nature.

Drone warfare today is integrated with a much larger strategic counterterrorism target—one in which, as in Afghanistan in the late 1990s, radical Islamist groups seize governance of whole populations and territories and provide not only safe haven, but also an honored central role to transnational terrorist groups. This is what current conflicts in Yemen and Mali threaten, in counterterrorism terms, and why the United States, along with France and even the UN, has moved to intervene militarily. Drone warfare is just one element of overall strategy, but it has a clear utility in disrupting terrorist leadership. It makes the planning and execution of complex plots difficult if only because it is hard to plan for years down the road if you have some reason to think you will be struck down by a drone but have no idea when. The unpredictability and terrifying anticipation of sudden attack, which terrorists have acknowledged in communications, have a significant impact on planning and organizational effectiveness.

This is all subject to objections, of course, and the objections generally fall into three categories: unnecessary, ineffective, or counterproductive.

There are some who argue that drone warfare is unnecessary because the right approach is simply to defend the homeland from within the homeland; among liberals this is often a way of saying, fight terrorists with law enforcement and criminal law, while among some conservatives it corresponds closely with the resurgence of right-wing isolationism.

Other critics argue that drone warfare is ineffective because killing one operational commander merely means that another rises to take his place. This is the source of the oft-heard remark that drone warfare is a "whack-a-mole" strategy: Kill one here and another pops up there. Drone warfare is nothing more than a tactic masquerading as a strategy, it is said. Worse, it indulges one of the oldest and most seductive quests of modern military technology, the one that says you can win a war from the air alone.

The whack-a-mole criticism is wildly overstated and, as a matter of terrorist leadership, simply not true. Captured terrorist communications show that qualified and experienced operational commanders are not so easy to come by. One can argue that the failure to carry off large-scale attacks in the West is the result of the defensive hardening of targets and better homeland security, which is certainly true; but culling the ranks of terrorist leaders and the resulting inability to plan another 9/11 is also critical.

4. Blowback

The most prominent critique today, however, is that drone warfare is counterproductive because it produces "blowback." What is blowback?

Blowback comprises the supposed bad consequences of drones that swamp the benefits, if any, of drone warfare itself— the anger of villagers whose civilian relatives have been killed, for instance, or the resentment among larger populations in

Pakistan or Yemen over drone strikes. The anger, we are told, is fanned by Islamist preachers, local media, and global Web communities, and then goes global in the *ummah* about the perceived targeting of Muslims and Islam. This leads to radicalization and membership recruitment where the strikes take place. Or maybe it leads to independently organized violence— perhaps the case of the Boston bombers, though it is too early to say. All this bad public perception outweighs whatever tactical value, if any, drone strikes might have.

Blowback can never be dismissed, because it might be true in some cases. But even when true, it would exist as a matter of degree, to be set against the benefits of the drone strikes themselves. By definition, blowback is a second-order effect, and its diffuse nature makes its existence more a matter of subjective judgment than any other evaluation of drone warfare. As a hypothesis, the possibility of blowback arises in two distinct settings: "narrow" counterinsurgency and "broad" global counterterrorism.

The narrow blowback hypothesis concerns those in communities directly affected by global counterterrorism drone strikes while the United States is trying to carry out a ground-level counterinsurgency campaign. The question is whether civilians, women and children especially, are being killed by drones in such numbers—because collateral damage is a fact, including from drone strikes—that they make these local communities even more fertile ground for anti-American operations. Do the drone strikes make things unacceptably more difficult for ground forces attempting to carry out a hearts-and-minds campaign to win over the local population?

Direct and immediate concerns about villagers' perceptions during the counterinsurgencies in Iraq and Afghanistan led, at some points, to extraordinary (from the standpoint of lawful targeting and acceptable collateral damage) measures against using air power and even infantry to fire back at insurgents. But local counterinsurgency is not the long-term concern today; global counterterrorism is. Village-level resentments fueling recruitment might be a concern, but this type of blowback matters far less in terms of war fighting when the United States no longer has infantry in those places (and is no longer making its counterterrorism policy rest upon the chimera of a stable, democratic Afghanistan).

It is sharply contested, to say the least, whether and to what extent drone strikes are creating blowback among villagers, or whether and to what extent, as a former British soldier recently returned from Afghanistan remarked to me, villagers are sad to see the Taliban commander who just insisted on marrying someone's young daughter blown up in an airstrike. There is also debate about the degree to which villagers are aware that the American drones are undertaking strikes that the Pakistani government might otherwise undertake. Critics often neglect to focus on the Pakistani government's regular and brutal assaults in the tribal zones. Despite a general perception that all of Pakistan is united against drone strikes, voices in the Pakistani newspapers have often made note that the tribal areas fear the Pakistani army far more than they fear U.S. drones, because, despite mistakes and inevitable civilian casualties, they see them as smaller and more precise. But the blunt reality is that as the counterinsurgency era ends for U.S. forces, narrow blowback concerns about whether villages might be sufficiently provoked against American infantry are subsiding.

That leaves the broader claim of *global* blowback—the idea that drone campaigns are effectively creating transnational terrorists as well as sympathy for their actions. That could always be true and could conceivably outweigh all other concerns. But the evidence is so diffuse as to be pointless. Do Gallup polls of the general Pakistani population indicate overwhelming resentment about drone strikes—or do they really suggest that more than half the country is unaware of a drone campaign at all? Recent polls found the latter to be the case. Any causal connections that lead from supposed resentments to actual terrorist recruitment are contingent and uncertain. Discussing global blowback is also an easy stance for journalists writing about U.S. counterterrorism—Mark Mazzetti's new book, *The Way of the Knife*, is a good example—because it automatically frames an oppositional narrative, one with dark undertones and intimations of unattractive, unintended consequence. The blowback argument is also peculiarly susceptible to raising the behavioral bar the United States must meet in order to keep the local population happy enough not to embrace suicide bombing and terrorism. It defines terrorist deviancy down, while U.S. and Western security behaviors are always defined up.

From a strategic standpoint, however, the trouble with the blowback theory is simple: It will always counsel doing nothing rather than doing something. It's the kibitzer's lazy objection. Whether one knows a lot or a little about the action and its possible blowback consequences, whether one has an axe to grind or is reasonably objective, one can always offer the blowback scenario.

There might be situations in which to give it priority; Gregory Johnsen, a Yemen expert, for example, says that a particular form of strike in Yemen causes blowback because it hits low-level fighters whose families cannot understand the American justification. (The response is, usually, that we are effectively fighting as the air arm of the Yemen government against its insurgents, including its low-level fighters.) That bears attention; whether it outweighs the strategic concern of supporting the Yemeni government, which does have to fight even low-level insurgents who in effect offer protection to the transnational terrorist wing, is another question. But we should consider it carefully.

Blowback is a form of the precautionary principle. But it's awfully difficult to conduct war, after all, on the basis of "first do no harm." As it happens, the United States once had a commander driven largely by considerations of blowback from a restive local population. His name was George McClellan. If he had not been replaced by Abraham Lincoln, the Union would have lost the Civil War.

[. . .]

*Kenneth Anderson is a professor of international law at American University and a member of the Task Force on National Security and Law at the Hoover Institution.

Anderson, Kenneth. "The Case for Drones (excerpt)." *Commentary,* July/August 2014. https://www.commentarymagazine.com/articles/the-case-for-drones/.

Statement of Farea Al-Muslimi

STATEMENT OF FAREA AL-MUSLIMI*

BEFORE THE SENATE JUDICIARY COMMITTEE,
SUBCOMMITTEE ON THE CONSTITUTION, CIVIL RIGHTS,
AND HUMAN RIGHTS

*"Drone Wars: The Constitutional and Counterterrorism
Implications of Targeted Killing"*

APRIL 23, 2013

Thank you very much, Chairman Durbin and Ranking Member Cruz, for holding this hearing and inviting me here today. I first visited the U.S. Capitol 6 years ago as a 16 year-old, high school exchange student and later to brief congressional staffers on issues related to Yemen. It is a tremendous honor for me to return to the United States Senate to testify today.

My name is Farea Al-Muslimi. I am from Wessab, a remote mountain village in Yemen, about nine hours' drive from my country's capital, Sana'a. Most of the world has never heard of Wessab. But just six days ago, my village was struck by a drone, in an attack that terrified thousands of simple, poor farmers. The drone strike and its impact tore my heart, much as the tragic bombings in Boston last week tore your hearts and also mine.

I have visited locations where U.S. targeted killing strikes have hit their intended targets. And I have visited sites where the U.S. strikes missed their targets and instead killed or injured innocent civilians. I have spoken with grieving family members and angry villagers. I have seen Al Qaeda in the Arabian Peninsula ("AQAP") use U.S. strikes to promote its agenda and try to recruit more terrorists.

I am here today to talk about the human costs and consequences of targeted killing by the United States in Yemen.

My Background

My family lives off the fruit, vegetables, and livestock we raise on our farms. We raise cows, goats, sheep, and hens. My father has been a farmer all his life. His income rarely exceeds $200 per month. He learned to read late in life, but my mother never did.

I have 12 living siblings. I should actually have 19, but we lost seven of my brothers and sisters. Some passed away in delivery due to a lack of quality medical services in our village. Others passed away when they were still young for the same reasons.

My life changed forever in the 9th grade when I was awarded a scholarship from the U.S. State Department. The scholarship gave me an opportunity to study English for one year at Amideast, the American English Center in Yemen. This scholarship gave me new opportunities and allowed me to see the world beyond my village for the first time.

I was later awarded a State Department scholarship to the Youth and Exchange Study program, which aims to build peace and understanding between the American people and people in Muslim countries. That scholarship allowed me to spend a year living with an American family and attending an American high school. The year I spent at Rosamond High School in Rosamond, California was one of the richest and best years of my life.

I made exceptional friends with my American classmates and had the most interesting and enriching experience one could imagine. I filled my days spending time with my American friends, learning about American culture, visiting churches almost every Sunday, learning about Christianity for the first time in my life, managing the school's basketball team, walking the Relay for Life, and even participating in a trick or treat at Halloween. In school, I won the Academic Excellence award in my U.S. History class, even ahead of my American classmates.

The most exceptional experience was coming to know someone who ended up being like a father and is my best friend in the United States. He was a member of the U.S. Air Force. Most of my year was spent with him and his family. He came to the mosque with me and I went to church with him. He taught me about his experiences in America and I taught him about my life in Yemen. We developed an amazing friendship that overcame our very different backgrounds.

Through a third scholarship from the U.S. State Department—the Tomorrow's Leaders scholarship—I was able to go to the most prestigious university in the Middle East, the American University of Beirut, where I recently graduated. The Tomorrow's Leaders scholarship enabled me to complete my undergraduate studies in Public Policy.

Working in Yemen as a Journalist, Speaker, and Activist

I will carry the experiences of my time in America with me for the rest of my life. As a high school student, I served as an ambassador to America for the Yemeni people. After that year, however, I returned home and became an ambassador for Americans to my country. I will happily retain this role for the rest of my life. I am a defender of the American values I learned when I studied and lived in the United States.

Today, I am a writer, speaker, and freelance journalist. I have worked with many local, regional, and international non-governmental organizations, including the National Democratic Institute for International Affairs, USAID, and Resonate! Yemen. At the age of 17, I was elected chairman of the Supporting Democracy Committee in the Yemeni Youth Consultative Council.

One of the most rewarding experiences I have had has been working as a "fixer" for international journalists in Yemen and Beirut. This work has allowed me to help the world learn about the experiences of my friends and neighbors. Most of my work with international journalists has been in the southern provinces of Abyan, Aden, Al-dhalea and Lahj—three of the areas where the United States has focused its so-called "war on terror."

A Drone Strike in My Home Village

Just six days ago, this so-called war came straight to my village. As I was thinking about my testimony and preparing to travel to the United States to participate in this hearing, I learned that a missile from a U.S. drone had struck the village where I was raised. Ironically, I was sitting with a group of American diplomats in Sana'a at a farewell dinner for a dear American friend when the strike happened. As I was leaving my American friends, both of my mobile phones began to receive a storm of text messages and calls.

For almost all of the people in Wessab, I'm the only person with any connection to the United States. They called and texted me that night with questions that I could not answer: Why was the United States terrifying them with these drones? Why was the United States trying to kill a person with a missile when everyone knows where he is and he could have been easily arrested?

My village is beautiful, but it is very poor and in a remote part of Yemen. Even though the region it is in is about the same size of Bahrain, there isn't a single meter of asphalt road in it. Developmental projects by the central government rarely reach my village and humanitarian aid from international organizations like USAID never does. I know that most people have never heard of Wessab. But I could never have imagined that it would be the location of a drone strike.

My understanding is that Hameed Meftah, who is also known as Hameed Al-Radmi, was the target of the drone strike. Many people in Wessab know Al-Radmi. Earlier on the night he was killed, he was reportedly in the village meeting with the General Secretary of Local Councilors, the head of the local government. A person in the village told me that Al-Radmi had also met with security and government officials at the security headquarters just three days prior to the drone strike. Yemeni officials easily could have found and arrested Al-Radmi.

After the strike, the farmers in Wessab were afraid and angry. They were upset because they know Al-Radmi but they did not know that he was a target, so they could have potentially been with him during the missile strike. Some of the people that were with Al-Radmi when he was killed were never affiliated with AQAP and only knew Al-Radmi socially. The farmers in my village were angry because Al-Radmi was a man with whom government security chiefs had a close connection. He received cooperation from and had an excellent relationship with the government agencies in the village. This made him look legitimate and granted him power in the eyes of those poor farmers, who had no idea that being with him meant they were risking death from a U.S. drone.

The people in my village wanted Al-Radmi to be captured, so that they could question him and find out what he was doing wrong so they could put an end to it. They still don't have an answer to that question. Instead, all they have is the psychological fear and terror that now occupies their souls. They fear that their home or a neighbor's home could be bombed at any time by a U.S. drone.

In the past, most of Wessab's villagers knew little about the United States. My stories about my experiences in America, my American friends, and the American values that I saw for myself helped the villagers I talked to understand the America that I know and love. Now, however, when they think of America they think of the terror they feel from the drones that hover over their heads ready to fire missiles at any time.

I personally don't even know if it is safe for me to go back to Wessab because I am someone who people in my village associate with America and its values. I don't know whether it is safe to travel to visit my mom because the roads are dangerous.

There is nothing villagers in Wessab needed more than a school to educate the local children or a hospital to help decrease the number of women and children dying every day. Had the United States built a school or hospital, it would have instantly changed the lives of my fellow villagers for the better and been the most effective counterterrorism tool. And I can almost certainly assure you that the villagers would have gone to arrest the target themselves.

Instead of first experiencing America through a school or a hospital, most people in Wessab first experienced America through the terror of a drone strike. What radicals had previously failed to achieve in my village, one drone strike accomplished in an instant: there is now an intense anger and growing hatred of America.

For me personally, it is deeply troubling, astonishing, and challenging to reconcile that the very same hand that taught me English, awarded me scholarships, and dramatically improved my life is the hand that droned my village, terrified my people, and now makes it harder for them to believe the good things that I tell them about America and my American friends. It is especially frustrating to me because all the United States needed to do was identify Al-Radmi as a target, so that he could've been arrested without the injuries, destruction, and death caused by the drone strike.

Visiting with Victims of Targeted Killings

In my work with foreign journalists, I have visited many areas struck by drones or warplanes that residents believe were dispatched as part of the targeted killing program conducted by the United States. I have traveled most frequently to Abyan, an area in southern Yemen, which had been seized in early 2011 by Ansar Al-Sharia, a group aligned with AQAP. One of my trips to Abyan, with National Public Radio, was in mid-January 2012, just two days after the area was freed from AQAP. Traveling in the area was dangerous, both because some AQAP members had simply gone underground by shaving their beards and remaining in town, and because we did not know whether we might find ourselves in a place where a drone might strike next.

In Abyan and other places in Yemen, I visited many locations where local residents were suffering from the consequences of targeted killing operations. I have met with dozens of civilians who were injured during drone strikes and other air attacks. I have met with relatives of people who were killed by drone strikes as well as numerous eyewitnesses. They have told me how these air strikes have changed their lives for the worse.

In early March 2013, I was working with *Newsweek* in Abyan when I met the mother of a boy named Muneer Muhammed. Muneer, an 18 year old boy, transported goods for shops via his donkey in the local souk of Ja'ar town. He had recently been engaged and was preparing for his wedding. Muneer was at work when a missile hit and killed him in May 2012.

At the time of strike, Muneer's mother was in Lahj. She told me that she could not attend her son's funeral or even see him before he was buried, due to the heavy fighting between the government forces and Ansar Al-Shariah along the road between Lahj and Abyan. In fact, the last time this grieving mother saw her son was when she was shown his dead body on a video from a random eyewitness's phone. She told me, in tears, that if she ever meets the individual who shot the missile, she will "crunch him into pieces" in her mouth.

The people with whom we spoke in Abyan told us that Muneer was not a member of AQAP. But that has not stopped AQAP from trying to use his death to recruit supporters to their cause. Local residents told us that they approached one of Muneer's relatives urging him to join AQAP in order to seek revenge for Muneer's death.

Days after Abyan was freed from AQAP control in June 2012, I met a fisherman named Ali Al-Amodi in a hospital in Aden. The day before, his house in Shaqra, on the sea side of Abyan, was targeted by a U.S. air strike. Al-Amodi told me that he stood helplessly as his 4 year old son and 6 year old daughter died in his arms on the way to the hospital.

Al-Amodi had no links with AQAP. He and other locals said that his house was targeted by mistake. In that same strike, four other children and one woman were killed. Witnesses said none were militants.

Later in June 2012, I visited Al-Makhzan, a town outside of Ja'ar, where a drone strike targeting Nader Al-Shadadi took place. Al-Shadadi is identified by the Yemeni government as a terrorist and a leader of Ansar Al-Shariah. He has been targeted at least three times in different places, but the strikes have missed him every time. This time, it targeted his aunt's house. Neighbors say he was not there, and his aunt's only son was killed. There is no evidence that the son was affiliated with AQAP.

Ma'mon, a 12 year old boy who lives next door and witnessed the aftermath of the strike, had tears in his eyes when he told me how the sound of the strike woke him up that morning. Referring to the drones, he told me how "we hear them every night" and that he is afraid each day that they "will come back."

In Aden, I spoke with Saleh Bin Fareed, one of the tribal leaders present on December 17, 2009 at the site where a U.S. cruise missile targeted the village of Al-Majalah in Lawdar, Abyan. In the poor village that day, more than 40 civilians were killed, including four pregnant women. Bin Fareed was one of the first people to the scene. He and others tried to rescue civilians. He told me their bodies were so decimated that it was impossible to differentiate between the children, the women, and their animals. Some of these innocent people were buried in the same grave as animals.

Widespread Impact of Targeted Killing in Yemen

The killing of innocent civilians by U.S. missiles in Yemen is helping to destabilize my country and create an environment from which AQAP benefits. Every time an innocent civilian is killed or maimed by a U.S. drone strike or another targeted killing, it is felt by Yemenis across the country. These strikes often cause animosity towards the United States and create a backlash that undermines the national security goals of the United States. The U.S. strikes also increase my people's hatred against the central government, which is seen as propped up by the Persian Gulf governments and the United States.

I know that some policy makers in the United States and Yemen claim that AQAP does not use drone strikes as a tool to recruit more people to their cause. This is incorrect. The case of the Toaiman family in Mareb, as reported by NPR based on a trip in which I participated, is one specific example. The Toaiman's oldest son joined AQAP hoping to avenge the death of his father, an innocent civilian killed by a drone strike in October 2011. The son has 28 brothers waiting to do so as well. One of his youngest brothers, a 9 year old, carries a picture of a plane in his pocket. The boy openly states that he wants revenge and identifies his father's killer as "America."

But the main issue is not whether AQAP recruits more terrorists because of drone strikes. AQAP's power and influence has never been based on the number of members in its ranks. AQAP recruits and retains power through its ideology, which relies in large part on the Yemeni people believing that America is at war with them.

Another argument I frequently hear is that drones are more effective than ground forces. But the Yemeni government has not made a serious effort to use ground forces against AQAP in my country. For example, the Counter Terrorism Unit of the Central Security Forces, which was funded and trained by the United States, did not even engage in the fight against AQAP when AQAP controlled the main cities of Abyan for more than a year until mid-2012. On the roads surrounding Abyan, AQAP was fought by poorly equipped, underage soldiers. In fact, I have never seen such a poorly armed and shabby looking army as the one I saw in Abyan. It is well known that the Yemeni Army has more military equipment and better-trained soldiers around other governorates in the south, where AQAP does not have a strong presence.

Air Strikes Complicate Internal Yemeni Dynamics

Whether targeted killings strikes are carried out by U.S. forces or Yemeni forces at the United States' request often makes little difference, especially when strikes kill innocent civilians. Yemenis already have a strained relationship with their own armed forces because of the internal conflicts in our country. (Even though I just turned 23, I have lived through nine wars in my life: six in Sada, one in the southern provinces in 1994, the recent conflict in Abyan, and the 2011 conflict in Sana'a. The U.S.

targeted killing program is the 10th war I have lived through.) The fact that innocent civilians are dying and the Yemeni army is receiving so much support from the United States strains that relationship even more.

All of this is happening at a critical moment in Yemen, which is being governed by a transitional president after our president of 33 years, Ali Abdullah Saleh, was forced from office during a popular uprising. The transitional phase seeks to maintain national cohesion and unity, but anger and distrust linger underneath the surface, creating ideal conditions for AQAP to grow and undermine progress. AQAP exploited similar divisions in 2011 at the start of the popular uprising. As the central government sought to squelch peaceful protests in Sana'a, the Abyan province fell into the hands of AQAP.

To be clear, the United States is not the only foreign country trying to influence events on the ground in Yemen. The Houthis, a group that is supported by Iran, have been reportedly working to make Yemen's president look like a U.S. puppet, in order to undermine his administration and hinder a peaceful transition. Yemen's transitional president, Abdu Rabu Mansour Hadi, has publicly endorsed U.S. drone strikes, which are widely despised by the Yemeni people. That endorsement was a gift for all the opposition groups wanting to discredit Hadi, whether those groups are aligned with Iran or even AQAP. As President Hadi declared his support for U.S. drone strikes, the Houthis gained credibility in the eyes of thousands of Yemenis.

In another, perverse sense, targeted killings further the goals of AQAP. What AQAP fighters ultimately demand, according to their ideology and distortion of Islam, is heaven and martyrdom. In their minds, when they are targeted and killed by a drone strike, that's exactly what they receive. Instead of effectively combating AQAP's ideology through a comprehensive approach that includes economic and social development, as well as ideological tactics, air strikes amount to a military-only solution.

The drone strikes are the face of America to many Yemenis. If America is providing economic, social and humanitarian assistance to Yemen, the vast majority of the Yemeni people know nothing about it. Everyone in Yemen, however, knows about America and its drones. Again, this allows AQAP to convince more individuals that America is at war with Yemen.

Drone strikes also distract Yemenis from AQAP, which is the real enemy. They focus all the attention on the sky to the neglect of everything else. Because of drone strikes, ordinary Yeminis who are not affiliated with AQAP live in fear of being targeted. This fear permeates our country and it is shared by the youngest and oldest Yeminis. A middle age man from Rada'a, in central Yemen, said in an interview recently: "In the past, mothers used to tell their kids to go to bed or I will call your father. Now, they say, 'Go to bed or I will call the planes.'"

The U.S. War Against AQAP Is a War of Mistakes

If it's not already clear from my testimony today, let me say this very plainly: I hate AQAP. I don't support their ideology. I don't like the way they have distorted my religion. And I despise their methods. The fight against AQAP, however, is not a traditional war. And I fear that these air strikes undermine the United States' effort to defeat AQAP and win the hearts and minds of the Yemeni people. You can't win this war by simply killing more people on the other side. Rather, I see the war against AQAP as a war of mistakes. The fewer mistakes you make, the more likely you are to win. Simply put, with drone strikes, the United States has made more mistakes than AQAP.

To be clear, I am not only referring to the mistake of killing innocent civilians. Of course, the death of an innocent civilian is the most tragic mistake of all. Nevertheless, even when no civilians are harmed, the United States makes a huge mistake when missiles fail to reach their intended target. Drone strikes that miss their targets make these terrorists look brave. They become role models, simply by evading weapons being launched by the greatest military power on earth. Perhaps the greatest source of satire, ridicule, and propaganda against the United States and Yemeni governments occurs when they claim to have killed ranking terrorists, like Saeed Al-Shahri or Nader Al-Shadadi, only to be proven wrong days later.

The United States and Yemeni government could make it harder for terrorists to get the critical support they need and also prevent more civilians from dying by announcing the AQAP members on their lists. I know this would have helped in my village. As a tribal leader from Rada'a, Soliman Al-homikani, told me last month in Sana'a, "[i]f I knew that this person was AQAP, I would never have let him get into my house or even to the area. But since I have no idea who is Qaeda and who is not, I let them in my house, as some have done, and they get targeted: militants and uninformed citizens."

Another lesson is worth mentioning here: AQAP paid the owner of the house in Ja'ar 38,000 Saudi riyals as compensation for causing damage to her house after the air strike. As far as I know, the U.S. government has never paid any sort of compensation to civilian victims in my country and the Yemeni government has paid next to nothing. Here, again, AQAP scores points in the propaganda war while the United States and Yemen do not.

Conclusion and Recommendations

I don't know if there is anyone on Earth who feels more thankful to America than me. In my heart I know that I can only repay the opportunities, friendship, warmth, and exposure your country provided me by being their ambassador to Yemenis for the rest of my life, just as I was an ambassador for Yemenis in America. I strongly believe that I have helped improve America's image, perhaps in ways that an official ambassador or other diplomat cannot. I have access to ordinary Yemenis. For me, helping the people of my country understand and know the America that I have experienced is a passion and not a career.

I have to say that the drone strikes and the targeted killing program have made my passion and mission in support of America almost impossible in Yemen. In some areas of Yemen, the anger against America that results from the strikes makes it dangerous for me to even acknowledge having visited America, much less testify how much my life changed thanks to the State Department scholarships. It's sometimes too dangerous to even admit that I have American friends.

Late last year, I was with an American colleague from an international media outlet on a tour of Abyan. Suddenly, locals started to become paranoid. They were moving erratically and frantically pointing toward the sky. Based on their past experiences with drone strikes, they told us that the thing hovering above us—out of sight and making a strange humming noise—was an American drone. My heart sank. I was helpless. It was the first time that I had earnestly feared for my life, or for an American friend's life in Yemen. I was standing there at the mercy of a drone.

I also couldn't help but think that the operator of this drone just might be my American friend with whom I had the warmest and deepest friendship in America. My mind was racing and my heart was torn. I was torn between the great country that I know and love and the drone above my head that could not differentiate between me and some AQAP militant. It was one of the most divisive and difficult feelings I have ever encountered.

That feeling, multiplied by the highest number mathematicians have, gripped me when my village was droned just days ago. It is the worst feeling I have ever had. I was devastated for days because I knew that the bombing in my village by the United States would empower militants. Even worse, I know it will make people like Al-Radmi look like a hero, while I look like someone who has betrayed his country by supporting America.

As someone who has lived and worked on this issue very closely, I cannot help but feel that the American and Yemen governments are losing the war against AQAP. Even when drone strikes target and kill the right people, it is at the expense of creating the many strategic problems I have discussed today. Every tactical success is at the expense of creating more strategic problems. I do, however, believe that things can still be fixed. If the United States wants to win the battle against AQAP in Yemen, I strongly suggest that it consider taking the following steps:

- Stop all the targeted killing strikes.

- Announce the names of those already on the "kill list," so that innocent civilians can stay out of harm's way.

- Issue an official apology to the families of all civilians killed or injured by targeted killing strikes.

- Compensate the families of innocent civilians killed or injured by strikes conducted or authorized by the United States.

- In every village where there has been a targeted killing, build a school or hospital so that the villagers' only experience with America will not be the death and destruction caused by an American missile.

Thank you very much.

*Farea Al-Muslimi is a Yemeni activist and journalist.

U.S. Congress. Senate Subcommittee on the Constitution, Civil Rights, and Human Rights of the Senate Committee of the Judiciary. *Drone Wars: The Constitutional and Counterterrorism Implications of Targeted Killing. Statement of Farea Al-Muslimi.* 113th Cong. Sess. 1. April 23, 2013. http://www.lawfareblog.com/wp-content/uploads/2013/04/04-23-13Al-MuslimiTestimony.pdf.

How Drones Help Al Qaeda

by Ibrahim Mothana*

"Dear Obama, when a U.S. drone missile kills a child in Yemen, the father will go to war with you, guaranteed. Nothing to do with Al Qaeda," a Yemeni lawyer warned on Twitter last month. President Obama should keep this message in mind before ordering more drone strikes like Wednesday's, which local officials say killed 27 people, or the May 15 strike that killed at least eight Yemeni civilians.

Drone strikes are causing more and more Yemenis to hate America and join radical militants; they are not driven by ideology but rather by a sense of revenge and despair. Robert Grenier, the former head of the C.I.A.'s counterterrorism center, has warned that the American drone program in Yemen risks turning the country into a safe haven for Al Qaeda like the tribal areas of Pakistan—"the Arabian equivalent of Waziristan."

Anti-Americanism is far less prevalent in Yemen than in Pakistan. But rather than winning the hearts and minds of Yemeni civilians, America is alienating them by killing their relatives and friends. Indeed, the drone program is leading to the Talibanization of vast tribal areas and the radicalization of people who could otherwise be America's allies in the fight against terrorism in Yemen.

The first known drone strike in Yemen to be authorized by Mr. Obama, in late 2009, left 14 women and 21 children dead in the southern town of al-Majala, according to a parliamentary report. Only one of the dozens killed was identified as having strong Qaeda connections.

Misleading intelligence has also led to disastrous strikes with major political and economic consequences. An American drone strike in May 2010 killed Jabir al-Shabwani, a prominent sheik and the deputy governor of Marib Province. The strike had dire repercussions for Yemen's economy. The slain sheik's tribe attacked the country's main pipeline in revenge. With 70 percent of the country's budget dependent on oil exports, Yemen lost over $1 billion. This strike also erased years of progress and trust-building with tribes who considered it a betrayal given their role in fighting Al Qaeda in their areas.

Yemeni tribes are generally quite pragmatic and are by no means a default option for radical religious groups seeking a safe haven. However, the increasing civilian toll of drone strikes is turning the apathy of tribal factions into anger.

The strikes have created an opportunity for terrorist groups like Al Qaeda in the Arabian Peninsula and Ansar al-Sharia to recruit fighters from tribes who have suffered casualties, especially in Yemen's south, where mounting grievances since the 1994 civil war have driven a strong secessionist movement.

Unlike Al Qaeda in Iraq, A.Q.A.P. has worked on gaining the support of local communities by compromising on some of their strict religious laws and offering basic services, electricity and gas to villagers in the areas they control. Furthermore, Iran has seized this chance to gain more influence among the disgruntled population in Yemen's south.

And the situation is quite likely to get worse now that Washington has broadened its rules of engagement to allow so-called signature strikes, when surveillance data suggest a terrorist leader may be nearby but the identities of all others targeted is not known. Such loose rules risk redefining "militants" as any military-age males seen in a strike zone.

Certainly, there may be short-term military gains from killing militant leaders in these strikes, but they are minuscule compared with the long-term damage the drone program is causing. A new generation of leaders is spontaneously emerging in furious retaliation to attacks on their territories and tribes.

This is why A.Q.A.P. is much stronger in Yemen today than it was a few years ago. In 2009, A.Q.A.P. had only a few hundred members and controlled no territory; today it has, along with Ansar al-Sharia, at least 1,000 members and controls substantial amounts of territory.

Yemenis are the ones who suffer the most from the presence of Al Qaeda, and getting rid of this plague is a priority for the majority of Yemen's population. But there is no shortcut in dealing with it. Overlooking the real drivers of extremism and focusing solely on tackling their security symptoms with brutal force will make the situation worse.

Only a long-term approach based on building relations with local communities, dealing with the economic and social drivers of extremism, and cooperating with tribes and Yemen's army will eradicate the threat of Islamic radicalism.

Unfortunately, liberal voices in the United States are largely ignoring, if not condoning, civilian deaths and extrajudicial killings in Yemen—including the assassination of three American citizens in September 2011, including a 16-year-old. During George W. Bush's presidency, the rage would have been tremendous. But today there is little outcry, even though what is happening is in many ways an escalation of Mr. Bush's policies.

Defenders of human rights must speak out. America's counterterrorism policy here is not only making Yemen less safe by strengthening support for A.Q.A.P., but it could also ultimately endanger the United States and the entire world.

*Ibrahim Mothana, a writer and activist, was a cofounder of the Watan Party in Yemen. He died in 2013.

Mothana, Ibrahim. "How Drones Help Al Qaeda." *New York Times,* op-ed, June 13, 2012. http://www.nytimes.com/2012/06/14/opinion/how-drones-help-al-qaeda.html?_r=1&.

The United States' Bloody Messes in Yemen

by Hooria Mashhour*

December 12 was supposed to be a day of celebration for the al-Ameri family. A young bride traveled to her wedding with her relatives in Bayda province, Yemen. But in a few dark seconds their celebrations were eviscerated. A U.S. drone fired at the wedding procession, destroying five vehicles and most of their occupants. Not even the bride's car, ornately decorated in flowers for the occasion, was spared from the carnage. Senior Yemeni officials later admitted that the strike was a "mistake."

Some mistake: Though the bride survived, the strike is said to have killed at least 14 civilians and injured 22 others, over a third of them seriously. This marks the largest death toll by a drone strike in Yemen since the drone war's inception. It is also the largest death toll by U.S. strike since December 2009, when a U.S. cruise missile killed 41 civilians in al-Majala, including 14 women and 21 children.

In the wake of the killing, a wave of outrage has swept the country. The Yemeni government rushed to meet community elders, seeking to negotiate a quiet settlement for the killing of the bride's loved ones. But the bereaved villagers rejected the overtures and instead demanded that Yemen's president, Abed Rabbo Mansour Hadi, stop U.S. drones before they would sit at any negotiating table.

On its side, rather than forthrightly address its role in these grim events, the U.S. government has issued no admission of responsibility, nor any apology. It has left the Yemeni government to clean up another bloody mess.

Only recently, we had cause to hope for better. In November, Yemeni civil engineer Faisal bin Ali Jaber traveled over 7,000 miles to the U.S. in search of answers. He met congressmen, senators, and even some White House officials to tell them how U.S. missiles incinerated his nephew and brother-in-law at his son's wedding last year. In that strike, the U.S. killed two potential allies—one an imam who regularly preached against al-Qaeda; the other one of the town's few policemen. Jaber received heartfelt condolences from many lawmakers. Yet no official was prepared to explain why his relatives were killed, or why the U.S. administration would not acknowledge its mistake.

This is not the first time a U.S. drone has killed civilians in Bayda. On Sept. 2, 2012, a U.S. plane hit a village shuttle near Radda. The vehicle was full of villagers carrying their day's shopping. As usual, the initial press coverage labelled the dead as "al-Qaeda militants," but when the relatives threatened to deliver the bodies to the president's gates, the Yemeni government was forced to concede that all 12 of those people killed were civilians. Among the victims, a pregnant woman and three children were laid to rest.

The use of drones in Yemen might appear a simple, quick-fix option for President Obama. But as Nabeel Khoury, former U.S. deputy chief of mission to Yemen, recently wrote, "Drone strikes take out a few bad guys to be sure, but they also kill a large number of innocent civilians. Given Yemen's tribal structure, the U.S. generates roughly forty to sixty new enemies for every AQAP [al-Qaeda in the Arabian Peninsula] operative killed by drones."

Let me be clear: I, like the vast majority of my countrymen, reject terrorism. All of us were repulsed by recent footage of a gruesome attack on a Yemeni defense ministry hospital. We agree that our fight against extremist groups cannot be won without a variety of efforts, including robust law enforcement. But more often than not, U.S. drone strikes leave families bereaved and villages terrified. Drones tear at the fabric of Yemeni society. Wronged and angry men are just the sort extreme groups like AQAP find easiest to recruit.

Our president may reassure the United States of his support for drone strikes but the reality is that no leader can legitimately approve the extrajudicial killing of his own citizens. Moreover, he does so in the face of Yemeni consensus. This August, Yemen's National Dialogue Conference—which President Obama has praised—decided by a 90 percent majority that the use of drones in Yemen should be criminalised.

Yemeni legislators are aware that the drone war is deeply unpopular. Since the Dec. 12 strike, our parliament has unanimously voted to ban drone flights in Yemeni airspace, declaring them a "grave breach" of the country's sovereignty. For a country so often divided, this unanimity from Yemen's most representative bodies testifies to the strength of opinion against drones. But their calls have thus far met only with more bombings from the skies. How can the people of Yemen build trust in their fledgling democracy when our collective will is ignored by democracy's greatest exponent?

*Hooria Mashhour is Yemen's minister for human rights.

Mashhour, Hooria. "The United States' Bloody Messes in Yemen." *Washington Post*, opinion piece, January 14, 2014. http://www.washingtonpost.com/opinions/hooria-mashhour-the-united-states-bloody-messes-in-yemen/2014/01/14/c21dfcec-7653-11e3-b1c5-739e63e9c9a7_story.html.

My Drone War

by Pir Zubair Shah*

"We don't even sit together to chat anymore," the Taliban fighter told me, his voice hoarse as he combed his beard with his fingers. We were talking in a safe house in Peshawar as the fighter and one of his comrades sketched a picture of life on the run in the borderlands of Waziristan. The deadly American drones buzzing overhead, the two men said, had changed everything for al Qaeda and its local allies.

The whitewashed two-story villa bristled with activity. Down the hall from my Taliban sources sat an aggrieved tribal elder and his son in one room and two officers from Pakistan's powerful Inter-Services Intelligence (ISI) Directorate in another. I had gathered them all there to make sense of what had become the signature incident of the war in Afghanistan and Pakistan: an American drone strike, one of the first ordered on the watch of the new U.S. president, Barack Obama. The early 2009 strike had killed a local elder, along with his son, two nephews, and a guest in the South Waziristan town of Wana. Several sources had told me the family was innocent, with no connections to the Taliban or al Qaeda. But traveling to Waziristan had become too dangerous even for me, a reporter who had grown up there. So instead I had brought Waziristan to Peshawar, renting rooms for my sources in the guesthouse. I had just one night to try to figure out what had happened.

I spent the night running from room to room, assembling the story in pieces. On the first floor sat the dead elder's brother and nephew, who told me what little they knew of the incident. On the second floor, the ISI officers, over whiskey and lamb tikka, described their work helping U.S. intelligence agents sort out targets from among the images relayed back from the drones. Then there were the two Taliban fighters, whom I had first met in Waziristan in 2007. One had been a fixer for the Haqqani network, skilled at smuggling men and materiel from Pakistan into Afghanistan. The other drew a government salary as an employee of Pakistan's agriculture department but worked across the border as an explosives expert; he had lost a finger fighting the allied forces in Afghanistan. None of the men in the house knew the others were there.

The two fighters described how the militants were adapting to this new kind of warfare. The Taliban and al Qaeda had stopped using electronic devices, they told me. They would no longer gather in huge numbers, even in mosques to pray, and spent their nights outside for safety, a life that was wearing thin. "We can't sleep in the jungle the whole of our lives," one told me. Gradually, a picture of a rare incident came into focus: a deadly strike that had mistakenly taken out a man with no connection to al Qaeda or the Taliban.

This is how it has gone with the drone war, a beat I have covered for six years, first for *Newsday* and then the *New York Times*. By the time I left Pakistan in the summer of 2010, the job had become nearly impossible, though it had always been a dauntingly difficult story to tell. The drone campaign is one of the U.S. government's most secret programs. Although the most authoritative study on the subject, by the New America Foundation last year, calculated that 283 drone strikes had occurred in the Afghanistan-Pakistan border region since 2004, Obama never even publicly acknowledged them until this past January. Making matters still more difficult, the targets are in one of the world's most inaccessible areas, one that has traditionally been out of bounds for outsiders and where the state of Pakistan has nominal or no governing authority. It is an environment in which accurate reporting is an often unattainable goal, where confusion, controversies, and myths proliferate.

Although the drone campaign has become the linchpin of the Obama administration's counterterrorism strategy in Central Asia—and one it is increasingly exporting to places such as Yemen and the Horn of Africa—we know virtually nothing about it. I spent more than half a decade tracking this most secret of wars across northern Pakistan, taking late-night calls from intelligence agents, sorting through missile fragments at attack sites, counting bodies and graves, interviewing militants and victims. I dodged bullets and, once, an improvised explosive device. At various times I found myself imprisoned by the Taliban and detained by the Pakistani military. Yet even I can say very little for certain about what has happened.

The evening of June 18, 2004, was a sweltering one in South Waziristan, and the 27-year-old local Taliban leader, Nek Muhammad Wazir, had decided to eat dinner in the courtyard of his house in the village of Kari Kot, along with his two brothers and two bodyguards. Muhammad's satellite phone rang, and he picked it up. Moments later, a missile streaked through the compound and exploded, killing all five men.

At the time, no one in the Pakistani public or media knew that it was a drone. The government would say nothing, and everyone else attributed Muhammad's killing either to a Pakistani military operation—after all, soldiers had gone looking for him without success on six occasions—or to the work of U.S. forces across the border in Afghanistan. A Taliban fighter who was within earshot of the explosion told me later that the militants were totally taken by surprise. "There was a noise in the air before, and then we heard the explosion," he recalled. The villagers, however, supplied the explanation: They collected the fragments of the missile, on which was printed in black, "Made in USA."

Then, in late 2005, a similarly mysterious explosion killed Abu Hamza Rabia, a high-ranking Egyptian member of al Qaeda, outside North Waziristan's capital city, Miram Shah. President Pervez Musharraf refused to explain what had happened, saying only that he was "200 percent" sure Rabia was dead. But a local reporter named Hayatullah Khan, who lived in the next village over from where Rabia was killed, had gone to the site to sift through the rubble. Amid the debris were pieces of a Hellfire missile. He took pictures, which swiftly appeared in newspapers around the world.

The photographs directly contradicted the statements of Musharraf's government, which had variously claimed that Pakistani forces killed Rabia or that the militants blew themselves up by accident. The following month, Khan was abducted by gunmen. His body was found six months later near the Afghan border with handcuffs on his wrists; he had been shot in the back, apparently while trying to escape. When I visited his family in North Waziristan a year later, Khan's brother told me he blamed the ISI.

In January 2006, shortly after Khan's disappearance, I got an early-morning phone call at my home in Islamabad from a colleague at *Newsday*, where I was then working as a fixer and bureau manager. There had been another drone strike in the

Bajaur tribal area, he told me; could I go investigate? I picked up a friend who worked for the BBC and drove north to Bajaur to see my first drone strike. It would be the first newspaper story to appear under my own byline—and my first experience covering the drone war.

As we drove into Damadola, a farming village sprawled across a wide valley, I spotted the bodies of a cow and a calf, splayed out underneath a tree with their eyes wide open. Nearby were the fresh ruins of three houses.

The drone's presumed target had been Osama bin Laden's deputy, Ayman al-Zawahiri, who had been rumored to be in the area. I arrived on the scene ahead of most other reporters, and the families of the victims took me to see their newly dug graves. "All those killed, including women and children, are from this village," a villager told me as he showed me the burial site. "There were no foreigners here." Then I noticed something odd: Although I counted 13 graves, the locals would only tell me the names of seven women and children who had been killed. When it came to the men, they were silent. Later, a Pakistani official told me foreigners had indeed been present, including Zawahiri, though he had left some time before the missile hit. Drones were not yet common, but the fugitive al Qaeda No. 2 had long since become accustomed to moving quickly from place to place.

It was in September 2006 that I heard a drone for the first time, flying over the mud-walled village of Ali Khel, a couple of miles west of Miram Shah. It was a hot summer night, too hot in the house of the building-contractor friend with whom I was staying, so I had gone out to sleep in the open along with several laborers who worked for him. The men were telling me about their travels in Afghanistan, how they would cross the border to fight for the Taliban and then return after a week or two to North Waziristan to work and make some money. Then I heard the buzzing, far above our heads—like a bee, but heavier and unceasing, drifting in and out of earshot. The laborers said nothing.

On the other side of the Tochi River, in the village of Khatai, lived a famous Taliban commander whom the Pakistani military had once tried to kill. The operation had been a debacle; the military lost at least two senior officers, and hundreds of soldiers found themselves besieged not only by Taliban fighters but by the local villagers. But the small, lethal machine flying far overhead had accomplished what the Pakistani soldiers could not. "Nowadays he doesn't live here all the time," my host that night said as he pointed toward the commander's nearby compound. "There are drones in the air now."

Taliban fighters speaking a Waziri dialect of Pashto call the drones bhungana—"the one that produces a bee-like sound." Their local adversaries call them ababeel—the name of a bird mentioned in the Quran, sent by God to defend the holy city of Mecca from an invading army by hurling small stones from its mouth. Over the several days I spent in Ali Khel I became accustomed to their sound. It was there all the time. During the day it was mostly absorbed into the hum of daily life, but in the calm of the night the buzzing was all you heard.

This kind of reporting trip, risky as it was, had become increasingly necessary, given the cagey and outright confusing response by the Pakistani government to the escalating air war over its territory. When news of the early attacks got out, officials were evasive, suggesting that the militants had been killed while making explosives in their compounds. Then, after a drone strike took out a madrasa in the Bajaur tribal area in October 2006, killing more than 80 people, the government claimed that Pakistani bombers had done the job. Militants responded that

November with a suicide bombing of a military barracks in the Dargai area of Malakand district, killing 42 soldiers and wounding dozens more.

The government learned its lesson, retreating back into ambiguity. From that moment on, only the residents of the areas targeted by the drones would have a clear understanding of what was happening—but those areas were mostly beyond the reach of the media.

If the conduct of the drone war is mysterious, the terrain over which it is fought is not, at least to me—I have known it all my life. I was born in South Waziristan, to parents from two different Pashtun tribes, in a town that had been famous in the British colonial era for its gun and knife factories. My ancestors had come from Afghanistan as preachers, and I had taken my first steps as a child in the Afghan city of Khost, just across the border, where my maternal grandfather lived.

After graduating from university in Islamabad in 2001, I had returned to the tribal regions to prepare for my civil service exam. As unthinkable as it seems now, it was then the most peaceful, tranquil place I knew, and I spent my evenings in Bajaur studying with a college professor in preparation for a career in Pakistan's foreign service. During the days I would travel with my uncle, a government irrigation engineer, to villages in the area, meeting the residents and elders.

As the media poured into Afghanistan and Pakistan after the 9/11 attacks, someone with my background and English-language skills was suddenly very much in demand, and I got my first job in *Newsday*'s Islamabad bureau. On my trips back to Waziristan, I saw the landscape of my childhood transforming into a war zone. By 2004, people I had known there in my youth were on all sides of the region's worsening conflict, in the Taliban and al Qaeda, as well as the Pakistani military and intelligence services.

As the Pakistani military operations started to expand from one tribal area to the next, reporting on the ground went from difficult to impossible. I found myself working more and more over the phone, canvassing the contacts I had made during my travels in the region. When it came to the drone attacks, some of my sources would have access to the site of the strike and would tell me what really happened. I soon learned that the official version of the story was usually the least reliable. The military often had the same access problem I did and was itself relying on secondary sources.

The Taliban started adapting, too. The militants had come to realize that the increasingly effective drone strikes made them look weak, and they began getting rid of the evidence as fast as they could. After every attack they would cordon off the area and remove the bodies of the dead, making it difficult to verify who and how many people had been killed. Going to the site of a drone attack became a futile exercise; only a very few local reporters known for their deference to the Taliban were given any meaningful access.

I made my last visit to Waziristan in June 2007. By then, people there knew I worked for an American newspaper; fearing for my safety, my family discouraged me from going. The military was turning away representatives of foreign news organizations, and the Taliban had grown increasingly paranoid—a fact I learned the hard way a year later.

It was a hot, sunny day in July 2008, and I had set out from Peshawar with a photographer to report on the Taliban in the Mohmand tribal area, where the group had taken over a series of marble quarries. After meeting up with a local guide, we arrived in the village of Ziarat and headed toward the local Taliban checkpoint. We had dressed in the traditional salwar kameez and had worn hats in an effort to blend in. My photographer was from Karachi, though, and I worried that his presence would mark us as outsiders. I asked him to stay near the car while I ventured out to the checkpoint, where I interviewed a contractor working in the mines. As I was about to finish my interview, I saw my photographer approaching, so I wrapped up the conversation and hustled him back to the car. But it was too late. A bearded man shouted at us—he had seen the photographer's camera bag.

We were escorted away from the main road in our car, a Talib riding alongside us with a rifle. The Taliban held us in a prison in the base of a mountain, guarded by young volunteers from a nearby village. When we arrived, all our belongings, including our cell phones and money, were confiscated. But we were treated well—better, at any rate, than the prisoners we saw chained up in the neighboring rooms.

In the evening two Taliban came to our room. "Who is the Waziristani?" one of them asked. I said it was me, and I followed them into a half-destroyed room elsewhere in the compound. "Tell us who really you are," one of them said. They looked through the contacts in my cell phone, demanding to know why they included the commander of the Frontier Corps, the regional U.S.-trained paramilitary force the Taliban were fighting. The questioning went on for three days. I told them I was a reporter. My Waziristan connections were of some help, but they posed a risk too: I knew the local Taliban had recently attacked my family's village in the nearby district of Tank, killing more than a dozen of my relatives. I didn't want them to know that I knew.

Finally, Abdul Wali, the local Taliban leader, arrived and, satisfied that we were who we said we were, ordered our release. They had to be vigilant, he told us. "People come here under the guise of journalists and photographers, and they either take pictures of our locations and pass them on to the authorities or drop a SIM [card] to facilitate a drone strike," he said. "You never know who is a reporter and who is a spy."

Among Waziristan's residents, "I will drone you" has by now entered the vocabulary of day-to-day conversation as a morbid joke. The mysterious machines buzzing far overhead have become part of the local folklore. "I am looking for you like a drone, my love," goes a romantic Pashto verse I've often heard the locals recite. "You have become Osama; no one knows your whereabouts."

But it was only when WikiLeaks released its cache of U.S. State Department cables beginning in late 2010 that Pakistanis learned just how complicit their government has been in the drone campaign. A February 2008 cable from the embassy in Islamabad reported that Pakistan's Army chief, Gen. Ashfaq Parvez Kayani, met with the U.S. Centcom commander, Adm. William Fallon, and asked the U.S. military for "continuous Predator coverage of the conflict area" in South Waziristan, where the Pakistani Army was fighting the militants at the time. "Kayani knows full well that the strikes have been precise (creating few civilian casualties) and targeted primarily at foreign fighters" in Waziristan, asserted a February 2009 cable signed by Anne Patterson, then the U.S. ambassador.

In an August 2008 meeting with Patterson, Prime Minister Yousuf Raza Gilani—the same man who, after Navy SEALs dropped into Pakistan to raid bin Laden's compound last year, warned that "Pakistan reserves the right to retaliate with full force"—gave Patterson his go-ahead for a drone campaign in Pakistan's tribal regions. "I don't care if they do it as long as they get the right people," he told her, according to a U.S. cable. "We'll protest in the National Assembly and then ignore it."

Eventually, the disclosures prompted a response: In March of last year, Pakistani Maj. Gen. Ghayur Mehmood, the commander in North Waziristan, appeared before reporters in Miram Shah and told them, "Myths and rumors about U.S. Predator strikes and the casualty figures are many, but it's a reality that many of those being killed in these strikes are hard-core elements, a sizable number of them foreigners. Yes, there are a few civilian casualties in such precision strikes, but a majority of those eliminated are terrorists, including foreign terrorist elements." It was an unusually candid public statement on the drone strikes from a high-ranking Pakistani official. Mehmood also provided something else that had until then been missing: official numbers. According to the government's figures, he said, 164 drone strikes had taken place since 2007, killing 964 terrorists: 793 locals and 171 foreigners. The dead included Arabs, Chechens, Filipinos, Moroccans, Tajiks, and Uzbeks. The figures also confirmed the dramatic escalation of the drone war. In 2007, the government said, a single drone strike had killed a single militant. In 2010, the strikes had killed 423.

Some such admission was probably inevitable; the revelations in the WikiLeaks cables and Pakistan's obvious inability to stop the attacks put the government in a position where it had to say something. Arguing that the drones were killing real terrorists was the best option available (though a military spokesman still tried to distance the Army from Mehmood's statements, saying they reflected only the general's opinion).

But it was also an acknowledgment of defeat: The secret war has become a lot less secret. At first, the tribal areas of Pakistan had seemed to present the perfect testing ground for a remote-controlled military strategy; it is a land set apart from its own country and mostly inaccessible to the international media and human rights groups, a place where violations of international law and civilian casualties go mostly uninvestigated. It is, in short, a black hole. But even as the Obama administration was increasingly embracing the drones as an alternative to the boots-on-the-ground military actions it inherited from its predecessor, its secret war was becoming as much a political liability as a precision weapon.

As the strikes have continued, they have given rise to a narrative that explains away the country's worsening radicalization and extremist violence as a product of the drones—a narrative that has served as a bargaining chip for Pakistani leaders in their dealings with the United States as they once again raise the price of Pakistan's cooperation in the war. (After a November 2011 incident in Mohmand district in which NATO forces mistakenly killed Pakistani soldiers, the first thing Pakistan demanded was the evacuation of the Shamsi air base in Baluchistan province, which had been used by the Americans for launching drones over the tribal areas; pictures of the emptied base immediately flashed across the Pakistani media.) In reality, the country's worsening anti-Americanism is driven more by the portrayal of the drones in the Pakistani media, which paints them as a scourge targeting innocent civilians, than by the drones themselves. Few Pakistanis have actually visited the tribal areas or even know much about them. Until the United States and Pakistan come clean about the program, though, it is an image that will persist, worsening the frictions within Pakistan's already divided society and between the United States and Pakistan.

That's too bad, because in reality Pakistanis are deeply torn about the drones. For every anti-American rant they inspire—the recent meteoric rise of Imran Khan, the cricketer turned politician, owes a great deal to his strong opposition to the drone strikes—there is also a recognition that these strikes from the sky have their purpose. At times, they have outright benefited the Pakistani state, as in the summer of 2009, when a drone attack killed Baitullah Mehsud, the leader of a militant alliance in Waziristan who was suspected of masterminding former Prime Minister Benazir Bhutto's 2007 assassination—Pakistan's Enemy No. 1, but a villain of less consequence to the United States.

Residents of the tribal areas are similarly conflicted. Many favor the drone strikes over the alternatives, such as military operations or less selective bombardments by Pakistani bombers and helicopter gunships. Better a few houses get vaporized than an entire village turned into refugees. Even the brother of the elder I brought to the Peshawar guesthouse said as much, allowing that "in our case, it might be faulty intelligence or mischief by someone" that had caused the strike that killed his brother. Regardless, he said, "I would always go for the drones."

Either way, they are now a fact of life in a secret war that is far from over. Once I called a source—a Taliban commander in one of the tribal areas. His brother picked up the phone and told me that the commander was asleep. It was noon, and I remarked that it was an odd time for a nap. "There are drones in the sky," the brother laughingly replied, "so he is not feeling well."

*Pir Zubair Shah is a Pakistani journalist. In 2009, he shared the Pulitzer Prize for international reporting.

Shah, Pir Zubair. "My Drone War." *Foreign Policy,* February 27, 2012. http://www.foreignpolicy.com/articles/2012/02/27/my_drone_war.

Republished with the permission of Foreign Policy; permission conveyed through Copyright Clearance Center, Inc.

Recommendations and Report of the Task Force on US Drone Policy
(excerpt)

by Stimson Center*

Innovation and Anxiety

Throughout human history, the ability to project force across significant distances has been a sought-after military capability, and innovations in the creation and use of long-distance weapons have at times enabled major social and political shifts.

Perhaps for this reason, significant innovations in long-distance weapons have frequently been greeted with decidedly mixed feelings. In the Middle Ages, for instance, feudal elites feared that the crossbow—which could be used even by minimally trained peasants, and was capable of shooting armor-piercing bolts—would upend the chivalric social order, rendering irrelevant knightly martial skills and suits of armor.[1] Depicted in medieval illuminated manuscripts as a weapon of demons, the crossbow was banned by Pope Urban in 1096. It proved too temptingly useful a weapon to ignore, however; by 1139, the Second Lateran Council of Pope Innocent II "prohibit[ed] under anathema that murderous art of crossbowmen and archers, which is hateful to God"—but only when "employed against

Christians and Catholics."[2] Eventually, crossbows were deemed acceptable for use in "just" wars.[3]

A few hundred years later, the advent of gunpowder weapons made both the crossbow and longbow obsolete. In 1453, Byzantine Constantinople fell to the heavy artillery of the Ottoman Sultan Mehmed II, stunning the Christian world. Although the West soon embraced gunpowder warfare, it was not without ambivalence: In *Henry VI, Part I*, Shakespeare's Hotspur recalls a courtier complaining of the "villainous salt-petre . . . digged/ Out of the bowels of the harmless Earth" to create "these vile guns." In 1605, Cervantes' Don Quixote denounced artillery as a "devilish invention," allowing "a base cowardly hand to take the life of the bravest gentleman," with bullets "coming nobody knows how or from whence."[4]

In our own era, the development of lethal unmanned aerial vehicles (UAVs) has generated similar consternation. Like the crossbow, the longbow, the cannon, the machine gun, the long-distance bomber and the cruise missile, UAVs—also referred to as "remotely piloted aircraft" (RPAs) or, more colloquially, as "drones"—are often viewed as a military "game-changer," offering soldiers and policymakers expanded tactical options against a broad array of targets.[5] And like other long-distance weapon innovations from times past, lethal UAVs have been both praised and vilified.

UAV Attributes and Uses

UAVs share some distinct attributes, which have made them attractive for military and counterterrorist operations:[6]

- *Persistence*: UAVs have the ability to loiter over a specific area for extended periods of time, allowing them to capture and collect more information[7] and allowing the user to observe, evaluate and act quickly.[8]

- *Precision*: In military applications, UAVs' sensor technology can provide for more precise information collection that facilitates more accurate targeting as well as battlefield and non-battlefield surveillance.

- *Operational Reach*: Because of longer flying times, UAVs can be used to project force from afar in environments that may otherwise be inaccessible or too dangerous for manned operations.

- *Force protection*: UAVs allow the user to have a military presence in areas that otherwise would be impossible politically, capacity/resource prohibitive, too dangerous to risk being shot down, or topographically inhospitable.

- *Stealth*: While today's UAVs can be readily detected by sophisticated air defense systems, most UAVs are relatively small, quiet and capable of being flown at high enough altitudes to avoid detection by the individuals being surveilled or targeted.

UAVs have substantial value for a wide range of military and intelligence tasks. On the battlefield, both weaponized and nonweaponized UAVs can protect and aid soldiers in a variety of ways. They can be used for reconnaissance purposes, for instance, and UAVs also have the potential to assist in the detection of chemical, biological, radiological and nuclear weapons, as well as ordinary explosives.[9] Weaponized UAVs can be used to provide close air support to soldiers engaged in combat.[10]

[...]

Military UAVs are also employed for disaster relief and humanitarian assistance purposes: Air Force UAVs provided vital imagery after the 2010 earthquake in Haiti[11] and the typhoon that devastated the Philippines in November 2013,[12] and Air National Guard UAVs assisted firefighters combatting wildfires in California in August 2013.[13]

Over the past decade, weaponized UAVs have also become a widely used tool for countering geographically diffuse terrorist networks. With their low profile and relative fuel efficiency— and without the constraints of pilot fatigue—a typical UAV can spend more "time on target" than manned aircraft, enabling better intelligence-gathering and greater targeting precision, and potentially reducing the risk of civilian casualties in missile strikes.[14] The use of UAVs also allows the United States to honor the preferences of partner nations that may be amenable to US missile strikes against targets in their territory, but unwilling to allow a sizeable US military presence on the ground. Better still, from a force protection perspective, lethal UAVs enable the United States to strike targets in dangerous and inaccessible areas with no short-term risk to US personnel.

Unmanned aerial vehicles have been used extensively in Afghanistan and Iraq, for intelligence, surveillance and recon-naissance (ISR) purposes, to carry out strikes and to provide close air support to ground troops. They have also become a weapon of choice for counterterrorism strikes in regions where US troops are not engaged in ground combat. Between 2004 and 2014, US UAV strikes in Pakistan are estimated to have killed approximately 2,000 to 4,000 people, while US strikes in Yemen are estimated to have killed several hundred people.[15] A small number of UAV strikes are believed to have occurred in Somalia, and there are also unconfirmed reports of US UAV strikes in a handful of other countries, including Mali and the Philippines.

[...]

Task Force Conclusions

[...]

We believe that UAVs should be neither glorified nor demonized. It is important to take a realistic view of UAVs, recognizing both their continuities with more traditional military technologies and the new tactics and policies they enable.

In general, we believe that the political and media discourse on UAVs has been characterized by a number of significant misconceptions. [...]

Specifically, we note that most US military UAVs are not weaponized, and only a tiny fraction of US government UAV missions involve targeted UAV strikes outside of traditional, territorially defined battlefields such as those in Afghanistan, Iraq and Libya. Further, UAVs are not US "super-weapons": while their use has led to significant tactical successes, they are not "strategic" weapons, and they currently have substantial vulnerabilities as well as strengths. Contrary to popular belief, UAVs are not necessarily cheaper than manned aircraft, and the United States does not have a monopoly on UAV technologies or an ability to predict all potential countermeasures; indeed, there is reason to fear the rapid and uncontrolled proliferation of UAV technologies developed in other states, along with the rapid evolution of technologies designed to counter UAVs. Finally, we address the widespread but erroneous belief that UAV strikes are apt to cause disproportionate civilian casualties, together with the claim that UAVs "turn killing into a video game."

[We] note that while UAVs, as such, present few new moral or legal issues, the availability of lethal UAV technologies has enabled US policies that likely would not have been adopted in the absence of UAVs. In particular, UAVs have enabled the United States to engage in the cross-border use of lethal force against targeted individuals in an unprecedented and expanding way.

In our view, the expanding use of targeted killings outside of hot battlefields raises numerous concerns, some strategic and some legal and ethical.

[...]

Targeted Strikes Outside of Traditional Battlefields

The availability of weaponized UAVs almost surely has led US decision-makers to adopt counterterrorism tactics that probably would have been deemed too risky or politically unacceptable had UAVs not been an option.

Specifically, if lethal UAVs were not an option, we doubt that the United States would have engaged in nearly as many targeted strikes against suspected terrorists in places such as Pakistan and Yemen.[16] In such contexts, airstrikes using manned aircraft would generally be viewed as creating an unacceptably high risk of civilian casualties.[17] Raids involving US forces on the ground— including special operations forces—would create a similar risk of unintended civilian casualties, and would also create a risk of significant US casualties. Finally, the relative invisibility of UAVs enables relative deniability, often a convenience to host nations that are unwilling to appear to have welcomed a US military presence inside their territory.

The existence of weaponized UAVs did not "cause" the United States to engage in targeted killings of terror suspects outside of traditional territorially bounded battlefields, but it seems reasonable to conclude that their existence *enabled* a significantly expanded US campaign of targeted cross-border strikes against suspected terrorists.[18] [...]

[...]

Lethal UAVs, Targeted Strikes and Strategic Risk

Strategically, we are concerned that the administration's heavy reliance on targeted killings as a pillar of US counterterrorism strategy rests on questionable assumptions and risks increasing instability and escalating conflicts.

In certain circumstances, targeted strikes against particular individuals may have enormous strategic value. This is particularly likely to be true when the individuals in question possess and are likely to utilize unique knowledge and skills, whether those skills are technical or organizational in nature. At times, strikes against key terrorist operatives and agents might be critical to preventing an imminent attack; similarly, in some circumstances killing specified individuals may have a deterrent or demoralizing effect on other operatives or potential recruits.

But while tactical strikes may have helped keep the homeland free of major terrorist attacks, existing evidence indicates that both Sunni and Shia Islamic extremist groups have grown in scope, lethality and influence in the broader area of operations in the Middle East, Africa and South Asia. Prior to 9/11 such extremist groups operated in a generally confined geographic area near the Afghanistan/Pakistan border. Today, such groups operate from Nigeria to Mali, to Libya, to the Sinai, to Syria, to Iraq, to Pakistan, Afghanistan and beyond, and there is no indication that a US strategy to destroy al-Qaida has curbed the rise of Sunni Islamic extremism, deterred the establishment of Shia Islamic extremist groups or advanced long-term US security interests.

The use of targeted UAV strikes to gain tactical advantage has led to some successes in various geographic areas of operations, but evidence about the scope, number, and lethality of terrorist attacks worldwide suggest that al-Qaida elements still have a broad reach and, potentially, a decades-long lifespan. These weapons will be part of that struggle, but they will not defeat the broader strategic threat. In fact, evidence suggests that the broader strategic struggle against terrorist entities is not succeeding.[19]

Furthermore, US targeted strikes also create new strategic risks. These include:

Possible Erosion of the Norm of Sovereignty

The growing use of UAVs outside of hot battlefields may erode the norm of state sovereignty in ways ultimately harmful to US interests. While the US use of manned aircraft or special operations raids would also raise sovereignty concerns if used for cross-border targeted killings, the relative greater frequency of US UAV strikes[20] increases the odds that a foreign state or elements within it will consider its sovereignty to have been infringed upon.[21]

Currently, US UAV strikes in Pakistan and Yemen appear to have been carried out with the actual or tacit consent of those states' governments,[22] but that consent appears somewhat ambiguous. In the case of Pakistan, for instance, both parliament and the courts[23] have declared US UAV strikes unlawful violations of Pakistan sovereignty, a sentiment that has been echoed by some executive branch representatives,[24] even as other Pakistani executive branch officials continue to offer intermittent cooperation with US strikes. In the case of Yemen, many Yemenis feel that the president, Abd Rabbuh Mansur Hadi, who approved US UAV strikes, does not represent the views of the population.

The US government takes the view that it has a legal right to use force in the territories of foreign sovereign states when those states are "unwilling or unable" to take what the United States considers appropriate action to eliminate what it sees as imminent threats. But inevitably, assessments of what constitutes an imminent threat to the United States and what would constitute appropriate action are somewhat subjective in nature; the United States may view the use of force as justified even when US allies and partners do not. The US use of force in sovereign nations whose consent is questionable or nonexistent may encourage other states to follow suit with their own military platforms or even commercial entities.[25]

Blowback

Civilian casualties, even if relatively few, can anger whole communities, increase anti-US sentiment and become a potent recruiting tool for terrorist organizations.[26]

Even strikes that kill only terrorist operatives can cause great resentment, particularly in contexts in which terrorist recruiting efforts rely on tribal loyalties or on an economically desperate population.

Friends, family and fellow tribe members of those attacked or harmed in strikes may become hostile to the United States, and, over years, their hostility may cost the United States in terms of foreign cooperation, hostility to US travelers and foreign business and support for terrorism. UAV "hunter-killer" operations may also go against the larger counterterrorism and counterinsurgency strategy of attempting to gain support of local populations to deter them from supporting al-Qaida and associated forces.[27] Even where strikes kill only legitimate targets, the perceived insult to sovereignty—in places such as Pakistan and Yemen and among fellow tribe members of the dead—sparks bitterness, feelings of nationalism or other forms of identity politics violently hostile to US military operations or Americans.[28]

As retired Army Gen. Stanley McChrystal, former International Security Assistance Force (ISAF) commander in Afghanistan, has noted, "The resentment created by American use of unmanned strikes . . . is much greater than the average American appreciates. They are hated on a visceral level, even by people who've never seen one or seen the effects of one." The unmanned strikes, McChrystal says, create a "perception of American arrogance that says, 'Well we can fly where we want, we can shoot where we want, because we can.'"[29]

UAV strikes by the United States have also generated a backlash in countries not directly affected by the strikes, in part due to the perception that such strikes cause excessive civilian deaths, and in part due to concerns about sovereignty, transparency, accountability and other human rights and rule of law issues. (These are discussed more fully below.) In February 2014, for instance, the European Parliament voted 534-49 for a resolution condemning US drone strikes, asserting that "thousands of civilians have reportedly been killed or seriously injured by drone strikes [but] these figures are difficult to estimate, owing to lack of transparency and obstacles to effective investigation."[30] The resolution went on to call for EU member states to "oppose and ban the practice of extrajudicial targeted killings [and] ensure that the member states, in conformity with their legal obligations, do not perpetrate unlawful targeted killings or facilitate such killings by other states."[31]

National officials, parliamentarians and thought leaders in numerous allied countries and at the United Nations have questioned or condemned US targeted strikes.[32] While US officials may take the view that such criticisms are based on erroneous information or an incorrect reading of the applicable law, the fact remains that when allies and partners do not support US policies, we pay a price. The price may be direct—allies may be unwilling to share intelligence data crucial to targeting, for instance, for fear of incurring legal liability in their own courts or for fear of domestic political consequences—or it may be indirect—anger at US targeted strikes may translate into lower levels of cooperation with unrelated US diplomatic initiatives. Either way, the risk of international backlash against US strikes needs to be factored in as we evaluate the strategic value of targeted strikes.

Slippery Slope

The increasing use of lethal UAVs may create a slippery slope leading to continual or wider wars. The seemingly low-risk and low-cost missions enabled by UAV technologies may encourage the United States to fly such missions more often, pursuing targets with UAVs that would be deemed not worth pursuing if manned aircraft or special operations forces had to be put at risk. For similar reasons, however, adversarial states may be quicker to use force against American UAVs than against US manned aircraft or military personnel: shooting down an unmanned airframe may not carry the same implications, either in terms of other states' domestic politics or in terms of foreign relations, which might make other nations more willing to shoot down US UAVs, increasing the risk of tit-for-tat escalation.[33]

UAVs also create an escalation risk insofar as they may lower the bar to enter a conflict, without increasing the likelihood of a satisfactory outcome. For example, the terrorists that US UAVs tend to be used to hunt are often mostly motivated by localized conflicts occurring in states with fractured political orders. The use of UAVs to track and kill such individuals does not repair the political rifts that give rise to terrorist violence. If US targeted killing campaigns fail to eradicate all threats of extremism, this may create a perceived policy failure. This, in turn, may create domestic political pressures to continue or escalate the use of lethal force, leading US UAV hunter-killer missions to continue indefinitely.

The US use of lethal UAVs for targeted strikes outside of hot battlefields is likely to be imitated by other states as well. While the United States enjoys temporary dominance in its ability to deploy lethal UAVs effectively—which can be effective in part because of the United States' broader and more integrated ISR capabilities—other states are catching up, and may soon find themselves tempted to deploy lethal UAVs in similar fashion. Such potential future increase in the use of lethal UAV strikes by foreign states may cause or increase instability, and may increase further the risk of widening conflicts in regions around the globe.

In recent years, US targeted strikes involving UAVs have gone from a relative rarity to a relatively common practice in Pakistan and Yemen. As the number of strikes increases, so too does the strategic risk.

To the best of our knowledge, however, the US executive branch has yet to engage in a systematic cost-benefit analysis of targeted UAV strikes as a routine counterterrorism tool.[34] There are numerous non-kinetic means of combatting terrorism; some of these—e.g., efforts to disrupt terrorist communications and finances—can easily be combined with targeted strikes, while others—e.g., efforts to build friendly relationships with local communities and inspire cooperation—may not be combined as easily.

A serious counterterrorism strategy needs to consider carefully, and reassess constantly, the balance between kinetic action and other counterterrorism tools, and the potential unintended consequences of increased reliance on lethal UAVs, including erosion of sovereignty norms, blowback and the possibility of prolonging or escalating conflict and instability.[35]

NOTES

(Notes have been renumbered.)

1. Nolan, Cathal J. The Age of Wars of Religion, 1000-1650: An Encyclopedia of Global Warfare and Civilization. Westport: Greenwood Press, 2006, 200. Accessed June 2, 2014. http://books.google.com/books?id=1h9zzSH-NmwC&lpg=PA200&ots=SJ8khQ7Mo7&dq=crossbow%20banned%20pope%20urban&pg=PA200#v=onepage&q=crossbow%20banned%20pope%20urban&f=false.

2. Eternal Word Television Network. "Second Lateran Council (1139)." Accessed June 2, 2014. http://www.ewtn.com/library/COUNCILS/LATERAN2.HTM.

3. Nolan, Cathal J. The Age of Wars of Religion, 1000-1650: An Encyclopedia of Global Warfare and Civilization. Westport: Greenwood Press, 2006, 200. Accessed June 2, 2014. http://books.google.com/books?id=1h9zzSH-NmwC&lpg=PA200&ots=SJ8khQ7Mo7&dq=crossbow%20banned%20pope%20urban&pg=PA200#v=onepage&q=crossbow%20banned%20pope%20urban&f=false.

4. Fuller, J.F.C. Armament & History: The Influence of Armament of History From the Dawn of Classical Warfare to the End of the Second World War. New York: First Da Capo Press, 1998, 91-92.

5. Whoever first brings a technological innovation to the battlefield often enjoys a step function advantage over its foes as long as it monopolizes that technology. This advantage boosts the confidence of the innovator and affects conduct on and off the battlefield for the length of the monopoly. Consider the dominant position of the United States in the four-year period that ran from 1945, when it used the atomic bomb against Japan, until 1949, when the Soviet Union successfully tested its own atomic weapon. During this period, American diplomacy benefited from its nuclear monopoly. Like all warfare innovations, however, the monopoly was short-lived. The technology proliferated and within a short time several countries were operating at a new, more lethal level. Recently, the United States has enjoyed a localized monopoly in UAVs in the uncontested theaters of Iraq and Afghanistan, and even across Southwest Asia outside of the combat zones. This monopoly has provided the United States a similar step function capability increase in terms of persistence and operational reach of force.

6. Needless to say, many of the same attributes that make UAVs valuable for military purposes also render them valuable in domestic law enforcement, counter-drug operations and border protection; UAVs also have numerous other civilian and commercial applications, ranging from crop inspection to wilderness search and rescue operations. See: Bennett, Brian. "FBI has been using drones since 2006, watchdog agency says." Los Angeles Times, September 26, 2013. Accessed June 3, 2014. http://www.latimes.com/nation/nationnow/la-na-nn-fbi-using-drones-2006-20130926-story.html.

7. Consider the "Gorgon Stare," a persistent wide area surveillance system utilized by the MQ-9 Reaper, provides video imaging of a large area of land, yet still providing useful on the ground detail (Gorgon Stare: Persistent Wide Area Airborne Surveillance (WAAS) System. Beavercreek, OH: Sierra Nevada Corporation. Accessed June 3, 2014. http://www.sncorp.com/pdfs/isr/gorgon_stare.pdf.) Furthermore, UAVs can

also focus on a smaller area for a long period of time, providing ISR for upwards of 24-hours. ISR data is often integrated with other surveillance technology, including satellites, U-2 and RC-135s. See: US Department of Defense. Intelligence Science Board. Office of the Under Secretary of Defense for Acquisition, Technology, and Logistics. Integrating Sensor-Collected Intelligence. By Defense Science Board and Intelligence Science Board Task Force. November 2008. Accessed June 2, 2014. http://www.fas.org/irp/agency/dod/dsb/sensors.pdf.

8. UAVs can significantly reduce the length of the command chain and shorten the kill chain (i.e., find, fix, track, target, engage) by improving the ability of the pilot to seek out the target and immediately fire—a process which for manned aviation takes two or more different aircraft and significant coordination. In general, UAV technologies have increased the ability of higher headquarters to make short-cycle decisions and impact the close-in fight literally by remote control. Simultaneously, lower echelon units now have greater access than ever to the same external information as higher headquarters and, aided by the use of locally controlled UAVs, are able to dominate greater battle space and better appreciate their own situation.

9. Johns Hopkins Applied Physics Laboratory. "APL Quick Response Created New Tool to Assess Nuclear Power Plant Crisis." News & Media. Last modified February 20, 2012. Accessed June 2, 2014. http://www.jhuapl.edu/newscenter/stories/st120220.asp.

10. In the past, warfighters on the ground under imminent threat would have to navigate a complicated command hierarchy to call for air support. The soldier on the ground would have to relay coordinates to a Forward Air Controller (FAC), who would then talk the pilot's eyes onto a target in an extremely hostile environment. These missions have always been very dangerous for the pilot, who has to fly low and avoid multiple threats, and also for people on the ground. It is a human-error rich environment, and even today, it is not uncommon for the wrong coordinates to be relayed, resulting in the deaths of friendlies or innocent civilians. To ease these difficulties, DARPA is currently investigating how to replace the FAC and the pilot by a weaponized UAV that will be commanded by the soldier on the ground with a smartphone. See: Defense Advanced Research Projects Agency (DARPA). "Persistent Close Air Support (PCAS)." Programs. Accessed June 2, 2014. http://www.darpa.mil/Our_Work/TTO/Programs/Persistent_Close_Air_Support_(PCAS).aspx.

11. Hodge, Nathan. "U.S. Diverts Spy Drone from Afghanistan to Haiti." Wired, January 15, 2010. Accessed June 2, 2014. http://www.wired.com/2010/01/pentagon-shares-earthquake-images-from-highflying-spy-drone/.

12. Everstine, Brian. "Drones Play Role in Disaster Response." Air Force Times, November 26, 2013. Accessed June 2, 2014. http://www.airforcetimes.com/article/20131126/NEWS/311260021/Drones-playrole-disaster-response.

13. Danigelis, Alyssa. "Predator Drone Joins Yosemite Wildfire Fight." Discovery News, August 29, 2013. Accessed June 2, 2014. http://news.discovery.com/earth/weather-extreme-events/predator-drone-joins-yosemite-wildfire-fight-130829.htm; UAVs also have enormous potential as a law enforcement tool. UAVs are already used by the US Drug Enforcement Agency and by US Customs and Border Patrol, but police and other state and local law enforcement officials may also find future uses for UAVs, including replacing snipers and chase cars, observing drug-dealing hot-spots and employment in hostage scenarios. See: Whitlock, Craig, and Craig Timberg. "Border-patrol drones being borrowed by other agencies more often than previously known." The Washington Post, January 14, 2014. Accessed June 3, 2014. http://www.washingtonpost.com/world/national-security/border-patrol-drones-being-borrowed-by-other-agencies-more-often-than-previouslyknown/2014/01/14/5f987af0-7d49-11e3-9556-4a4bf7bcbd84_story.html.

14. UAVs' internal surveillance systems provide accurate and precise imagery and video for targeting. Combined with long loitering time, the employment of UAVs allow pilots to fire on the target when they are certain both of the target and that non-combatants are not present—improving the assurance of proportionality and discrimination.

15. With little information provided by the administration regarding collateral damage, various organizations have attempted to collate information from a variety of different sources in order to provide estimates of the number of casualties from each drone strike, and the possible status of each victim — militant, leader, or civilian. Three organizations lead this effort: The Bureau of Investigative Journalism (BIJ), The New America Foundation (NAF) and The Long War Journal (LWJ). While the three datasets do not vary drastically in their estimates of the total number of deaths and civilian casualties, they do vary in their classifications of those deaths — including in terminology used and in number of strikes listed. The terminology used by each organization to identify those killed in the strikes varies from "civilian," "possible civilian," "militant," "alleged militant" or "unknown." For example BIJ

predominately uses the terms "alleged militants" to classify casualties when those killed are presumed to be affiliated with terrorist groups, whereas LWJ and NAF use "militant" without the qualifier. BIJ does not use the term militant directly because, [it] "do[es] not know who the majority of the dead are. However, field reports form journalists, government officials and militant sources often provide clear suggestions that they are allegedly militants." NAF uses the term militant "to describe all organized, named groups that bear arms and that are not part of Pakistani, Somali or Yemeni military, police, paramilitary or militia forces." NAF states that "if two or more news reports label the dead as 'militants,' while others call them 'people' or some other neutral term, we have labeled them as militants." They note the same two-source method for their classification of civilians as well. When the "majority of reports do not refer to the dead as 'civilians,' 'women' or 'children,' but one media outlet does," NAF then labels the casualties as "unknown." The LWJ, however, does not provide detailed information explaining its methodology of classifying those killed. See: Data Comparison of Casualties from Pakistan UAV Strikes in 2011. Washington DC: Stimson Center, October 2013. Accessed June 2, 2014. http://www.stimson.org/images/uploads/reporting_on_civilian_casualties_from_targeted_strikes_in_pakistan.pdf.

16. It is impossible to say this with complete certainty, of course. Perhaps US political decision-makers would have decided that the threat posed by al-Qaida and its associates was grave enough to justify the same number of targeted strikes carried out by manned aircraft or by special operations forces, even with the higher risk of casualties.

17. Lewis, Michael. "Drones: Actually the Most Humane Form of Warfare Ever." Atlantic, August 21, 2013. Accessed June 4, 2014. http://www.theatlantic.com/international/archive/2013/08/drones-actuallythe-most-humane-form-of-warfare-ever/278746/.

18. While the number of US drone strikes appears to have decreased in 2013, the use of drones in particular areas have seen sharp increases at particular intervals since 2004. See: The Long War Journal. "Charting the Data for US Airstrikes in Pakistan, 2004–2014." Last modified October 10, 2013. Accessed October 11, 2013. http://www.longwarjournal.org/pakistan-strikes.php.

19. Jordan, Jenna. Attacking the Leader, Missing the Mark: Why Terrorist Groups Survive Decapitation Strikes. International Security 38, no. 4 (Spring 2014): 7-38. Accessed June 4, 2014. http://muse.jhu.edu/

login?auth=0&type=summary&url=/journals/international_security/
v038/38.4.jordan.pdf.

20. "Of the estimated 465 non-battlefield targeted killings undertaken by
    the United States since November 2002, approximately 98 percent
    were carried out by drones." See: Kreps, Sarah. "The Foreign Pol-
    icy Essay: Preventing the Proliferation of Armed Drones." Lawfare
    Blog, April 13, 2014. Accessed June 2, 2014. http://www.lawfareblog
    .com/2014/04/the-foreign-policy-essay-preventing-the-proliferation-
    of-armed-drones/.

21. While non-lethal UAVs have come under less scrutiny than lethal
    UAVs, ISR UAVs could be used increasingly in non-permissive air-
    space, impinging on other country's sovereignty.

22. Somalia still has no national government capable of exercising control
    over all of Somalia's territory. According to reports, the African Union
    and Somali government only controls small portions of the country
    outside of Mogadishu, including of eastern Somalia and areas on the
    border of Ethiopia. Somaliland and Puntlab in the north have respec-
    tively declared independence or semi-autonomy, and major portions of
    the south remain in the hands of the Islamists. See: "Who are Somalia's
    al-Shabab?" BBC News, May 16, 2014. Accessed June 2, 2014. http://
    www.bbc.com/news/world-africa-15336689.

23. See, e.g., Mullen, Daniel. "Pakistan Court Declares US Drone Strikes
    Illegal." Jurist, May 9, 2013. Accessed June 2, 2014. http://jurist.org/
    paperchase/2013/05/pakistan-court-declares-drone-strikes-illegal-
    directs-foreign-ministry-to-introduce-resolution-in-un.php.

24. See, e.g., 2012 comments by Pakistani ambassador to the UN in Geneva,
    Zamir Akram, calling for an end to the "totally counterproductive attacks"
    by the US in Pakistan. See: Bowcott, Owen. "Drone Strikes Threaten 50
    Years of International Law, Says UN Rapporteur." The Guardian, June 21,
    2012. Accessed June 2, 2014. http://www.theguardian.com/world/2012/
    jun/21/drone-strikes-international-law-un; see also Nauman, Qasim.
    "Pakistan condemns U.S. drone strikes." Reuters, June 4, 2012. Accessed
    June 2, 2014. http://www.reuters.com/article/2012/06/04/us
    -pakistan-usa-drones-idUSBRE8530MS20120604.

25. Consider, for instance, the situation in Crimea and Eastern Ukraine: the
    United States recognizes the Ukrainian authorities in Kiev as the legiti-
    mate government in these regions, but Russia views Crimea as part of
    Russia, and Eastern Ukraine as arguably independent or autonomous
    with regard to Kiev. It is hardly a stretch to imagine Russia using lethal

UAVs to carry out strikes against pro-Kiev forces in Crimea or Eastern Ukraine on the grounds that Kiev's consent is unnecessary and it is the Russians who are the sole arbiters of who can give consent and what constitutes a sovereignty violation. Indeed, in a variety of ways Russia is already exploiting ambiguities in the notion of sovereignty and consent partially created by US actions (e.g, to deploy Russian troops in disputed areas of Ukraine).

26. See, e.g., "The political message [sent out by UAV strikes] emphasizes the disparity in power between the parties and reinforces popular support for the terrorists, who are seen as David fighting Goliath. Moreover, by resorting to military force rather than to law enforcement, targeted killings might strengthen the sense of legitimacy of terrorist operations, which are sometimes viewed as the only viable option for the weak to fight against a powerful empire." See: Blum, Gabriella, and Philip Heymann. Laws, Outlaws and Terrorists. Cambridge, MA: The MIT Press, 2010.

27. A 2012 Pew Research poll found that in every country, except India and the United States, a larger percentage of the population disapproved of United States UAV strikes than approved of them. See: Global Opinion of Obama Slips, International Policies Faulted. Washington, DC: Pew Research Center Global Attitudes Project, June 13, 2012. Accessed March 12, 2014. http://www.pewglobal.org/2012/06/13/global-opinion-of-obama-slips-international-policies-faulted/.

28. According to one 2012 poll, 74% of Pakistanis say they view the US as their "enemy." See: Byman, Daniel. "Why Drones Work: The Case for Washington's Weapon of Choice." Foreign Affairs (July/August 2013). Accessed June 2, 2014. http://www.foreignaffairs.com/articles/139453/daniel-byman/why-drones-work. Posen, Barry. "The Case for Restraint." The American Interest 3, no. 1 (November/December 2007); Pape, Robert. Bombing to Win: Air Power and Coercion in War. Ithaca, NY: Cornell University Press, 1995; see also Alexander, David. "Retired General Cautions Against Overuse of "Hated" Drones." Reuters, January 7, 2013. Accessed June 2, 2014. http://www.reuters.com/article/2013/01/07/us-usa-afghanistan-mcchrystal-idUSBRE90608O20130107.

29. Alexander, David. "Retired General Cautions Against Overuse of "Hated" Drones." Reuters, January 7, 2013. Accessed June 2, 2014. http://www.reuters.com/article/2013/01/07/us-usa-afghanistan-mcchrystal-idUSBRE90608O20130107.

30. European Parliament. Joint Motion for a Resolution-On the Use of Armed Drones. 2014. Accessed June 2, 2014. http://www.reprieve. org.uk/media/downloads/2014_01_27_PUB_European_Parliament_ resolution_on_use_of_drones.pdf.

31. Ibid.

32. Christof Heyns, the UN special rapporteur on extrajudicial killings, summary or arbitrary executions, has asserted that US targeted strikes threaten the entire international legal system, for instance, and claims that some US strikes may constitute "war crimes." The UN Special Rapporteur on Terrorism and Human Rights has raised similar concerns. See: Bowcott, Owen. "Drone Strikes Threaten 50 Years of International Law, Says UN Rapporteur." Guardian, June 21, 2012. Accessed June 2, 2014. http://www. theguardian.com/world/2012/jun/21/ drone-strikes-international-law-un.

33. As Sarah Kreps and Micah Zenko note, "Countries will not be deterred from launching drone attacks simply because an adversary has drones in its arsenal, too. If anything, the inherent advantages of drones—most of all, not placing pilots or ground forces at risk of being killed or captured—have lowered the threshold for the use of force." See: Kreps, Sarah, and Micah Zenko. "The Next Drone Wars: Preparing for Proliferation." Foreign Affairs (March/April 2014). Accessed June 2, 2014. http://www .foreignaffairs.com/articles/140746/sarah-kreps-and-micah-zenko/ the-next-drone-wars.

34. Some external studies have sought to assess the value of UAV strikes. See, e.g., 2013 Army War College study finding that drone strikes in Pakistan had no apparent effect on levels of insurgent violence in Afghanistan, but that "strikes that kill militants in Pakistan are associated with increases in subsequent insurgent violence in the country. This fact could be creating a dynamic in which all insurgent organizations, even those that have few grievances against United States and the government of Pakistan or that engage in low levels of violence, feel threatened by the drones and seek support from other insurgent organizations that do have as their goal undermining the US position in the region." (Walsh, James Igoe. The Effectiveness of Drone Strikes in Counterinsurgency and Counterterrorism Campaigns. Carlisle, PA: US Army War College Strategic Studies Institute, September 2013. Accessed June 3, 2014. http://www.strategicstudiesinstitute.army.mil/pubs/display. cfm?pubID=1167.) Others, such as Daniel Byman, have argued for the effectiveness of such strikes. See, e.g., Byman, Daniel. "Why Drones Work." Foreign Affairs (July/August 2013). Accessed June 3, 2014.

http://www.foreignaffairs.com/articles/139453/daniel-byman/why-drones-work; Johnston, Patrick B. and Anoop K. Sarbahi. "The Impact of U.S. Drone Strikes on Terrorism in Pakistan and Afghanistan." Patrick Johnston, February 11, 2014. Accessed June 3, 2014. http://patrickjohnston.info/materials/drones.pdf; also see generally Oliver, Christopher, "Are Drone Strikes Effective in Afghanistan and Pakistan? On the dynamics of violence between the United States and the Taliban." Journalist's Resource, February 12, 2013. Accessed June 3, 2014. http://journalistsresource.org/studies/international/foreign-policy/are-drone-strikes-effective-in-afghanistan-pakistan-violence-united-states-taliban#.

35. E.g., one issue that must be considered is whether UAV strikes have begun to have diminishing marginal returns. CNN's Correspondent and New America Foundation expert Peter Bergen notes that "The CIA drone campaign in Pakistan has killed 58 militant leaders... [and] Thirty-five militant leaders have also been killed in Yemen. Meanwhile, at least 339 civilians have been killed as well as at least 2,200 foot soldiers in militant groups in Pakistan and Yemen. At least 230 other people were reported killed..." Strikes that kill senior leaders may have greater benefits than strikes that kill lower-level "foot soldiers"; similarly, strikes that might be strategically justifiable at Time A may be less so at Time B. We do not believe there is a single answer to the question of whether US targeted strikes do more harm than good: we believe that targeted strikes can, in some circumstances, be strategically valuable, while in other circumstances they may do as much harm as good. We are concerned, however, that US decision-makers have focused mainly on the tactical value of UAV strikes, at a moment when their overall strategic value in Yemen and Pakistan may be dwindling (and when further strikes may even be counterproductive). See: Bergen, Peter. "Drones Will Fill the Sky." CNN, May 13, 2014. Accessed June 4, 2014. http://www.cnn.com/2014/05/13/opinion/bergen-armed-drones-key-future-warfare/index.html?utm_source=feedburner&utm_medium=feed&utm_campaign=Feed%3A+rss%2Fcnn_latest+%28RSS%3A+Most+Recent%29.

*The **Stimson Center** is a nonprofit and nonpartisan think tank that finds pragmatic solutions to global security challenges.

Stimson Center. "Recommendations and Report of the Task Force on US Drone Policy (exerpt)." 2nd ed. Washington, D.C.: Stimson Center, forthcoming.

RECOMMENDATIONS AND REPORT OF THE TASK FORCE ON US DRONE POLICY, 2nd Edition, Task Force co-chairs Gen. John P. Abizaid (US Army, Ret.) and Rosa Brooks, © The Stimson Center.

Limiting Armed Drone Proliferation

by Micah Zenko and Sarah Kreps*

Introduction

The use of unmanned aerial systems—commonly referred to as drones—over the past decade has revolutionized how the United States uses military force. As the technology has evolved from surveillance aircraft to an armed platform, drones have been used for a wide range of military missions: the United States has successfully and legitimately used armed drones to conduct hundreds of counterterrorism operations in battlefield zones, including Afghanistan, Iraq, and Libya. It has also used armed drones in non-battlefield settings, specifically in Pakistan, Yemen, Somalia, and the Philippines. Collectively, these strikes have eliminated a number of suspected terrorists and militants from Asia to Africa at no cost in terms of U.S. casualties, an advantage of drones over manned platforms that has made them attractive to many other states. However, non-battlefield strikes have drawn criticism, particularly those conducted under the assertion that they are acts of self-defense.

Though the United States remains the lead actor in terms of possessing and using armed drones, the rest of the world is quickly catching up. Russia, China, Iran, South Korea, and

Taiwan, for example, have begun to develop increasingly sophisticated indigenous drone capabilities. Other countries, including Pakistan, Turkey, Saudi Arabia, and the United Arab Emirates (UAE), have publicized their intent to purchase them.

The direct consequences of armed drone proliferation on U.S. national security are several years out, but the policymaking decisions that will shape those consequences confront the Obama administration today. How the United States uses armed drones and for what purposes will contribute to the norms that will influence how states use them in the future. Under the leadership of the United States, norms regarding the proliferation and use of weapons—from nuclear and biological weapons to blinding lasers and antipersonnel landmines—have been overwhelmingly adopted and followed. Similar efforts should be made for the proliferation and use of armed drones, even if not all states abide by these norms. U.S. export policy will determine, to a certain extent, which states acquire what types of armed drones, and will set expectations about appropriate exports by other armed drone producers. If the United States reinforces multilateral institutions designed to limit armed drone proliferation, it will have the ability to shape the constraints that other states will face when acquiring drones.

Persistent media attention tends not to differentiate between armed and commercial drones, but rather homogenizes all types, despite the fact that armed drones will be more destabilizing. Though the armed drones acquired by states in the near term likely will not have capabilities equal to those of the United States, their effects will still be destabilizing. States that acquire armed drones will likely use them as probes and for limited attacks in international waters and across borders, against domestic threats, and, potentially, for even more lethal missions, including delivering weapons of mass destruction (WMDs). Although other vehicles, such as trucks and manned civilian aircraft, can also be used to deliver WMDs, the ability of drones to hover and wait for the opportune moment in which they can produce maximum effect confers uniquely lethal capabilities. If the United States delays and forgoes the opportunity to establish rules of the road for the use of armed drones and to constrain their proliferation, there will be grave consequences for U.S. interests, in terms of the prevention of armed conflict, promotion of human rights, strengthening of international norms and legal frameworks, and the future of warfare.

Subsequently, the United States should pursue a strategy that limits the proliferation of armed drones and promotes their use in a manner consistent with international law and norms, and that does not threaten U.S. interests or allies. The strategy should consider foreseeable destabilizing or deadly missions over the next decade and beyond, but remain flexible enough should unprecedented uses and missions emerge. Such a strategy will be difficult to execute and require sustained high-level attention from the Obama administration and its successors. Given that many states want to acquire armed drones, and drone producers outside the drone transfer regime, such as China and Israel, are already exporting drones, the need for implementation is all the more pressing.[1] Such a strategy would serve U.S. national interests in the following ways:

- Minimize the proliferation of the most capable and lethal drones to countries that are conflict prone.

- Reduce the potential for militarized disputes between states that could lead to an escalation of armed conflict in unstable regions.

- Decrease the likelihood that states and nonstate actors will use armed drones against the United States and its allies.

- Establish a more widely accepted legal and operational basis for conducting drone strikes to ensure that countries do not use armed drones in ways that threaten the United States or its allies.

- Increase the likelihood that internationally accepted norms and rules for armed drone exports and use will be adopted by emerging drone powers.

[. . .]

How Drones Are Different and Can Destabilize

Drones should be treated as a distinct class of weapons. They have unique properties that lead them to be used, and defended against, in ways that are destabilizing. In November 2013, Canada's chief of defense staff, General Thomas Lawson, made a claim that is commonplace among military officials: "If a kinetic round is propelled toward a confirmed enemy for strategic purposes by a rifle, by an artillery piece, by an aircraft manned, or by an aircraft unmanned, any of those that end up with a desired effect is a supportable point of view."[15] Similarly, in May 2012, then chief of staff of the U.S. Air Force, General Norton Schwartz declared, "If it is a legitimate target, then I would argue that the manner in which you engage that target, whether it be close combat or remotely, is not a terribly relevant question."[16] This premise is technically true and consistent with military officials' efforts to demystify drones, reduce public opposition to them, and integrate them into their armed services. However, these assumptions overlook the unique advantages of armed drones, which raise the prospect for moral hazard, where governments are more willing to use them over other weapons platforms because the associated costs and risks are assumed to be comparably lower. Indeed, the Obama administration commissioned a separate review of U.S. drone export policies, precisely because the vast majority of U.S. officials believe that it is a distinct weapons system.[17]

The attractiveness of armed drones stems from three inherent advantages. First, the typical MALE drone can persist over a target for up to fourteen hours without being refueled, which provides a continuous monitoring of the situation below. In contrast, manned aircraft can neither loiter nor fly repeatedly over an area of interest for more than four to six hours due to fuel or pilot limitations. Second, with a missile attached to the surveillance platform, the responsiveness of armed drones when time-sensitive targets appear in the operator's view is unmatched. Moreover, drone-fired missiles can be diverted by the weapons system operator at the last moment if noncombatants enter the likely blast radius.[18] Third, and most important, unmanned systems do not place human pilots or ground forces at risk of being killed or captured in hostile environments. Such advantages have made drones the "weapon of choice" of the United States for killing suspected terrorists.[19]

The inherent advantages of drones will not alone make traditional interstate warfare more likely—such conflicts are relatively rare anyway, with only one active interstate conflict in both 2012 and 2013.[20] Nor will the probable type, quantity, range, and lethality of armed drones that states possess in coming decades make a government more likely to attempt to defeat an opposing army, capture or control foreign territory, or remove a foreign leader from power. However, misperceptions over the use of armed drones increase the likelihood of militarized disputes with U.S. allies, as well as U.S. military forces, which could lead to an escalating crisis and deeper U.S. involvement. Though surveillance drones can be used to provide greater stability between countries by monitoring ceasefires or disputed borders, armed drones will have destabilizing consequences. Arming a drone, whether by design or by simply putting a crude payload on an unarmed drone, makes it a weapon, and thereby a direct national security threat for any state whose border it breaches.

INCREASED FREQUENCY OF INTERSTATE AND INTRASTATE FORCE

For the United States, drones have significantly reduced the political, diplomatic, and military risks and costs associated with the use of military force, which has led to a vast expansion of lethal operations that would not have been attempted with other weapons platforms. Aside from airstrikes in traditional conflicts such as Libya, Iraq, and Afghanistan—where one-quarter of all International Security Assistance Force (ISAF) airstrikes in 2012 were conducted by drones—the United States has conducted hundreds in non-battlefield settings: Pakistan (approximately 369), Yemen (approximately 87), Somalia (an estimated 16), and the Philippines (at least 1, in 2006).[21] Of the estimated 473 non-battlefield targeted killings undertaken by the United States since November 2002, approximately 98 percent were carried out by drones. Moreover, despite maintaining a "strong preference" for capturing over killing suspected terrorists since September 2011, there have been only 3 known capture attempts, compared with 194 drone strikes that have killed an estimated 1,014 people, 86 of whom were civilians.[22]

Senior U.S. civilian and military officials, whose careers span the pre– and post–armed drone era, overwhelmingly agree that the threshold for the authorization of force by civilian officials has been significantly reduced. Former secretary of defense Robert Gates asserted in October 2013, for example, that armed drones allow decision-makers to see war as a "bloodless, painless, and odorless" affair, with technology detaching leaders from the "inevitably tragic, inefficient, and uncertain" consequences of war.[23] President Barack Obama admitted in May 2013 that the United States has come to see armed drones "as a cure-all for terrorism," because they are low risk and instrumental in "shielding the government" from criticisms "that a troop deployment invites."[24] Such admissions from leaders of a democratic country with a system of checks and balances point to the temptations that leaders with fewer institutional checks will face.

President Obama and his senior aides have stated that the United States is setting precedents with drones that other states may emulate.[25] If U.S. experience and Obama's cautionary words are any guide, states that acquire armed drones will be more willing to threaten or use force in ways they might not otherwise, within both interstate and intrastate contexts.

States might undertake cross-border, interstate actions less discriminately, especially in areas prone to tension. As is apparent in the East and South China Seas, nationalist sentiments and the discovery of untapped, valuable national resources can make disputes between countries more likely. In such contested areas, drones will enable governments to undertake strike missions or probe the responses of an adversary—actions they would be less inclined to take with manned platforms. According to the Central Intelligence Agency (CIA), there are approximately 430 bilateral maritime boundaries, most of which are not defined by formal agreements between the affected states.[26]

Beyond the cases of East Asia, other cross-border flash-points for conflict where the low-risk proposition of drone strikes would be tempting include Russia in Georgia or Ukraine, Turkey in Syria, Sudan within its borders, and China on its western periphery. In 2013, a Chinese counternarcotics official revealed that his bureau had considered attempting to kill a drug kingpin named Naw Kham, who was hiding in a remote region in northeastern Myanmar, by using a drone carrying twenty kilograms of dynamite. "The plan was rejected, because the order was to catch him alive," the official recalled.[27] With armed drones, China might make the same calculation that the United States has made—that killing is more straightforward than capturing—in choosing to target ostensibly high-threat individuals with drone strikes. China's demonstrated willingness to employ armed drones against terrorists or criminals outside its borders could directly threaten U.S. allies in the region, particularly if the criterion China uses to define a terrorist does not align with that of the United States or its allies.

Domestically, governments may use armed drones to target their perceived internal enemies. Most emerging drone powers have experienced recent domestic unrest. Turkey, Russia, Pakistan, and China all have separatist or significant opposition movements (e.g., Kurds, Chechens, the Taliban, Tibetans, and Uighurs) that presented political and military challenges to their rule in recent history. These states already designate individuals from these groups as "terrorists," and reserve the right to use force against them. States possessing the lower risk—compared with other weapons platforms—capability of armed drones could use them more frequently in the service of domestic pacification, especially against time-sensitive targets that reside in mountainous, jungle, or other inhospitable terrain. Compared with typical methods used by military and police forces to counter insurgencies, criminals, or terrorists—such as ground troops and manned aircraft—unmanned drones provide significantly greater real-time intelligence through their persistent loiter time and responsiveness to striking an identified target.

INCREASED RISK OF MISPERCEPTION AND ESCALATION

Pushing limits in already unstable regions is complicated by questions raised regarding rules of engagement: how would states respond to an armed drone in what they contend is their sovereign airspace, and how would opposing sides respond to counter-drone tactics? Japanese defense officials claim that shooting down Chinese drones in what Japan contends is its airspace is more likely to occur than downing manned aircraft because drones are not as responsive to radio or pilot warnings, thereby raising the possibility of an escalatory response.[28] Alternatively, Japan might misidentify a Chinese manned fighter as an advanced drone and fire on it, especially if the aircraft's radar signature is not sufficiently distinctive or if combat drones routinely fly over the disputed area.

Thus, the additional risks associated with drone strikes, combined with the lack of clarity on how two countries would react to an attempted downing of a drone, create the potential for miscalculation and subsequent escalation. As U.S. Air Force commanders in South Korea noted, a North Korean drone equipped with chemical agents would not have to kill many or even any people on the peninsula to terrorize the population and escalate tensions.[29] This scenario points to the spiraling escalatory dynamic that could be repeated—likely intensified in the context of armed drones—in other tension-prone areas, such as the Middle East, South Asia, and Central and East Africa, where the mix of low-risk and ambiguous rules of engagement is a recipe for escalation. Not all of these contingencies directly affect U.S. interests, but they would affect treaty allies whose security the United States has an interest in maintaining. Compared with other weapons platforms, current practice repeatedly demonstrates that drones make militarized disputes more likely due to a decreased threshold for the use of force and an increased risk of miscalculation.

INCREASED RISK OF LETHALITY

The proliferation of armed drones will increase the likelihood of destabilizing or devastating one-off, high-consequence attacks. In March 2013, Senator Dianne Feinstein (D-CA) observed of drones: "In some respects it's a perfect assassination weapon. . . . Now we have a problem. There are all these nations that want to buy these armed drones. I'm strongly opposed to that."[30] The worst-case contingency for the use of armed drones, albeit an unlikely circumstance, would be to deliver weapons of mass destruction. Drones are, in many ways, the perfect vehicle for delivering biological and chemical agents.[31] A WMD attack, or even the assassination of a political leader, another troubling though unlikely circumstance, would have tremendous consequences for regional and international stability.

Deterring such drone-based attacks will depend on the ability of the United States and other governments to accurately detect and attribute them. Technical experts and intelligence analysts disagree about the extent to which this will be possible, but the difficulties lie in the challenges of detecting drones (they emit small radar, thermal, and electron signatures, and can fly low), determining who controlled it (they can be programmed to fly to a preset GPS coordinate), or assigning ownership to a downed system (they can be composed of commercial, off-the-shelf components).[32]

It is equally noteworthy that civilian officials or military commanders have almost always used armed drones in ways beyond their initially intended applications. Drones do not simply fulfill existing mission requirements; they create new and unforeseen ones, and will continue to do so in the future. Furthermore, U.S. officials would be misguided to view future uses of armed drones solely through the prism of how the United States has used them—for discrete military operations in relatively benign air-defense environments. The potential for misperception is compounded by the fact that few governments seeking or acquiring armed drones have publicly articulated any strategy for how they will likely use them. Conversely, the uncertainty about how other countries will use drones provides the United States with an opportunity to shape drone doctrines, especially for U.S. allies interested in procuring drones from U.S. manufacturers.

[...]

NOTES

1. "Israeli Unmanned Aerial Systems," Frost & Sullivan, May 20, 2013.

[...]

15. Tom Lawson, remarks at the Center for Strategic and International Studies, November 26, 2013.

16. Norton A. Schwartz, "Pragmatic Steps for Global Security," remarks at the Stimson Center, May 1, 2012.

17. Interviews with U.S. government officials.

18. Certain missiles fired from other weapons platforms can also be diverted, but as a matter of practice, they rarely are. Missiles fired from drones are diverted much more frequently.

19. Daniel Byman, "Why Drones Work: The Case for Washington's Weapon of Choice," *Foreign Affairs*, July/August 2013.

20. Lotta Themner and Peter Wallensteen, "Armed Conflicts, 1946–2012," *Journal of Peace Research*, 50:4, July 2, 2013, p. 510.

21. Bill Roggio and Alexander Mayer, "Charting the Data for U.S. Airstrikes in Pakistan, 2004–2014," *Long War Journal*, last updated December 25, 2013; Bill Roggio and Bob Barry, "Charting the Data for U.S. Airstrikes in Yemen, 2002–2014," *Long War Journal*, last updated June 5, 2014; "Yemen: Reported U.S. Covert Action 2001–2011," Bureau of Investigative Journalism, March 29, 2012; "Yemen: Reported U.S. Covert Action 2012," Bureau of Investigative Journalism, May 8, 2012; "Yemen: Reported U.S. Covert Actions 2013," Bureau of Investigative Journalism, January 3, 2013; "Yemen: Reported U.S. Covert Actions 2014," Bureau of Investigative Journalism, updated June 4, 2014; Mark Mazzetti, *The Way of the Knife: The CIA, a Secret Army, and a War at the Ends of the Earth* (New York: Penguin Press, 2013), p. 134.

22. Average based on ranges provided by New America Foundation (NAF) and Bureau of Investigative Journalism through June 2014.

23. Greg Jaffe, "Former Defense Secretary Gates Warns Against Lure of Drone Warfare," *Washington Post*, October 23, 2013.

24. Jason Koebler, "Obama: Administration Saw Drone Strikes as 'Cure-All' for Terrorism," *U.S. News and World Report*, May 23, 2013.

25. John O. Brennan, "The Ethics and Efficacy of the President's Counterterrorism Strategy," Wilson Center, April 30, 2012; and Mark Bowden, *The Finish: The Killing of Osama Bin Laden* (New York: Atlantic Monthly Press, 2012), p. 262.

26. *The World Factbook 2013–14*, Central Intelligence Agency, 2013.

27. Liu Chang, "Manhunt for Deadly Drug Kingpin," *Global Times*, February 19, 2013.

28. Itsunori Onodera, "Press Conference by the Defense Minister," Japan Ministry of Defense, September 10, 2013; and "Defense Ministry Working on Protocol to Shoot Down Encroaching Drones," *Asahi Shimbun*, October 2, 2013.

29. Interview with senior U.S. Air Force official stationed in South Korea, April 2014.

30. Breanna Edwards, "Dianne Feinstein: Time to Set Drone Rules," *Politico*, March 7, 2013. Indeed Feinstein has been a strong opponent of selling armed variants of drones, including to NATO allies.

31. Dennis M. Gormley, "Limiting the Unintended Consequences of Unmanned Air System Proliferation," *Whitehead Journal of Diplomacy & International Relations*, Winter/Spring 2013, pp. 67–79.

32. David Sanger and William Broad, "Pentagon Study Finds Agencies Ill Equipped to Detect Foreign Nuclear Efforts," *New York Times*, January 24, 2014.

[…]

*Micah Zenko is the Douglas Dillon fellow in the Center for Preventive Action at the Council on Foreign Relations.

Sarah Kreps is a Stanton nuclear security fellow at the Council on Foreign Relations.

Zenko, Micah, and Sarah Kreps. *Limiting Armed Drone Proliferation*. Council Special Report No. 69. New York: Council on Foreign Relations Center for Preventive Action, 2014, 3–5, 8–13.

Used by permission.

PART 2:

Are They Ethical?

What are the potential risks or benefits of using armed drones and engaging in targeted killings? Can drones be an ethical choice of weapon because they may enable improved targeting precision and thus lead to fewer civilian deaths? If drones do enable better targeting, might they still have other moral risks? Might they result in killing becoming too easy and more frequent? Should the ethical question be asked about "drones" in the abstract or does the better question address how they are currently used by the United States?

Jane Mayer, in "The Predator War," provides background on the program and the ethical issues it raises. She notes that some commentators have been concerned that drones may facilitate a "Playstation mentality" around killing and that some contend that remote killing is unethical. In "Confessions of a Drone Warrior," journalist Matthew Power interviews former drone operator Brandon Bryant, who explains that being involved in the strikes left him traumatized—suggesting that while drone operators may be physically distant from their targets, they may nevertheless be strongly emotionally affected by their role in killing.

National security journalist Scott Shane lays out the arguments of some moral philosophers that a "Moral Case for Drones" exists because drones can be used to minimize civilian harm. In "The Case for Drones," law professor Kenneth Anderson outlines a number of the primary ethical arguments made in favor of U.S. drone use, including that the remoteness "actually enables precision" because operators, not facing personal risk, can take more time and care in targeting and that drone warfare is currently "the best method available" to strike at terrorists.

However, professors John Kaag and Sarah Kreps argue in "The Moral Hazard of Drones" that drones may provide an easier way to kill and that this poses a moral hazard. And, in "Distant Death," journalist Conor Friedersdorf contends that U.S. drone use risks encouraging drone proliferation, facilitating more lethal and secret force, and that it has had negative effects on communities targeted by strikes. Friedersdorf also maintains that instead of responding morally when it does strike, the United States responds like a "hit-and-run driver," refusing to take responsibility.

As you read the articles in this section, consider the following questions:

- What ethical risks or benefits might armed drones entail? Are these risks and benefits unique or particular to drones or heightened with drones in some way?

- In what circumstances might drone strikes be morally justifiable? Do you think current U.S. practices are morally justifiable?

- What are the different moral issues raised specifically by "drones" as distinct from those raised by "targeted killings"?

The Predator War: What Are the Risks of the C.I.A.'s Covert Drone Program?

by Jane Mayer*

On August 5th, officials at the Central Intelligence Agency, in Langley, Virginia, watched a live video feed relaying closeup footage of one of the most wanted terrorists in Pakistan. Baitul-lah Mehsud, the leader of the Taliban in Pakistan, could be seen reclining on the rooftop of his father-in-law's house, in Zanghara, a hamlet in South Waziristan. It was a hot summer night, and he was joined outside by his wife and his uncle, a medic; at one point, the remarkably crisp images showed that Mehsud, who suffered from diabetes and a kidney ailment, was receiving an intravenous drip.

The video was being captured by the infrared camera of a Predator drone, a remotely controlled, unmanned plane that had been hovering, undetected, two miles or so above the house. Pakistan's Interior Minister, A. Rehman Malik, told me recently that Mehsud was resting on his back. Malik, using his hands to make a picture frame, explained that the Predator's targeters could see Mehsud's entire body, not just the top of his head. "It was a perfect picture," Malik, who watched the videotape later, said. "We used to see James Bond movies where he talked into his shoe or his watch. We thought it was a fairy tale. But this was fact!" The image remained just as stable when the

C.I.A. remotely launched two Hellfire missiles from the Predator. Authorities watched the fiery blast in real time. After the dust cloud dissipated, all that remained of Mehsud was a detached torso. Eleven others died: his wife, his father-in-law, his mother-in-law, a lieutenant, and seven bodyguards.

Pakistan's government considered Mehsud its top enemy, holding him responsible for the vast majority of recent terrorist attacks inside the country, including the assassination of former Prime Minister Benazir Bhutto, in December, 2007, and the bombing, last September, of the Marriott Hotel in Islamabad, which killed more than fifty people. Mehsud was also thought to have helped his Afghan confederates attack American and coalition troops across the border. Roger Cressey, a former counterterrorism official on the National Security Council, who is now a partner at Good Harbor, a consulting firm, told me, "Mehsud was someone both we and Pakistan were happy to see go up in smoke." Indeed, there was no controversy when, a few days after the missile strike, CNN reported that President Barack Obama had authorized it.

However, at about the same time, there was widespread anger after the *Wall Street Journal* revealed that during the Bush Administration the C.I.A. had considered setting up hit squads to capture or kill Al Qaeda operatives around the world. The furor grew when the *Times* reported that the C.I.A. had turned to a private contractor to help with this highly sensitive operation: the controversial firm Blackwater, now known as Xe Services. Members of the Senate and House intelligence committees demanded investigations of the program, which, they said, had been hidden from them. And many legal experts argued that, had the program become fully operational, it would have violated a 1976 executive order, signed by President Gerald R. Ford, banning American intelligence forces from engaging in assassination.

Hina Shamsi, a human-rights lawyer at the New York University School of Law, was struck by the inconsistency of the public's responses. "We got so upset about a targeted-killing program that didn't happen," she told me. "But the drone program *exists*." She said of the Predator program, "These are targeted international killings by the state." The program, as it happens, also uses private contractors for a variety of tasks, including flying the drones. Employees of Xe Services maintain and load the Hellfire missiles on the aircraft. Vicki Divoll, a former C.I.A. lawyer, who now teaches at the U.S. Naval Academy, in Annapolis, observed, "People are a lot more comfortable with a Predator strike that kills many people than with a throat-slitting that kills one." But, she added, "mechanized killing is still killing."

The U.S. government runs two drone programs. The military's version, which is publicly acknowledged, operates in the recognized war zones of Afghanistan and Iraq, and targets enemies of U.S. troops stationed there. As such, it is an extension of conventional warfare. The C.I.A.'s program is aimed at terror suspects around the world, including in countries where U.S. troops are not based. It was initiated by the Bush Administration and, according to Juan Zarate, a counterterrorism adviser in the Bush White House, Obama has left in place virtually all the key personnel. The program is classified as covert, and the intelligence agency declines to provide any information to the public about where it operates, how it selects targets, who is in charge, or how many people have been killed.

Nevertheless, reports of fatal air strikes in Pakistan emerge every few days. Such stories are often secondhand and difficult to confirm, as the Pakistani government and the military have tried to wall off the tribal areas from journalists. But, even if a precise account is elusive, the outlines are clear: the C.I.A. has joined the Pakistani intelligence service in an aggressive campaign to eradicate local and foreign militants, who have taken refuge in some of the most inaccessible parts of the country.

The first two C.I.A. air strikes of the Obama Administration took place on the morning of January 23rd—the President's third day in office. Within hours, it was clear that the morning's bombings, in Pakistan, had killed an estimated twenty people. In one strike, four Arabs, all likely affiliated with Al Qaeda, died. But in the second strike a drone targeted the wrong house, hitting the residence of a pro-government tribal leader six miles outside the town of Wana, in South Waziristan. The blast killed the tribal leader's entire family, including three children, one of them five years old. In keeping with U.S. policy, there was no official acknowledgment of either strike.

Since then, the C.I.A. bombardments have continued at a rapid pace. According to a just completed study by the New America Foundation, the number of drone strikes has risen dramatically since Obama became President. During his first nine and a half months in office, he has authorized as many C.I.A. aerial attacks in Pakistan as George W. Bush did in his final three years in office. The study's authors, Peter Bergen and Katherine Tiedemann, report that the Obama Administration has sanctioned at least forty-one C.I.A. missile strikes in Pakistan since taking office—a rate of approximately one bombing a week. So far this year, various estimates suggest, the C.I.A. attacks have killed between three hundred and twenty-six and five hundred and thirty-eight people. Critics say that many of the victims have been innocent bystanders, including children.

In the last week of September alone, there were reportedly four such attacks—three of them in one twenty-four-hour period. At any given moment, a former White House counterterrorism official says, the C.I.A. has multiple drones flying over Pakistan, scouting for targets. According to the official, "there are so many drones" in the air that arguments have erupted over which remote operators can claim which targets, provoking "command-and-control issues."

General Atomics Aeronautical Systems, the defense contractor that manufactures the Predator and its more heavily armed sibling, the Reaper, can barely keep up with the government's demand. The Air Force's fleet has grown from some fifty drones in 2001 to nearly two hundred; the C.I.A. will not divulge how many drones it operates. The government plans to commission hundreds more, including new generations of tiny "nano" drones, which can fly after their prey like a killer bee through an open window.

With public disenchantment mounting over the U.S. troop deployment in Afghanistan, and the Obama Administration divided over whether to escalate the American military presence there, many in Washington support an even greater reliance on Predator strikes. In this view, the U.S., rather than trying to stabilize Afghanistan by waging a counter-insurgency operation against Taliban forces, should focus purely on counterterrorism, and use the latest technology to surgically eliminate Al Qaeda leaders and their allies. In September, the conservative pundit George Will published an influential column in the Washington *Post*, "Time to Get Out of Afghanistan," arguing that "America should do only what can be done from offshore, using intelligence, drones, cruise missiles, air strikes and small, potent Special Forces units, concentrating on the porous 1,500-mile border with Pakistan, a nation that actually matters." Vice-President Joseph Biden reportedly holds a similar view.

It's easy to understand the appeal of a "push-button" approach to fighting Al Qaeda, but the embrace of the Predator program has occurred with remarkably little public discussion, given that it represents a radically new and geographically unbounded use of state-sanctioned lethal force. And, because of the C.I.A. program's secrecy, there is no visible system of accountability in place, despite the fact that the agency has killed many civilians inside a politically fragile, nuclear-armed country with which the U.S. is not at war. Should something go wrong in the C.I.A.'s program—last month, the Air Force lost control of a drone and had to shoot it down over Afghanistan—it's unclear what the consequences would be.

The Predators in the C.I.A. program are "flown" by civilians, both intelligence officers and private contractors. According to a former counterterrorism official, the contractors are "seasoned professionals—often retired military and intelligence officials." (The intelligence agency outsources a significant portion of its work.) Within the C.I.A., control of the unmanned vehicles is split among several teams. One set of pilots and operators works abroad, near hidden airfields in Afghanistan and Pakistan, handling takeoffs and landings. Once the drones are aloft, the former counterterrorism official said, the controls are electronically "slewed over" to a set of "reachback operators," in Langley. Using joysticks that resemble video-game controls, the reachback operators—who don't need conventional flight training—sit next to intelligence officers and watch, on large flat-screen monitors, a live video feed from the drone's camera. From their suburban redoubt, they can turn the plane, zoom in on the landscape below, and decide whether to lock onto a target. A stream of additional "signal" intelligence, sent to Langley by the National Security Agency, provides electronic means of corroborating that a target has been correctly identified. The

White House has delegated trigger authority to C.I.A. officials, including the head of the Counter-Terrorist Center, whose identity remains veiled from the public because the agency has placed him under cover.

People who have seen an air strike live on a monitor described it as both awe-inspiring and horrifying. "You could see these little figures scurrying, and the explosion going off, and when the smoke cleared there was just rubble and charred stuff," a former C.I.A. officer who was based in Afghanistan after September 11th says of one attack. (He watched the carnage on a small monitor in the field.) Human beings running for cover are such a common sight that they have inspired a slang term: "squirters."

Peter W. Singer, the author of "Wired for War," a recent book about the robotics revolution in modern combat, argues that the drone technology is worryingly "seductive," because it creates the perception that war can be "costless." Cut off from the realities of the bombings in Pakistan, Americans have been insulated from the human toll, as well as from the political and the moral consequences. Nearly all the victims have remained faceless, and the damage caused by the bombings has remained unseen. In contrast to Gaza, where the targeted killing of Hamas fighters by the Israeli military has been extensively documented—making clear that the collateral damage, and the loss of civilian life, can be severe—Pakistan's tribal areas have become largely forbidden territory for media organizations. As a result, no videos of a drone attack in progress have been released, and only a few photographs of the immediate aftermath of a Predator strike have been published.

The seeming unreality of the Predator enterprise is also felt by the pilots. Some of them reportedly wear flight suits when they operate a drone's remote controls. When their shifts end, of course, these cubicle warriors can drive home to have dinner with their families. Critics have suggested that unmanned systems, by sparing these combatants from danger and sacrifice, are creating what Sir Brian Burridge, a former British Air Chief Marshal in Iraq, has called "a virtueless war," requiring neither courage nor heroism. According to Singer, some Predator pilots suffer from combat stress that equals, or exceeds, that of pilots in the battlefield. This suggests that virtual killing, for all its sterile trappings, is a discomfiting form of warfare. Meanwhile, some social critics, such as Mary Dudziak, a professor at the University of Southern California's Gould School of Law, argue that the Predator strategy has a larger political cost. As she puts it, "Drones are a technological step that further isolates the American people from military action, undermining political checks on . . . endless war."

The advent of the Predator targeted-killing program "is really a sea change," says Gary Solis, who teaches at Georgetown University's Law Center and recently retired from running the law program at the U.S. Military Academy. "Not only would we have expressed abhorrence of such a policy a few years ago; we did." In July, 2001, two months before Al Qaeda's attacks on New York and Washington profoundly altered America's mind-set, the U.S. denounced Israel's use of targeted killing against Palestinian terrorists. The American Ambassador to Israel, Martin Indyk, said at the time, "The United States government is very clearly on record as against targeted assassinations. . . . They are extrajudicial killings, and we do not support that."

Before September 11th, the C.I.A., which had been chastened by past assassination scandals, refused to deploy the Predator for anything other than surveillance. Daniel Benjamin, the State Department's counterterrorism director, and Steven Simon, a former counterterrorism adviser, report in their 2002 book "The Age of Sacred Terror" that the week before Al Qaeda attacked the U.S. George Tenet, then the agency's director, argued that it would be "a terrible mistake" for "the Director of Central Intelligence to fire a weapon like this."

Yet once America had suffered terrorist attacks on its own soil the agency's posture changed, and it petitioned the White House for new authority. Within days, President Bush had signed a secret Memorandum of Notification, giving the C.I.A. the right to kill members of Al Qaeda and their confederates virtually anywhere in the world. Congress endorsed this policy, passing a bill called the Authorization for Use of Military Force. Bush's legal advisers modelled their rationale on Israel's position against terrorism, arguing that the U.S. government had the right to use lethal force against suspected terrorists in "anticipatory" self-defense. By classifying terrorism as an act of war, rather than as a crime, the Bush Administration reasoned that it was no longer bound by legal constraints requiring the government to give suspected terrorists due process.

In November, 2002, top Bush Administration officials publicly announced a successful Predator strike against an Al Qaeda target, Qaed Salim Sinan al-Harethi, a suspect in the 2000 bombing of the U.S.S. Cole. Harethi was killed after a Hellfire missile vaporized the car in which he and five other passengers were riding, on a desert road in Yemen. Paul Wolfowitz, then the Deputy Defense Secretary, praised the new tactic, telling CNN, "One hopes each time that you get a success like that, not only to have gotten rid of somebody dangerous but to have imposed changes in their tactics, operations, and procedures."

At first, some intelligence experts were uneasy about drone attacks. In 2002, Jeffrey Smith, a former C.I.A. general counsel, told Seymour M. Hersh, for an article in this magazine, "If they're dead, they're not talking to you, and you create more martyrs." And, in an interview with the Washington *Post*, Smith said that ongoing drone attacks could "suggest that it's acceptable behavior to assassinate people. . . . Assassination as a norm of international conduct exposes American leaders and Americans overseas."

Seven years later, there is no longer any doubt that targeted killing has become official U.S. policy. "The things we were complaining about from Israel a few years ago we now embrace," Solis says. Now, he notes, nobody in the government calls it assassination.

The Predator program is described by many in the intelligence world as America's single most effective weapon against Al Qaeda. In May, Leon Panetta, the C.I.A.'s director, referred to the Predator program as "the only game in town" in an unguarded moment after a public lecture. Counterterrorism officials credit drones with having killed more than a dozen senior Al Qaeda leaders and their allies in the past year, eliminating more than half of the C.I.A.'s twenty most wanted "high value" targets. In addition to Baitullah Mehsud, the list includes Nazimuddin Zalalov, a former lieutenant of Osama bin Laden; Ilyas Kashmiri, Al Qaeda's chief of paramilitary operations in Pakistan; Saad bin Laden, Osama's eldest son; Abu Sulayman al-Jazairi, an Algerian Al Qaeda planner who is believed to have helped train operatives for attacks in Europe and the United States; and Osama al-Kini and Sheikh Ahmed Salim Swedan, Al Qaeda operatives who are thought to have played central roles in the 1998 bombings of American embassies in East Africa.

Juan Zarate, the Bush counterterrorism adviser, believes that "Al Qaeda is on its heels" partly because "so many bigwigs" have been killed by drones. Though he acknowledges that Osama bin Laden and Ayman al-Zawahiri, the group's top leaders, remain at large, he estimates that no more than fifty members of Al Qaeda's senior leadership still exist, along with two to three hundred senior members outside the terror organization's "inner core."

Zarate and other supporters of the Predator program argue that it has had positive ripple effects. Surviving militants are forced to operate far more cautiously, which diverts their energy from planning new attacks. And there is evidence that the drone strikes, which depend on local informants for targeting information, have caused debilitating suspicion and discord within the ranks. Four Europeans who were captured last December after trying to join Al Qaeda in Pakistan described a life of constant fear and distrust among the militants, whose obsession with drone strikes had led them to communicate only with elaborate secrecy and to leave their squalid hideouts only at night. As the *Times* has reported, militants have been so unnerved by the drone program that they have released a video showing the execution of accused informants. Pakistanis have also been gripped by rumors that paid C.I.A. informants have been planting tiny silicon-chip homing devices for the drones in the tribal areas.

The drone program, for all its tactical successes, has stirred deep ethical concerns. Michael Walzer, a political philosopher and the author of the book "Just and Unjust Wars," says that he is unsettled by the notion of an intelligence agency wielding such lethal power in secret. "Under what code does the C.I.A. operate?" he asks. "I don't know. The military operates under a legal code, and it has judicial mechanisms." He said of the C.I.A.'s drone program, "There should be a limited, finite group of people who are targets, and that list should be publicly defensible and available. Instead, it's not being publicly defended. People are being killed, and we generally require some public justification when we go about killing people."

Since 2004, Philip Alston, an Australian human-rights lawyer who has served as the United Nations Special Rapporteur on Extrajudicial, Summary, or Arbitrary Executions, has repeatedly tried, but failed, to get a response to basic questions about the C.I.A.'s program—first from the Bush Administration, and now from Obama's. When he asked, in formal correspondence, for the C.I.A.'s legal justifications for targeted killings, he says, "they blew me off." (A C.I.A. spokesperson told me that the agency "uses lawful, highly accurate, and effective tools and tactics to take the fight to Al Qaeda and its violent allies. That careful, precise approach has brought major success against a very dangerous and deadly enemy.") Alston then presented a critical report on the drone program to the U.N. Human Rights Council, but, he says, the U.S. representatives ignored his concerns.

Alston describes the C.I.A. program as operating in "an accountability void," adding, "It's a lot like the torture issue. You start by saying we'll just go after the handful of 9/11 masterminds. But, once you've put the regimen for waterboarding and other techniques in place, you use it much more indiscriminately. It becomes standard operating procedure. It becomes all too easy. Planners start saying, 'Let's use drones in a broader context.' Once you use targeting less stringently, it can become indiscriminate."

Under international law, in order for the U.S. government to legally target civilian terror suspects abroad it has to define a terrorist group as one engaging in armed conflict, and the use of force must be a "military necessity." There must be no reasonable alternative to killing, such as capture, and to warrant death the target must be "directly participating in hostilities."

The use of force has to be considered "proportionate" to the threat. Finally, the foreign nation in which such targeted killing takes place has to give its permission.

Many lawyers who have looked at America's drone program in Pakistan believe that it meets these basic legal tests. But they are nevertheless troubled, as the U.S. government keeps broadening the definition of acceptable high-value targets. Last March, the Obama Administration made an unannounced decision to win support for the drone program inside Pakistan by giving President Asif Ali Zardari more control over whom to target. "A lot of the targets are nominated by the Pakistanis—it's part of the bargain of getting Pakistani coöperation," says Bruce Riedel, a former C.I.A. officer who has served as an adviser to the Obama Administration on Afghanistan and Pakistan. According to the New America Foundation's study, only six of the forty-one C.I.A. drone strikes conducted by the Obama Administration in Pakistan have targeted Al Qaeda members. Eighteen were directed at Taliban targets in Pakistan, and fifteen were aimed specifically at Baitullah Mehsud. Talat Masood, a retired Pakistani lieutenant general and an authority on security issues, says that the U.S.'s tactical shift, along with the elimination of Mehsud, has quieted some of the Pakistani criticism of the American air strikes, although the bombings are still seen as undercutting the country's sovereignty. But, given that many of the targeted Pakistani Taliban figures were obscure in U.S. counterterrorism circles, some critics have wondered whether they were legitimate targets for a Predator strike. "These strikes are killing a lot of low-level militants, which raises the question of whether they are going beyond the authorization to kill leaders," Peter Bergen told me. Roger Cressey, the former National Security Council official, who remains a strong supporter of the drone program, says, "The debate is that we've been doing this so long we're now bombing low-level guys who don't deserve a Hellfire missile up their ass." (In his view, "Not every target has to be a rock star.")

The Obama Administration has also widened the scope of authorized drone attacks in Afghanistan. An August report by the Senate Foreign Relations Committee disclosed that the Joint Integrated Prioritized Target List—the Pentagon's roster of approved terrorist targets, containing three hundred and sixty-seven names—was recently expanded to include some fifty Afghan drug lords who are suspected of giving money to help finance the Taliban. These new targets are a step removed from Al Qaeda. According to the Senate report, "There is no evidence that any significant amount of the drug proceeds goes to Al Qaeda." The inclusion of Afghan narcotics traffickers on the U.S. target list could prove awkward, some observers say, given that President Hamid Karzai's running mate, Marshal Mohammad Qasim Fahim, and the President's brother, Ahmed Wali Karzai, are strongly suspected of involvement in narcotics. Andrew Bacevich, a professor of history and international relations at Boston University, who has written extensively on military matters, said, "Are they going to target Karzai's brother?" He went on, "We should be very careful about who we define as the enemy we have to kill. Leaders of Al Qaeda, of course. But you can't kill people on Tuesday and negotiate with them on Wednesday."

Defining who is and who is not too tangential for the U.S. to kill can be difficult. John Radsan, a former lawyer in the C.I.A.'s office of general counsel, who is now a professor at William Mitchell College of Law, in St. Paul, Minnesota, says, "You can't target someone just because he visited an Al Qaeda Web site. But you also don't want to wait until they're about to detonate a bomb. It's a sliding scale." Equally fraught is the question of how many civilian deaths can be justified. "If it's Osama bin Laden in a house with a four-year-old, most people will say go ahead," Radsan says. "But if it's three or four children? Some say that's too many. And if he's in a school? Many say don't do it." Such judgment calls are being made daily by the C.I.A., which, Radsan points out, "doesn't have much experience with killing. Traditionally, the agency that does that is the Department of Defense."

Though the C.I.A.'s methodology remains unknown, the Pentagon has created elaborate formulas to help the military make such lethal calculations. A top military expert, who declined to be named, spoke of the military's system, saying, "There's a whole taxonomy of targets." Some people are approved for killing on sight. For others, additional permission is needed. A target's location enters the equation, too. If a school, hospital, or mosque is within the likely blast radius of a missile, that, too, is weighed by a computer algorithm before a lethal strike is authorized. According to the recent Senate Foreign Relations Committee report, the U.S. military places no name on its targeting list until there are "two verifiable human sources" and "substantial additional evidence" that the person is an enemy.

In Israel, which conducts unmanned air strikes in the Palestinian territories, the process of identifying targets, in theory at least, is even more exacting. Military lawyers have to be convinced that the target can't reasonably be captured, and that he poses a threat to national security. Military specialists in Arab culture also have to be convinced that the hit will do more good than harm. "You have to be incredibly cautious," Amos Guiora, a law professor at the University of Utah, says. From 1994 to 1997, he advised Israeli commanders on targeted killings in the Gaza Strip. "Not everyone is at the level appropriate for targeted killing," he says. "You want a leader, the hub with many spokes." Guiora, who follows the Predator program closely, fears that national-security officials here lack a clear policy and a firm definition of success. "Once you start targeted killing, you better make damn sure there's a policy guiding it," he says. "It can't be just catch-as-catch-can."

Daniel Byman, the director of Georgetown University's Center for Peace and Security Studies, argues that, when possible, "it's almost always better to arrest terrorists than to kill them. You get intelligence then. Dead men tell no tales." The C.I.A.'s killing of Saad bin Laden, Osama's son, provides a case in point. By the time that Saad bin Laden had reached Pakistan's tribal areas, late last year, there was little chance that any law-enforcement authority could capture him alive. But, according to Hillary Mann Leverett, an adviser to the National Security Council between 2001 and 2003, the Bush Administration would have had several opportunities to interrogate Saad bin Laden earlier, if it had been willing to make a deal with Iran, where, according to U.S. intelligence, he lived occasionally after September 11th. "The Iranians offered to work out an international framework for transferring terror suspects, but the Bush Administration refused," she said. In December, 2008, Saad bin Laden left Iran for Pakistan; within months, according to NPR, a Predator missile had ended his life. "We absolutely did not get the most we could," Leverett said. "Saad bin Laden would have been very, very valuable in terms of what he knew. He probably would have been a gold mine."

Byman is working on a book about Israel's experiences with counterterrorism, including targeted killing. Though the strikes there have weakened the Palestinian leadership, he said, "if you use these tools wrong, you can lose the moral high ground, which is going to hurt you. Inevitably, some of the intelligence is going to be wrong, so you're always rolling the dice. That's the reality of real-time intelligence."

Indeed, the history of targeted killing is marked by errors. In 1973, for example, Israeli intelligence agents murdered a Moroccan waiter by mistake. They thought that he was a terrorist who had been involved in slaughtering Israeli athletes at the Munich Olympics, a year earlier. And in 1986 the Reagan Administration attempted to retaliate against the Libyan leader Muammar Qaddafi for his suspected role in the deadly bombing of a disco frequented by American servicemen in Germany. The U.S. launched an air strike on Qaddafi's household. The bombs missed him, but they did kill his fifteen-month-old daughter.

The C.I.A.'s early attempts at targeting Osama bin Laden were also problematic. After Al Qaeda blew up the U.S. Embassies in Tanzania and Kenya, in August, 1998, President Bill Clinton retaliated, by launching seventy-five Tomahawk cruise missiles at a site in Afghanistan where bin Laden was expected to attend a summit meeting. According to reports, the bombardment killed some twenty Pakistani militants but missed bin Laden, who had left the scene hours earlier.

The development of the Predator, in the early nineteen-nineties, was supposed to help eliminate such mistakes. The drones can hover above a target for up to forty hours before refuelling, and the precise video footage makes it much easier to identify targets. But the strikes are only as accurate as the intelligence that goes into them. Tips from informants on the ground are subject to error, as is the interpretation of video images. Not long before September 11, 2001, for instance, several U.S. counterterrorism officials became certain that a drone had captured footage of bin Laden in a locale he was known to frequent in Afghanistan. The video showed a tall man in robes, surrounded by armed bodyguards in a diamond formation. At that point, drones were unarmed, and were used only for surveillance. "The optics were not great, but it was him," Henry Crumpton, then the C.I.A.'s top covert-operations officer for the region, told *Time*. But two other former C.I.A. officers, who also saw the footage, have doubts. "It's like an urban legend," one of them told me. "They just jumped to conclusions. You couldn't see his face. It could have been Joe Schmo. Believe me, no tall man with a beard is safe anywhere in Southwest Asia." In February, 2002, along the mountainous eastern border of Afghanistan, a Predator reportedly followed and killed three suspicious Afghans, including a tall man in robes who was thought to be bin Laden. The victims turned out to be innocent villagers, gathering scrap metal.

In Afghanistan and Pakistan, the local informants, who also serve as confirming witnesses for the air strikes, are notoriously unreliable. A former C.I.A. officer who was based in Afghanistan after September 11th told me that an Afghan source had once sworn to him that one of Al Qaeda's top leaders was being treated in a nearby clinic. The former officer said that he could barely hold off an air strike after he passed on the tip to his superiors. "They scrambled together an élite team," he recalled. "We caught hell from headquarters. They said 'Why aren't you moving on it?' when we insisted on checking it out first." It turned out to be an intentionally false lead. "Sometimes you're dealing with tribal chiefs," the former officer said. "Often, they say an enemy of theirs is Al Qaeda because they just want to get rid of somebody. Or they made crap up because they wanted to prove they were valuable, so that they could make money. You couldn't take their word."

The consequences of bad ground intelligence can be tragic. In September, a NATO air strike in Afghanistan killed between seventy and a hundred and twenty-five people, many of them civilians, who were taking fuel from two stranded oil trucks; they had been mistaken for Taliban insurgents. (The incident is being investigated by NATO.) According to a reporter for the *Guardian*, the bomb strike, by an F-15E fighter plane, left such a tangle of body parts that village elders resorted to handing out pieces of unidentifiable corpses to the grieving families, so that they could have something to bury. One Afghan villager told the newspaper, "I took a piece of flesh with me home and I called it my son."

Predator drones, with their superior surveillance abilities, have a better track record for accuracy than fighter jets, according to intelligence officials. Also, the drone's smaller Hellfire missiles are said to cause far less collateral damage. Still, the recent campaign to kill Baitullah Mehsud offers a sobering case study of the hazards of robotic warfare. It appears to have taken sixteen missile strikes, and fourteen months, before the C.I.A. succeeded in killing him. During this hunt, between two hundred and seven and three hundred and twenty-one additional people were killed, depending on which news accounts you rely upon. It's all but impossible to get a complete picture of whom the C.I.A. killed during this campaign, which took place largely in Waziristan. Not only has the Pakistani government closed off the region to the outside press; it has also shut out international humanitarian organizations like the International Committee for the Red Cross and Doctors Without Borders. "We can't get within a hundred kilometres of Waziristan," Brice de la Vingne, the operational coördinator for Doctors Without Borders in Pakistan, told me. "We tried to set up an emergency room, but the authorities wouldn't give us authorization."

A few Pakistani and international news stories, most of which rely on secondhand sources rather than on eyewitness accounts, offer the basic details. On June 14, 2008, a C.I.A. drone strike on Mehsud's home town, Makeen, killed an unidentified person. On January 2, 2009, four more unidentified people were killed. On February 14th, more than thirty people were killed, twenty-five of whom were apparently members of Al Qaeda and the Taliban, though none were identified as major leaders. On April 1st, a drone attack on Mehsud's deputy, Hakimullah Mehsud, killed ten to twelve of his followers instead. On April 29th, missiles fired from drones killed between six and ten more people, one of whom was believed to be an Al Qaeda leader. On May 9th, five to ten more unidentified people were killed; on May 12th, as many as eight people died. On June 14th, three to eight more people were killed by drone attacks. On June 23rd, the C.I.A. reportedly killed between two and six unidentified militants outside Makeen, and then killed dozens more people—possibly as many as eighty-six—during funeral prayers for the earlier casualties. An account in the Pakistani publication *The News* described ten of the dead as children. Four were identified as elderly tribal leaders. One eyewitness, who lost his right leg during the bombing, told Agence France-Presse that the mourners suspected what was coming: "After the prayers ended, people were asking each other to leave the area, as drones were hovering." The drones, which make a buzzing noise, are nicknamed *machay* ("wasps") by the Pashtun natives, and can sometimes be seen and heard, depending on weather conditions. Before the mourners could clear out, the eyewitness said, two drones started firing into the crowd. "It created havoc," he said. "There was smoke and dust everywhere. Injured people were crying and asking for help." Then a third missile hit. "I fell to the ground," he said.

The local population was clearly angered by the Pakistani government for allowing the U.S. to target a funeral. (Intelligence had suggested that Mehsud would be among the mourners.) An editorial in *The News* denounced the strike as sinking to the level of the terrorists. The Urdu newspaper *Jang* declared that Obama was "shutting his ears to the screams of thousands of women whom your drones have turned into dust." U.S. officials were undeterred, continuing drone strikes in the region until Mehsud was killed.

After such attacks, the Taliban, attempting to stir up anti-American sentiment in the region, routinely claims, falsely, that the victims are all innocent civilians. In several Pakistani cities, large protests have been held to decry the drone program. And, in the past year, perpetrators of terrorist bombings in Pakistan have begun presenting their acts as "revenge for the drone attacks." In recent weeks, a rash of bloody assaults on Pakistani government strongholds has raised the spectre that formerly unaligned militant groups have joined together against the Zardari Administration.

David Kilcullen, a counter-insurgency warfare expert who has advised General David Petraeus in Iraq, has said that the propaganda costs of drone attacks have been disastrously high. Militants have used the drone strikes to denounce the Zardari government—a shaky and unpopular regime—as little more than an American puppet. A study that Kilcullen co-wrote for the Center for New American Security, a think tank, argues, "Every one of these dead non-combatants represents an alienated family, a new revenge feud, and more recruits for a militant movement that has grown exponentially even as drone strikes have increased." His co-writer, Andrew Exum, a former Army Ranger who has advised General Stanley McChrystal in

Afghanistan, told me, "Neither Kilcullen nor I is a fundamentalist—we're not saying drones are not part of the strategy. But we are saying that right now they are part of the problem. If we use tactics that are killing people's brothers and sons, not to mention their sisters and wives, we can work at cross-purposes with insuring that the tribal population doesn't side with the militants. Using the Predator is a tactic, not a strategy."

Exum says that he's worried by the remote-control nature of Predator warfare. "As a military person, I put myself in the shoes of someone in FATA"—Pakistan's Federally Administered Tribal Areas—"and there's something about pilotless drones that doesn't strike me as an honorable way of warfare," he said. "As a classics major, I have a classical sense of what it means to be a warrior." An Iraq combat veteran who helped design much of the military's doctrine for using unmanned drones also has qualms. He said, "There's something important about putting your own sons and daughters at risk when you choose to wage war as a nation. We risk losing that flesh-and-blood investment if we go too far down this road."

Bruce Riedel, who has been deeply involved in these debates during the past few years, sees the choices facing Obama as exceedingly hard. "Is the drone program helping or hurting?" he asked. "It's a tough question. These are not cost-free operations." He likened the drone attacks to "going after a beehive, one bee at a time." The problem is that, inevitably, "the hive will always produce more bees." But, he said, "the only pressure currently being put on Pakistan and Afghanistan is the drones." He added, "It's really all we've got to disrupt Al Qaeda. The reason the Administration continues to use it is obvious: it doesn't really have anything else."

*Jane Mayer has been a *New Yorker* staff writer since 1995.

Mayer, Jane. "The Predator War: What Are the Risks of the C.I.A.'s Covert Drone Program?" *The New Yorker*, October 26, 2009. http://www.newyorker.com/magazine/2009/10/26/the-predator-war.

Used by permission.

Confessions of a Drone Warrior

by Matthew Power*

He was an experiment, really. One of the first recruits for a new kind of warfare in which men and machines merge. He flew multiple missions, but he never left his computer. He hunted top terrorists, saved lives, but always from afar. He stalked and killed countless people, but could not always tell you precisely what he was hitting. Meet the 21st-century American killing machine, who's still utterly, terrifyingly human.

From the darkness of a box in the Nevada desert, he watched as three men trudged down a dirt road in Afghanistan. The box was kept cold—precisely sixty-eight degrees—and the only light inside came from the glow of monitors. The air smelled spectrally of stale sweat and cigarette smoke. On his console, the image showed the midwinter landscape of eastern Afghanistan's Kunar Province—a palette of browns and grays, fields cut to stubble, dark forests climbing the rocky foothills of the Hindu Kush. He zoomed the camera in on the suspected insurgents, each dressed in traditional *shalwar kameez*, long shirts and baggy pants. He knew nothing else about them: not their names, not their thoughts, not the thousand mundane and profound details of their lives.

He was told that they were carrying rifles on their shoulders, but for all he knew, they were shepherd's staffs. Still, the directive from somewhere above, a mysterious chain of command that led straight to his headset, was clear: confirmed weapons. He switched from the visible spectrum—the muted grays and browns of "day-TV"—to the sharp contrast of infrared, and the insurgents' heat signatures stood out ghostly white against the cool black earth. A safety observer loomed behind him to make sure the "weapon release" was by the book. A long verbal checklist, his targeting laser locked on the two men walking in front. A countdown—three . . . two . . . one . . . —then the flat delivery of the phrase "missile off the rail." Seventy-five hundred miles away, a Hellfire flared to life, detached from its mount, and reached supersonic speed in seconds.

It was quiet in the dark, cold box in the desert, except for the low hum of machines.

He kept the targeting laser trained on the two lead men and stared so intently that each individual pixel stood out, a glowing pointillist dot abstracted from the image it was meant to form. Time became almost ductile, the seconds stretched and slowed in a strange electronic limbo. As he watched the men walk, the one who had fallen behind seemed to hear something and broke into a run to catch up with the other two. Then, bright and silent as a camera flash, the screen lit up with white flame.

Airman First Class Brandon Bryant stared at the scene, unblinking in the white-hot clarity of infrared. He recalls it even now, years later, burned into his memory like a photo negative: "The smoke clears, and there's pieces of the two guys around the crater. And there's this guy over here, and he's missing his right leg above his knee. He's holding it, and he's rolling around, and the blood is squirting out of his leg, and it's hitting the ground, and it's hot. His blood is hot. But when it hits the ground, it starts to cool off; the pool cools fast. It took him a long time to die. I just watched him. I watched him become the same color as the ground he was lying on."

That was Brandon Bryant's first shot. It was early 2007, a few weeks after his twenty-first birthday, and Bryant was a remotely-piloted-aircraft sensor operator—a "sensor" for short—part of a U.S. Air Force squadron that flew Predator drones in the skies above Iraq and Afghanistan. Beginning in 2006, he worked in the windowless metal box of a Ground Control Station (GCS) at Nellis Air Force Base, a vast sprawl of tarmac and maintenance hangars at the edge of Las Vegas.

The airmen kept the control station dark so they could focus on controlling their MQ-1B Predators circling two miles above the Afghan countryside. Bryant sat in a padded cockpit chair. He had a wrestler's compact build, a smooth-shaved head, and a piercing ice blue gaze frequently offset by a dimpled grin. As a sensor, his job was to work in tandem with the drone's pilot, who sat in the chair next to him. While the pilot controlled the drone's flight maneuvers, Bryant acted as the Predator's eyes, focusing its array of cameras and aiming its targeting laser. When a Hellfire was launched, it was a joint operation: the pilot pulled a trigger, and Bryant was responsible for the missile's "terminal guidance," directing the high-explosive warhead by laser to its desired objective. Both men wore regulation green flight suits, an unironic Air Force nod to the continuity of military decorum in the age of drone warfare.

Since its inception, the drone program has been largely hidden, its operational details gathered piecemeal from heavily redacted classified reports or stage-managed media tours by military public-affairs flacks. Bryant is one of very few people with firsthand experience as an operator who has been willing to talk openly, to describe his experience from the inside. While Bryant considers leakers like Chelsea Manning and Edward Snowden heroes willing to sacrifice themselves for their principles, he's cautious about discussing some of the details to which his top-secret clearance gave him access. Still, he is a curtain drawn back on the program that has killed thousands on our behalf.

Despite President Obama's avowal earlier this year that he will curtail their use, drone strikes have continued apace in Pakistan, Yemen, and Afghanistan. With enormous potential growth and expenditures, drones will be a center of our policy for the foreseeable future. (By 2025, drones will be an $82 billion business, employing an additional 100,000 workers.) Most Americans—61 percent in the latest Pew survey—support the idea of military drones, a projection of American power that won't risk American lives.

And yet the very idea of drones unsettles. They're too easy a placeholder or avatar for all of our technological anxieties— the creeping sense that screens and cameras have taken some piece of our souls, that we've slipped into a dystopia of disconnection. Maybe it's too soon to know what drones mean, what unconsidered moral and ethical burdens they carry. Even their shape is sinister: the blunt and featureless nose cone, like some eyeless creature that has evolved in darkness.

For Bryant, talking about them has become a sort of confessional catharsis, a means of processing the things he saw and did during his six years in the Air Force as an experimental test subject in an utterly new form of warfare.

Looking back, it was really little more than happenstance that had led him to that box in the desert. He'd been raised poor by his single mom, a public-school teacher in Missoula, Montana, and he struggled to afford tuition at the University of Montana.

In the summer of 2005, after tagging along with a buddy to the Army recruiting office, he wandered into the Air Force office next door. His friend got a bad feeling and bailed at the last minute, but Bryant had already signed his papers. In short order he was running around at Lackland Air Force Base during Warrior Week in the swelter of a Texas summer. He wasn't much for military hierarchy, but he scored high on his aptitude tests and was shunted into intelligence, training to be an imagery analyst. He was told he would be like "the guys that give James Bond all the information that he needs to get the mission done."

Most of the airmen in his intel class were funneled into the drone program, training at Creech Air Force Base in the sagebrush desert an hour north of Las Vegas. Bryant was told it was the largest group ever inducted. His sensor-operator course took ten weeks and led into "green flag" exercises, during which airmen piloted Predators and launched dummy Hellfires at a cardboard town mocked up in the middle of the desert. The missiles, packed with concrete, would punch through the derelict tanks and wrecked cars placed around the set. "It's like playing Dungeons & Dragons," says Bryant. "Roll a d20 to see if you hit your target." His training inspector, watching over his shoulder, would count down to impact and say, "Splash! You killed everyone."

Within a few months he "went off" to war, flying missions over Iraq at the height of the conflict's deadliest period, even though he never left Nevada.

His opening day on the job was also his worst. The drone took off from Balad Air Base, fifty miles outside Baghdad in the Sunni Triangle. Bryant's orders, delivered during a pre-shift mission briefing, were straightforward: a force-protection mission, acting as a "guardian angel" over a convoy of Humvees.

He would search out IEDs, insurgent activity, and other threats. It was night in the U.S. and already daylight in Iraq when the convoy rolled out.

From 10,000 feet, Bryant scanned the road with infrared. Traffic was quiet. Everything normal. Then he spotted a strange circle, glowing faintly on the surface of the road. A common insurgent's technique for laying IEDs is to douse a tire with gasoline, set it afire on a roadway, and dig up the softened tar beneath. The technique leaves a telltale heat signature, visible in infrared. Bryant, a fan of *The Lord of the Rings*, joked that it looked like the glowing Eye of Sauron.

Bryant pointed the spot out to the pilot, who agreed it looked like trouble. But when they tried to warn the convoy, they realized they couldn't. The Humvees had activated their radio jammers to disrupt the cell-phone signals used to remotely detonate IEDs. The drone crew's attempts at radio contact were as useless as shouting at the monitor. Brandon and his pilot patched in their flight supervisor to brainstorm a new way to reach them. They typed frantically back and forth in a group chat, a string of messages that soon included a cast of superiors in the U.S. and Iraq. Minutes passed, and the convoy rolled slowly toward the glowing circle. Bryant stared at the screen, heart pounding, scarcely breathing. The lead Humvee rolled across the eye. "Nothing happens," says Bryant. "And we're kind of like, maybe it was a mistake. Everyone's like *Whew*, good on you for spotting it, but we're glad that it wasn't what you thought it was." He remembers exhaling, feeling the nervous tension flow out of him.

"And the second vehicle comes along and *boom. . . .*"

A white flash of flame blossomed on the screen. Bryant was zoomed in as close as he could get, toggling his view between infrared and day-TV, watching in unblinking horror as the shredded Humvee burned. His headset exploded with panicked chatter from the ground in Iraq: *What the fuck happened? We've got guys down over here!* Frantic soldiers milled around, trying to pull people out of the smoldering wreckage. The IED had been tripped by either a pressure plate or manual detonation; the radio jammers would have done nothing to prevent it. Three soldiers were severely wounded, and two were killed.

"I kind of finished the night numb," Bryant says. "Then you just go home. No one talked about it. No one talked about how they felt after anything. It was like an unspoken agreement that you wouldn't talk about your experiences."

The pace of work in the box unraveled Bryant's sense of time. He worked twelve-hour shifts, often overnight, six days a week. Both wars were going badly at the time, and the Air Force leaned heavily on its new drone fleet. A loaded Predator drone can stay aloft for eighteen hours, and the pilots and sensors were pushed to be as tireless as the technology they controlled. (Bryant claims he didn't get to take leave for the first four years he served.)

Even the smell of that little shed in the desert got to Bryant. The hermetically sealed control center was almost constantly occupied—you couldn't take a bathroom break without getting swapped out—and the atmosphere was suffused with traces of cigarette smoke and rank sweat that no amount of Febreze could mask. One bored pilot even calculated the number of farts each cockpit seat was likely to have absorbed.

Mostly the drone crews' work was an endless loop of watching: scanning roads, circling compounds, tracking suspicious activity. If there was a "troops-in-contact" situation—a firefight, ground troops who call in a strike—Bryant's Predator could be called to the scene in minutes with its deadly payload. But usually time passed in a haze of banal images of rooftops, walled courtyards, or traffic-snarled intersections.

Sitting in the darkness of the control station, Bryant watched people on the other side of the world go about their daily lives, completely unaware of his all-seeing presence wheeling in the sky above. If his mission was to monitor a high-value target, he might linger above a single house for weeks. It was a voyeuristic intimacy. He watched the targets drink tea with friends, play with their children, have sex with their wives on rooftops, writhing under blankets. There were soccer matches, and weddings too. He once watched a man walk out into a field and take a crap, which glowed white in infrared.

Bryant came up with little subterfuges to pass the long hours at the console: sneaking in junk food, mending his uniforms, swapping off twenty-minute naps with the pilot. He mastered reading novels while still monitoring the seven screens of his station, glancing up every minute or two before returning to the page. He constructed a darkly appropriate syllabus for his occupation. He read the dystopian sci-fi classic *Ender's Game*, about children whose violent simulated games turn out to be actual warfare. Then came Asimov, Bryant pondering his Three Laws of Robotics in an age of Predators and Hellfires. *A robot may not injure a human being. . . .*

Bryant took five shots in his first nine months on the job. After a strike he was tasked with lingering over a site for several haunting hours, conducting surveillance for an "after-action report." He might watch people gather up the remains of those killed and carry them to the local cemetery or scrub the scene by dumping weapons into a river. Over Iraq he followed an insurgent commander as he drove through a crowded marketplace. The man parked in the middle of the street, opened his trunk, and pulled two girls out. "They were bound and gagged," says Bryant. "He put them down on their knees, executed them in the middle of the street, and left them there. People just watched it and didn't do anything." Another time, Bryant watched as a local official groveled in his own grave before being executed by two Taliban insurgents.

In the early months Bryant had found himself swept up by the Big Game excitement when someone in his squadron made "mind-blowingly awesome shots, situations where these guys were bad guys and needed to be taken out." But a deep ambivalence about his work crept in. Often he'd think about what life must be like in those towns and villages his Predators glided over, like buzzards riding updrafts. How would he feel, living beneath the shadow of robotic surveillance? "Horrible," he says now. But at first, he believed that the mission was vital, that drones were capable of limiting the suffering of war, of saving lives. When this notion conflicted with the things he witnessed in high resolution from two miles above, he tried to put it out of his mind. Over time he found that the job made him numb: a "zombie mode" he slipped into as easily as his flight suit.

Bryant's second shot came a few weeks after targeting the three men on that dirt road in Kunar. He was paired with a pilot he didn't much like, instructed to monitor a compound that intel told them contained a high-value individual—maybe a Taliban commander or Al Qaeda affiliate, nobody briefed him on the specifics. It was a typical Afghan mud-brick home, goats and cows milling around a central courtyard. They watched a corner of the compound's main building, bored senseless for hours. They assumed the target was asleep.

Then the quiet ended. "We get this word that we're gonna fire," he says. "We're gonna shoot and collapse the building. They've gotten intel that the guy is inside." The drone crew received no further information, no details of who the target was or why he needed a Hellfire dropped on his roof.

Bryant's laser hovered on the corner of the building. "*Missile off the rail.*" Nothing moved inside the compound but the eerily glowing cows and goats. Bryant zoned out at the pixels. Then, about six seconds before impact, he saw a hurried movement in the compound. "This figure runs around the corner, the outside, toward the front of the building. And it looked like a little kid to me. Like a little human person."

Bryant stared at the screen, frozen. "There's this giant flash, and all of a sudden there's no person there." He looked over at the pilot and asked, "Did that look like a child to you?" They typed a chat message to their screener, an intelligence observer who was watching the shot from "somewhere in the world"—maybe Bagram, maybe the Pentagon, Bryant had no idea—asking if a child had just run directly into the path of their shot.

"And he says, 'Per the review, it's a dog.'"

Bryant and the pilot replayed the shot, recorded on eight-millimeter tape. They watched it over and over, the figure darting around the corner. Bryant was certain it wasn't a dog.

If they'd had a few more seconds' warning, they could have aborted the shot, guided it by laser away from the compound. Bryant wouldn't have cared about wasting a $95,000 Hellfire to avoid what he believed had happened. But as far as the official military version of events was concerned, nothing out of the ordinary *had* happened. The pilot "was the type of guy to not argue with command," says Bryant. So the pilot's after-action report stated that the building had been destroyed, the high-value target eliminated. The report made no mention of a dog or any other living thing. The child, if there had been a child, was an infrared ghost.

The closest Bryant ever got to "real" combat—the roadside bombs and mortar fire experienced by combat troops—was after volunteering to deploy to Iraq. He spent the scorching summer and fall of 2007 stationed at the airfield in Balad, flying Predators on base-defense missions—scanning the area for insurgents. Some troops thanked the drone crews for being "angels in the sky," but more often they were the butt of jokes, mocked as "chair-borne rangers" who would "only earn a Purple Heart for burning themselves on a Hot Pocket."

Bryant struggled to square the jokes with the scenes that unfolded on his monitors. On one shift, he was told by command that they needed coordinates on an insurgent training compound and asked him to spot it. There was a firing range, and he watched as a group of fighters all entered the same building. One of the issues with targeting insurgents was that they often traveled with their families, and there was no way to tell who exactly was in any given building. Bryant lasered the building as he was ordered. Moments later, smoke mushroomed high into the air, a blast wave leveling the entire compound. An F-16, using Bryant's laser coordinates as guidance, had dropped a 1,000-pound bomb on the building—ten times the size of a Hellfire. "They didn't actually tell us that they were gonna blow it up," says Bryant. "We're like, 'Wow, that was nice of you to inform us of that.'"

In 2008, Bryant was transferred to a new post in "the shit-tiest place in the world," a drone squadron out of Cannon Air

Force Base in Clovis, New Mexico, where, Bryant says, "the air is not oxygen, it's basically cow shit." He continued as an operator for several more years, but his directive had changed. He was now mainly tracking high-value targets for the Joint Special Operations Command—the same secret-shrouded branch of the service that spearheaded the hunt for Osama bin Laden. "We were going after top dudes. They started showing us PowerPoint presentations on who these people are," he says. "Why we're after him, and what he did. I liked that. I liked being able to know shit like that."

Bryant has never been philosophically opposed to the use of drones—he sees them as a tool, like any other, that can be used for good ends, citing their potential use to fight poachers, or to monitor forest fires. For him it's about who controls them, and toward what ends. "It can't be a small group of people deciding how they're used," he says. "There's got to be transparency. People have to know how they're being used so they're used responsibly."

Transparency has not been the defining feature of U.S. drone policy over the last decade. Even as Bryant was being trained to operate drones in our very public wars in Iraq and Afghanistan, a parallel and clandestine drone war was being waged in places like Pakistan, Yemen and Somalia. Since 2004, the CIA has carried out hundreds of strikes in Pakistani territory, cutting secret deals with Pakistani intelligence to operate a covert assassination program. Another covert CIA drone base was operated from Saudi Arabia, launching strikes against militants in the lawless and mountainous interior of Yemen. While Bryant never flew for the CIA itself, their drone operators were drawn directly from the Air Force ranks.

While stationed in Clovis, among the highest-value targets Bryant's squadron hunted was Anwar al-Awlaki, the U.S.-born Yemeni imam and Al Qaeda recruiter. Al-Awlaki was ultimately killed by a CIA drone strike in Yemen in September 2011 (as was his 16-year-old son, Abdulrahman, a few weeks later). But Bryant claims his Air Force squadron "did most of the legwork" to pinpoint his location.

By 2011, Bryant had logged nearly 6,000 hours of flight time, flown hundreds of missions, targeted hundreds of enemies. He was in what he describes as "a fugue state of mind." At the entrance to his flight headquarters in Clovis, in front of a large bulletin board, plastered with photographs of targets like al-Awlaki, he looked up at the faces and asked: "What mother-fucker's gonna die today?"

It seemed like someone else's voice was speaking, some dark alter ego. "I knew I had to get out."

By the spring of 2011, almost six years after he'd signed on, Senior Airman Brandon Bryant left the Air Force, turning down a $109,000 bonus to keep flying. He was presented with a sort of scorecard covering his squadron's missions. "They gave me a list of achievements," he says. "Enemies killed, enemies captured, high-value targets killed or captured, stuff like that." He called it his diploma. He hadn't lased the target or pulled the trigger on all of the deaths tallied, but by flying in the missions he felt he had enabled them. "The number," he says, "made me sick to my stomach."

Total enemies killed in action: 1,626.

"After that first missile hit, I didn't really talk to anyone for a couple weeks." Bryant spoke to me while driving his beat-up black Dodge Neon in looping cursive circles around his hometown of Missoula. A yellow support-the-troops sticker on his bumper was obscured by a haze of road salt. The car's interior was festooned with patches from the different units he'd served with; in the back seat was a military pack stuffed with equal parts dirty laundry and bug-out gear. The gray midwinter sky weighed on a procession of strip malls and big-box stores; the snowy crenellations of the Bitterroot Range stretched far away to the south. He stared ahead as though watching the scene of his shot on an endless loop. "I didn't know what it meant to kill someone. And watching the aftermath, watching someone bleed out, because of something that I did?"

That night, on the drive home, he'd started sobbing. He pulled over and called his mother. "She just was like, 'Everything will be okay,' and I told her I killed someone, I killed people, and I don't feel good about it. And she's like, 'Good, that's how it should feel, you should never not feel that way.'"

Other members of his squadron had different reactions to their work. One sensor operator, whenever he made a kill, went home and chugged an entire bottle of whiskey. A female operator, after her first shot, refused to fire again even under the threat of court martial. Another pilot had nightmares after watching two headless bodies float down the Tigris. Bryant himself would have bizarre dreams where the characters from his favorite game, World of Warcraft, appeared in infrared.

By mid-2011, Bryant was back in Missoula, only now he felt angry, isolated, depressed. While getting a video game at a Best Buy, he showed his military ID with his credit card, and a teenage kid behind him in line spoke up. "He's like, 'Oh, you're in the military; my brother, he's a Marine, he's killed like thirty-six dudes, and he tells me about it all the time.' And I turn around and say, 'If you fucking ever talk like this to me again, I will stab

you. Don't ever disrespect people's deaths like that ever again.'"
The kid went pale, and Bryant took his game and left.

At the urging of a Vietnam veteran he met at the local VA office, Bryant finally went to see a therapist. After a few sessions, he just broke down: "I told her I wanted to be a hero, but I don't feel like a hero. I wanted to do something good, but I feel like I just wasted the last six years of my life." She diagnosed him with post-traumatic stress disorder.

It was an unexpected diagnosis. For decades the model for understanding PTSD has been "fear conditioning": quite literally the lasting psychological ramifications of mortal terror. But a term now gaining wider acceptance is "moral injury." It represents a tectonic realignment, a shift from a focusing on the violence that has been done to a person in wartime toward his feelings about what he has done to others—or what he's failed to do for them. The concept is attributed to the clinical psychiatrist Jonathan Shay, who in his book *Achilles in Vietnam* traces the idea back as far as the Trojan War. The mechanisms of death may change—as intimate as a bayonet or as removed as a Hellfire—but the bloody facts, and their weight on the human conscience, remain the same. Bryant's diagnosis of PTSD fits neatly into this new understanding. It certainly made sense to Bryant. "I really have no fear," he says now. "It's more like I've had a soul-crushing experience. An experience that I thought I'd never have. I was never prepared to take a life."

In 2011, Air Force psychologists completed a mental-health survey of 600 combat drone operators. Forty-two percent of drone crews reported moderate to high stress, and 20 percent reported emotional exhaustion or burnout. The study's authors attributed their dire results, in part, to "existential conflict." A later study found that drone operators suffered from the same levels of depression, anxiety, PTSD, alcohol abuse, and suicidal ideation as traditional combat aircrews. These effects appeared to spike at the exact time of Bryant's deployment, during the surge in Iraq. (Chillingly, to mitigate these effects, researchers have proposed creating a Siri-like user interface, a virtual copilot that anthropomorphizes the drone and lets crews shunt off the blame for whatever happens. *Siri, have those people killed.*)

In the summer of 2012, Bryant rejoined the Air Force as a reservist, hoping to get into the famed SERE program (Survival, Evasion, Resistance, Escape), where he would help train downed pilots to survive behind enemy lines. After so much killing, he wanted to save people. But after a severe concussion in a training accident, he dropped out and returned once more to Missoula. He walked with a cane, had headaches and memory lapses, and fell into a black depression.

During the worst of it, Bryant would make the rounds of Missoula's dozens of roughneck bars and drink himself to blackout on whiskey and cokes, vanishing for days or weeks on end. Many of those nights he would take his government-issued minus-forty-degree sleeping bag and pull into a parking lot in the middle of town next to the Clark Fork river. There's a small park with a wooden play structure there, built to look like a dragon with slides and ladders descending from it. He would climb to the little lookout deck at the top, blind drunk, and sleep there, night after night.

He doesn't remember much of that hazy period last summer, but his mother, LanAnn, does. Several times he had left a strange locked case sitting out on the kitchen table at her house, and she had put it back in the closet. The third day she woke to find the case open, with a loaded Sig Sauer P226 semi-automatic pistol lying out. Terrified that he might kill himself, she gave it to a friend with a locked gun safe. She'd only told her son about it a week earlier. He had no memory of any of it.

"I really thought we were going to lose him," LanAnn Bryant says now.

Something needed to change. Bryant hoped that by going to the press, people would understand drone crews' experience of war, that it was "more than just a video game" to them. In the fall, he spoke to a reporter for the German newsweekly *Der Spiegel*. The story was translated into English, and the British tabloid *Daily Mail* picked it up, posting it with the wildly inaccurate headline *drone operator followed orders to shoot a child . . . and decided he had to quit*. The story went viral.

The backlash from the drone community was immediate and fierce. Within days, 157 people on Bryant's Facebook page had de-friended him. "You are a piece of shit liar. Rot in hell," wrote a former Air Force comrade. In a sort of exercise in digital self-flagellation, Bryant read thousands of Reddit comments about himself, many filled with blistering vitriol and recrimination. "I read every single one of them," he says. "I was trying to just get used to the negative feelings." The spectrum of critics ranged from those who considered drone warfare a crime against humanity to combat veterans who thought Bryant was a whiner. He'd had death threats as well—none he took seriously—and other people said he should be charged with treason and executed for speaking to the media. On the day of one of our interviews, *The New York Times* ran an article about the military's research into PTSD among drone operators. I watched as he scanned a barrage of Facebook comments mocking the very idea that drone operators could suffer trauma:

> *I broke a fucking nail on that last mission!*

> *Maybe they should wear seatbelts*

> *they can claim PTSD when they have to do "Body Collection & Identification"*

And then Bryant waded in:

> *I'm ashamed to have called any of you assholes brothers in arms.*

> *Combat is combat. Killing is killing. This isn't a video game. How many of you have killed a group of people, watched as their bodies are picked up, watched the funeral, then killed them too?*

> *Yeah, it's not the same as being on the ground. So fucking what? Until you know what it is like and can make an intelligent meaningful assessment, shut your goddamn fucking mouths before somebody shuts them for you.*

Bryant's defense—a virtual battle over an actual war—left him seething at his keyboard. He says that when flying missions, he sometimes felt himself merging with the technology, imagining himself as a robot, a zombie, a drone itself. Such abstractions don't possess conscience or consciousness; drones don't care what they mean, but Bryant most certainly does. Now he plans to study to be an EMT, maybe get work on an ambulance, finally be able to save people like he always wanted. He no longer has infrared dreams, no longer closes his eyes and sees those strange polarized shadows flit across them.

Bryant closed his laptop and went out into the yard, tossing a tennis ball to his enormous bounding Japanese mastiff. Fingers of snow extended down through the dark forests of the Bitterroot, and high white contrails in the big sky caught the late-afternoon sunlight. The landscape of western Montana, Bryant observed, bears a striking resemblance to the Hindu Kush of eastern Afghanistan—a place he's seen only pixelated on a monitor. It was a cognitive dissonance he had often felt flying missions, as he tried to remind himself that the world was just as real when seen in a grainy image as with the naked eye, that despite being filtered through distance and technology, cause and effect still applied. This is the uncanny valley over which our drones circle. We look through them at the world, and ultimately stare back at ourselves.

*Matthew Power was an American journalist who wrote on a wide range of topics. He died in 2014.

Power, Matthew. "Confessions of a Drone Warrior." *GQ*, October 23, 2013. http://www.gq.com/news-politics/big-issues/201311/drone-uav-pilot-assassination.

The Moral Case for Drones

by Scott Shane*

For streamlined, unmanned aircraft, drones carry a lot of baggage these days, along with their Hellfire missiles. Some people find the very notion of killer robots deeply disturbing. Their lethal operations inside sovereign countries that are not at war with the United States raise contentious legal questions. They have become a radicalizing force in some Muslim countries. And proliferation will inevitably put them in the hands of odious regimes.

But most critics of the Obama administration's aggressive use of drones for targeted killing have focused on evidence that they are unintentionally killing innocent civilians. From the desolate tribal regions of Pakistan have come heartbreaking tales of families wiped out by mistake and of children as collateral damage in the campaign against Al Qaeda. And there are serious questions about whether American officials have understated civilian deaths.

So it may be a surprise to find that some moral philosophers, political scientists and weapons specialists believe armed, unmanned aircraft offer marked moral advantages over almost any other tool of warfare.

"I had ethical doubts and concerns when I started looking into this," said Bradley J. Strawser, a former Air Force officer and an assistant professor of philosophy at the Naval Postgraduate

School. But after a concentrated study of remotely piloted vehicles, he said, he concluded that using them to go after terrorists not only was ethically permissible but also might be ethically obligatory, because of their advantages in identifying targets and striking with precision.

"You have to start by asking, as for any military action, is the cause just?" Mr. Strawser said. But for extremists who are indeed plotting violence against innocents, he said, "all the evidence we have so far suggests that drones do better at both identifying the terrorist and avoiding collateral damage than anything else we have."

Since drone operators can view a target for hours or days in advance of a strike, they can identify terrorists more accurately than ground troops or conventional pilots. They are able to time a strike when innocents are not nearby and can even divert a missile after firing if, say, a child wanders into range.

Clearly, those advantages have not always been used competently or humanely; like any other weapon, armed drones can be used recklessly or on the basis of flawed intelligence. If an operator targets the wrong house, innocents will die.

Moreover, any analysis of actual results from the Central Intelligence Agency's strikes in Pakistan, which has become the world's unwilling test ground for the new weapon, is hampered by secrecy and wildly varying casualty reports. But one rough comparison has found that even if the highest estimates of collateral deaths are accurate, the drones kill fewer civilians than other modes of warfare.

Avery Plaw, a political scientist at the University of Massachusetts, put the C.I.A. drone record in Pakistan up against the ratio of combatant deaths to civilian deaths in other settings.

Mr. Plaw considered four studies of drone deaths in Pakistan that estimated the proportion of civilian victims at 4 percent, 6 percent, 17 percent and 20 percent respectively.

But even the high-end count of 20 percent was considerably lower than the rate in other settings, he found. When the Pakistani Army went after militants in the tribal area on the ground, civilians were 46 percent of those killed. In Israel's targeted killings of militants from Hamas and other groups, using a range of weapons from bombs to missile strikes, the collateral death rate was 41 percent, according to an Israeli human rights group.

In conventional military conflicts over the last two decades, he found that estimates of civilian deaths ranged from about 33 percent to more than 80 percent of all deaths.

Mr. Plaw acknowledged the limitations of such comparisons, which mix different kinds of warfare. But he concluded, "A fair-minded evaluation of the best data we have available suggests that the drone program compares favorably with similar operations and contemporary armed conflict more generally."

By the count of the Bureau of Investigative Journalism in London, which has done perhaps the most detailed and skeptical study of the strikes, the C.I.A. operators are improving their performance. The bureau has documented a notable drop in the civilian proportion of drone casualties, to 16 percent of those killed in 2011 from 28 percent in 2008. This year, by the bureau's count, just three of the 152 people killed in drone strikes through July 7 were civilians.

The drone's promise of precision killing and perfect safety for operators is so seductive, in fact, that some scholars have raised a different moral question: Do drones threaten to lower the threshold for lethal violence?

"In the just-war tradition, there's the notion that you only wage war as a last resort," said Daniel R. Brunstetter, a political scientist at the University of California at Irvine who fears that drones are becoming "a default strategy to be used almost anywhere."

With hundreds of terrorist suspects killed under President Obama and just one taken into custody overseas, some question whether drones have become not a more precise alternative to bombing but a convenient substitute for capture. If so, drones may actually be encouraging unnecessary killing.

Few imagined such debates in 2000, when American security officials first began to think about arming the Predator surveillance drone, with which they had spotted Osama bin Laden at his Afghanistan base, said Henry A. Crumpton, then deputy chief of the C.I.A.'s counterterrorism center, who tells the story in his recent memoir, "The Art of Intelligence."

"We never said, 'Let's build a more humane weapon,'" Mr. Crumpton said. "We said, 'Let's be as precise as possible, because that's our mission—to kill Bin Laden and the people right around him.'"

Since then, Mr. Crumpton said, the drone war has prompted an intense focus on civilian casualties, which in a YouTube world have become harder to hide. He argues that technological change is producing a growing intolerance for the routine slaughter of earlier wars.

"Look at the firebombing of Dresden, and compare what we're doing today," Mr. Crumpton said. "The public's expectations have been raised dramatically around the world, and that's good news."

*Scott Shane is a national security reporter for the *New York Times*.

Shane, Scott. "The Moral Case for Drones." News Analysis. *New York Times*, July 14, 2012. http://www.nytimes.com/2012/07/15/sunday-review/the-moral-case-for-drones.html?_r=0.

The Case for Drones (excerpt)

by Kenneth Anderson*

1. When Obama Embraced Drone Warfare

[. . .]

[The use of drones for targeted killings] has worked far better than anyone expected. It is effective, and has rightfully assumed an indispensable place on the list of strategic elements of U.S. counterterrorism-on-offense.

But it is not only a strategy of effectiveness, convenience, and necessity. Drone warfare offers ethical advantages as well, allowing for increased discrimination in time, manner, and targeting not available via any other comparable weapon platform. As such, it lends civilians in the path of hostilities vastly greater protection than does any other fighting tool. Drone warfare is an honorable attempt to seek out terrorists and insurgents who hide among civilians.

The expansion into automated and robotic military equipment owes much to the ethical impulse to create new technologies of discrimination when fighting enemies for whom unwitting civilian shields were their main materiel of war. Moreover, these are weapons that gain much of their discrimination in use from the fact that U.S. forces are *not* directly at personal risk and are thus able to take time to choose a moment to attack when civilians might be least at risk. Remoteness—the fact that the drone user is nowhere near the target, as the pilot is probably sitting in an air-conditioned room in Nevada—actually enables precision.

Ethical and effective—and yet today drone warfare is coming under increasingly strong public attack as being neither. Opponents of drones are seeking to raise the political costs of drone warfare to the United States, portraying it as a symbol of an arrogant, reprobate superpower dating back to the days of the "ugly American." Steve Coll, writing in the *New Yorker*, says drone use is "unnervingly reminiscent of Eisenhower's enthusiasm for poisoning schemes and coup plots." And though, in a recent Gallup poll, two-thirds of those surveyed said they supported drone strikes, there is no question that the political, legal, and moral legitimacy of drone warfare is increasingly at risk. The delegitimators are the international community, both its UN officials and NGO advocates; a sizable portion of academic international lawyers; much of the elite international media; and Obama's American left.

These delegitimators also include a number of conservatives and Republicans, chief among them Kentucky Senator Rand Paul. [...]

[...]

2. How Drone Warfare Works

Drone warfare consists of two distinct things. The first is a technology of war—the drone itself, such as the Predator, a "remotely piloted aerial vehicle" originally designed for pure surveillance. As a surveillance aircraft, it is slow-speed, but (in terms of manned aircraft) it has immensely long "loiter" times over the object of interest, clocking in many hours circling at slow speed. It is noisy, sometimes visible, and vulnerable to any enemy with even a minimal air-defense system. But it was not designed for use against highly developed military powers, but for the surveillance of technologically unsophisticated but potentially dangerous actors lacking such capabilities. From a strategic standpoint, the drone offers unparalleled "persistence" around its target—persistence that can last months on end and can outstrip what a human team might monitor on the ground, even if undetected, apart from other air systems.

This feature of Predators and Reapers—the two forms of drones really at issue today—enables the second aspect of drone warfare: targeted killing, a method of using force that takes advantage of drone technology. But drones and targeted killing are not the same thing: One is a technology and weapon platform, the other a way to use it. Targeted killing can be done not only with drones, but with human teams, too, as seen most dramatically in the Bin Laden raid by the Navy SEALs.

Similarly, drones are useful for more than targeted killing. They have broad, indeed rapidly expanding, military functions as a weapons platform—as evidenced in counterinsurgency strikes in Pakistan, Afghanistan, and Yemen against *groups* of fighters, not only individuals. This is conventional targeting of hostile forces in conventional conflict, just like one would see with a manned war plane. They have much in common. The pilot of a manned craft is often far away from the target, as would be a drone pilot—over the horizon or many miles away. Unlike the drone pilot, however, he might have minimal situational awareness of the actual events on the ground at the target—his knowledge may be nothing more than instrument data. A drone pilot may in fact have far greater visual and other sensor data than the pilot of a manned craft without handling the distractions caused by the work to keep a high-speed jet in the air.

The most offensively foolish (though endlessly repeated) objection raised against drones was the one made by Jane Mayer in her influential 2009 *New Yorker* article, "The Predator War": that drone pilots are so distant from their targets that they encourage a "push-button," video-game mentality toward killing. The professional military find the claim bizarre, and it fails to take into account the other kinds of weapons and platforms in use. Note, the pilot of a manned craft is often thousands of feet away and a mile above a target looking at a tiny coordinates screen. And what of the sailor, deep in the below-decks of a ship, or a submarine, firing a cruise missile with no awareness of any kind about the target hundreds of miles away?

For that matter, the common perception of drones as a sci-fi combination of total surveillance and complete discretion in where and when to strike is simply wrong. The drone *pilot* might sit in Nevada, but the drone itself has a limited range, requires an airstrip, fuel, repairs, and 200 or so personnel to keep it in the air. All this physical infrastructure must be close to the theater of operations. Stress rates among drone pilots are at least as high as those of manned aircraft pilots; they are far from having a desensitized attitude toward killing. This appears to be partially because these are not mere combat operations but fundamentally and primarily intelligence operations. Drone pilots engaged in targeted killing operations watch their targets from a very personal distance via sensor technology, through which they track intimate, daily patterns of life to gather information and, perhaps, to determine precisely the best moment to strike, when collateral damage might be least.

As one drone operator told me, it is not as if one sees the terrible things the target is engaged in doing that made him a target in the first place; instead, it feels, after a few weeks of observation, as though you are killing your neighbor.

In any case, the mentality of drone pilots in targeted-killing ops is irrelevant to firing decisions; they do not make decisions to fire weapons. The very existence of a remote platform, one with long loiter times and maximum tactical surveillance, enables decisions to fire by committee. And deliberately so, notes Gregory McNeal, a professor of law at Pepperdine University, who has put together the most complete study of the still largely secret decision-making process—the so-called disposition lists and kill matrix the *New York Times* has described in front page stories. It starts from the assessment of intelligence through meetings in which determinations, including layers of legal review, are made about whether a potential target has sufficient value and, finally, whether and when to fire the weapon in real time. The drone pilot is just a pilot.

Targeting is therefore a bureaucratized process that necessarily relies on judgment and estimations of many uncertainties. Its discretionary and bloodless nature alarms critics, as does its bureaucratic regularization. Yet it is essential to understand, as McNeal observes, that this is not fundamentally different from any other process of targeting that takes place in conventional war, save that it seeks to pinpoint the targets. Conventional war targeting, by contrast, seeks not individuals, but merely formations of hostile forces as groups. In either case, targeting is inherently intelligence-driven and a highly organized activity, whether in the military or across the broader national-security agencies.

Concerns about the nature of the warfare itself leads to a sharing and checking of that discretion among actors; in turn, this leads to committees' making decisions; and by the time this process of bureaucratic rationalization is complete, it looks like military targeting processes in conventional war, with an extra dollop of intelligence assessments, not some mysterious Star Chamber assassination committee. After all, any group of generals deciding where to hit the enemy in war is, by definition, a "kill list" committee.

[. . .]

5. The Ethical Objection

[. . .] The leading objection to drone warfare today is that it supposedly involves large, or "excessive," numbers of civilian casualties, and that the claims of precision and discrimination are greatly overblown. These are partly factual questions full of unknowns and many contested issues. The Obama administration did not help itself by offering estimates of civilian collateral damage early on that ranged absurdly from zero to the low two digits. This both squandered credibility with the media and, worse, set a bar of perfection—zero civilian collateral damage—that no weapon system could ever meet, while distracting people entirely from the crucial question of what standard civilian harms should be set against.

The most useful estimates of civilian casualties from targeted killing with drones come from the New America Foundation (NAF) and the Foundation for Defense of Democracies, which each keep running counts of strikes, locations, and estimates of total killed and civilian casualties. They don't pretend to know what they don't know, and rely on open sources and media accounts. There is no independent journalistic access to

Waziristan to help corroborate accounts that might be wrong or skewed by Taliban sources, Pakistani media, Pakistani and Western advocacy groups, or the U.S. or Pakistani governments. Pakistan's military sometimes takes credit for drone strikes against its enemies and sometimes blames drone strikes for its own air raids against villages. A third source of estimates, UK-based The Bureau of Investigative Journalism (TBIJ), comes up with higher numbers.

TBIJ (whose numbers are considered much too high by many knowledgeable American observers) came up with a range, notes Georgetown law professor and former Obama DOD official Rosa Brooks. The 344 known drone strikes in Pakistan between 2004 and 2012 killed, according to TBIJ, between "2,562 and 3,325 people, of whom between 474 and 881 were civilians." The NAF, she continues, came up with slightly lower figures, somewhere "between 1,873 and 3,171 people killed overall in Pakistan, of whom between 282 and 459 were civilians." (Media have frequently cited the total killed as though it were the civilians killed.) Is this a lot of civilians killed? Even accepting for argument's sake TBIJ's numbers, Brooks concludes, if you work out the "civilian deaths per drone strike ratio for the last eight years . . . on average, each drone strike seems to have killed between 0.8 and 2.5 civilians." In practical terms, adds McNeal, this suggests "less than three civilians killed per strike, and that's using the highest numbers" of any credible estimating organization.[1]

Whether any of this is "disproportionate" or "excessive" as a matter of the laws of war cannot be answered simply by comparing total deaths to civilian deaths, or civilian deaths per drone strike, however. Although commentators often leap to a conclusion in this way, one cannot answer the legal question of proportionality without an assessment of the military benefits anticipated. Moreover, part of the disputes over numbers involves not just unverifiable facts on the ground, but differences in legal views defining who is a civilian and who is a lawful target. The U.S. government's definition of those terms, following its long-standing views of the law of targeting in war, almost certainly differs from those of TBIJ or other liberal nongovernmental groups, particularly in Europe. Additionally, much of drone warfare today targets groups who are deemed, under the laws of war, to be part of hostile forces. Targeted killing aimed at individuated high-value targets is a much smaller part of drone warfare than it once was. The targeting of groups, however, while lawful under long-standing U.S. interpretations of the laws of war, might result in casualties often counted by others as civilians.

Yet irrespective of what numbers one accepts as the best estimate of harms of drone warfare, or the legal proportionality of the drone strikes, the moral question is simply, What's the alternative? One way to answer this is to start from the proposition that if you believe the use of force in these circumstances is lawful and ethical, then all things being equal as an ethical matter, the method of force used should be the one that spares the most civilians while achieving its lawful aims. If that is the comparison of moral alternatives, there is simply no serious way to dispute that drone warfare is the best method available. It is more discriminating and more precise than other available means of air warfare, including manned aircraft—as France and Britain, lacking their own drones and forced to rely on far less precise manned jet strikes, found over Libya and Mali—and Tomahawk cruise missiles.

A second observation is to look across the history of precision weapons in the past several decades. I started my career as a human-rights campaigner, kicking off the campaign to ban landmines for leading organizations. Around 1990, I had many conversations with military planners, asking them to develop more accurate and discriminating weapons—ones with smaller kinetic force and greater ability to put the force where sought. Although every civilian death is a tragedy, and drone warfare is very far from being the perfect tool the Obama administration sometimes suggests, for someone who has watched weapons development over a quarter century, the drone represents a steady advance in precision that has cut zeroes off collateral-damage figures.

Those who see only the snapshot of civilian harm today are angered by civilian deaths. But barring an outbreak of world peace, it is foolish and immoral not to encourage the development and use of more sparing and exact weapons. One has only to look at the campaigns of the Pakistani army to see the alternatives in action. The Pakistani military for many years has been in a running war with its own Taliban and has regularly attacked villages in the tribal areas with heavy and imprecise airstrikes. A few years ago, it thought it had reached an accommodation with an advancing Taliban, but when the enemy decided it wanted not just the Swat Valley but Islamabad, the Pakistani government decided it had no choice but to drive it back. And it did, with a punishing campaign of airstrikes and rolling artillery barrages that leveled whole villages, left hundreds of thousands without homes, and killed hundreds.

But critics do not typically evaluate drones against the standards of the artillery barrage of manned airstrikes, because their assumption, explicit or implicit, is that there is no call to use force at all. And of course, if the assumption is that you don't need or should not use force, then any civilian death by drones is excessive. That cannot be blamed on drone warfare, its ethics or effectiveness, but on a much bigger question of whether one ought to use force in counterterrorism at all.

6. The Ethical Objection, Globalized

The objection to civilian deaths draws out a related criticism: Why should the United States be able to conduct these drone strikes in Pakistan or in Yemen, countries that are not at war with America? What gives the United States the moral right to take its troubles to other places and inflict damage by waging war? Why should innocent Pakistanis suffer because the United States has trouble with terrorists?

The answer is simply that like it or not, the terrorists are in these parts of Pakistan, and it is the terrorists that have brought trouble to the country. The U.S. has adopted a moral and legal standard with regard to where it will conduct drone strikes against terrorist groups. It will seek consent of the government, as it has long done with Pakistan, even if that is contested and much less certain than it once was. But there will be no safe havens. If al-Qaeda or its affiliated groups take haven somewhere and the government is unwilling or unable to address that threat, America's very long-standing view of international law permits it to take forcible action against the threat, sovereignty and territorial integrity notwithstanding.

This is not to say that the United States could or would use drones anywhere it wished. Places that have the rule of law and the ability to respond to terrorists on their territory are different from weakly governed or ungoverned places. There won't be drones over Paris or London—this canard is popular among campaigners and the media but ought to be put to rest. But the vast, weakly governed spaces, where states are often threatened by Islamist insurgency, such as Mali or Yemen, are a different case altogether.

This critique often leads, however, to the further objection that the American use of drones is essentially laying the groundwork for others to do the same. Steve Coll wrote in the *New Yorker*: "America's drone campaign is also creating an ominous global precedent. Ten years or less from now, China will likely be able to field armed drones. How might its Politburo apply Obama's doctrines to Tibetan activists holding meetings in Nepal?"

The United States, it is claimed, is arrogantly exerting its momentary technological advantage to do what it likes. It will be sorry when other states follow suit. But the United States does not use drones in this fashion and has claimed no special status for drones. The U.S. government uses drone warfare in a far more limited way, legally and morally, and entirely within the bounds of international law. The problem with China (or Russia) using drones is that they might not use them in the same way as the United States. The drone itself is a tool. How it is used and against whom—these are moral questions. If China behaves malignantly, drones will not be responsible. Its leaders will be.

Finally, drone warfare is often objected to on the premise that the reduced risks to one's own soldiers might tempt political leaders to resort to force more than they should. As a moral objection, however, this is simply wrong. It is probably true that drone warfare makes it easier to use force—though the proposition that it is "too easy" depends entirely on whether one sees any particular use of force as just or unjust. While many assume that the use of force needs to be made more difficult, in the case of humanitarian intervention, where NATO countries are loath to risk their forces, one might say it is exactly the other way around.

In any case, it is an immoral argument that posits soldiers as mere means to pressure political leadership. Soldiers take risks against the enemy for reasons of military necessity. But they don't exist to put pressure on their own political leaders. That would be to use them as hostages.

It is a most remarkable state of affairs, however, that advocacy and campaigning groups—dedicated over the decades to demanding that war's risks to civilians be reduced—have so thoroughly bought into an argument that the fundamental problem of drones is that they threaten to make war less harmful to civilians as well as soldiers.

[…]

NOTE

1. An often cited report, "Living Under Drones," issued in 2012 by advocacy law clinics at NYU and Stanford law schools, does not merit the attention it has received. The study was solicited by a UK anti-drone organization, Reprieve, which helped organize the "study," and which then sat in on some interviews. A Pakistani group closely linked to Reprieve, the Foundation for Fundamental Rights, which is engaged in multiple lawsuits against the drone programs, selected the interviewees and also sat in on interviews; the interviewees included nine of FFR's own clients in its anti-drone lawsuits. The foundation also partly funded the study by paying for the transportation of interviewees. The report invents a peculiar and novel category—"experiential victims" of drones—apparently lacking enough direct family members killed or injured in actual drone strikes to make the numbers interesting. Crucially, this category includes "victims" who might have witnessed not a drone strike but merely drone surveillance, and also includes those who might be family members of a person from North Waziristan who might have witnessed something. In any case, those called "close family members" for purposes of establishing this "experiential" victimhood

include grandparents, parents, siblings, children, uncles, and cousins. All of this is plainly laid out in "Living Under Drones" and requires no special digging around for background facts; national-security columnist for PBS's *Need to Know*, Joshua Foust, walked through numerous methodological inadequacies of the report in an article for the *Atlantic* online on September 26, 2012.

*Kenneth Anderson is a professor of international law at American University and a member of the Task Force on National Security and Law at the Hoover Institution.

Anderson, Kenneth. "The Case for Drones (excerpt)." *Commentary*, July/August 2014. https://www.commentarymagazine.com/articles/the-case-for-drones/.

The Moral Hazard of Drones

*by John Kaag and Sarah Kreps**

As the debate on the morality of the United States' use of unmanned aerial vehicles ("U.A.V.'s," also known as drones) has intensified in recent weeks, several news and opinion articles have appeared in the media. Two, in particular, both published this month, reflect the current ethical divide on the issue. A feature article in Esquire by Tom Junod censured the "Lethal Presidency of Barack Obama" for the administration's policy of targeted killings of suspected militants; another, "The Moral Case for Drones," a news analysis by The Times' Scott Shane, gathered opinions from experts that implicitly commended the administration for replacing Dresden-style strategic bombing with highly precise attacks that minimize collateral damage.

Amid this discussion, we suggest that an allegory might be helpful to illustrate some of the many moral perils of drone use that have been overlooked. It shows that our attempts to avoid obvious ethical pitfalls of actions like firebombing may leave us vulnerable to other, more subtle, moral dangers.

While drones have become the weapons of our age, the moral dilemma that drone warfare presents is not new. In fact, it is very, very old:

Once upon a time, in a quiet corner of the Middle East, there lived a shepherd named Gyges. Despite the hardships in his life

Gyges was relatively satisfied with his meager existence. Then, one day, he found a ring buried in a nearby cave.

This was no ordinary ring; it rendered its wearer invisible. With this new power, Gyges became increasingly dissatisfied with his simple life. Before long, he seduced the queen of the land and began to plot the overthrow of her husband. One evening, Gyges placed the ring on his finger, sneaked into the royal palace, and murdered the king.

In his "Republic," Plato recounts this tale, but does not tell us the details of the murder. Still, we can rest assured that, like any violent death, it was not a pleasant affair. However, the story ends well, at least for Gyges. He marries the queen and assumes the position of king.

This story, which is as old as Western ethics itself, is meant to elicit a particular moral response from us: disgust. So why do we find Plato's story so appalling?

Maybe it's the way that the story replaces moral justification with practical efficiency: Gyges' being able to commit murder without getting caught, without any real difficulty, does not mean he is justified in doing so. (Expediency is not necessarily a virtue.)

Maybe it's the way that Gyges' ring obscures his moral culpability: it's difficult to blame a person you can't see, and even harder to bring them to justice.

Maybe it's that Gyges is successful in his plot: a wicked act not only goes unpunished, but is rewarded.

Maybe it's the nagging sense that any kingdom based on such deception could not be a just one: what else might happen in such a kingdom under the cover of darkness?

Our disgust with Gyges could be traced to any one of these concerns, or to all of them.

One might argue that the myth of Gyges is a suitable allegory to describe the combatants who have attacked and killed American civilians and troops in the last 10 years. A shepherd from the Middle East discovers that he has the power of invisibility, the power to strike a fatal blow against a more powerful adversary, the power to do so without getting caught, the power to benefit from his deception. These, after all, are the tactics of terrorism.

But the myth of Gyges is really a story about modern counterterrorism, not terrorism.

We believe a stronger comparison can be made between the myth and the moral dangers of employing precision guided munitions and drone technologies to target suspected terrorists. What is distinctive about the tale of Gyges is the ease with which he can commit murder and get away scot-free. The technological advantage provided by the ring ends up serving as the justification of its use.

Terrorists, whatever the moral value of their deeds, may be found and punished; as humans they are subject to retribution, whether it be corporal or legal. They may lose or sacrifice their lives. They may, in fact, be killed in the middle of the night by a drone. Because remote controlled machines cannot suffer these consequences, and the humans who operate them do so at a great distance, the myth of Gyges is more a parable of modern counterterrorism than it is about terrorism.

Only recently has the use of drones begun to touch on questions of morality. Perhaps it's because the answers to these questions appear self-evident. What could be wrong with the use of unmanned aerial vehicles? After all, they limit the cost of war, in terms of both blood and treasure. The U.S. troops who operate them can maintain safer stand-off positions in Eastern Europe or at home. And armed with precision-guided munitions, these drones are said to limit collateral damage. In 2009, Leon Panetta, who was then the director of the Central Intelligence Agency, said, U.A.V.'s are "very precise and very limited in terms of collateral damage . . . the only game in town in terms of confronting or trying to disrupt the al Qaeda leadership." What could be wrong with all this?

Quite a bit, it turns out.

Return, for a minute, to the moral disgust that Gyges evokes in us. Gyges also risked very little in attacking the king. The success of his mission was almost assured, thanks to the technological advantage of his ring. Gyges could sneak past the king's guards unscathed, so he did not need to kill anyone he did not intend on killing. These are the facts of the matter.

What we find unsettling here is the idea that these facts could be confused for moral justification. Philosophers find this confusion particularly abhorrent and guard against it with the only weapon they have: a distinction. The "fact-value distinction" holds that statements of fact should never be confused with statements of value. More strongly put, this distinction means that statements of fact do not even *imply* statements of value. "Can" does not imply "ought." To say that we *can* target individuals without incurring troop casualties does not imply that, we *ought* to.

This seems so obvious. But, as Peter W. Singer noted earlier this year in The Times, when the Obama administration was asked why continued U.S. military strikes in the Middle East did not constitute a violation of the 1973 War Powers Resolution, it responded that such activities did not "involve the presence of U.S. ground troops, U.S. casualties or a serious threat thereof." The justification of these strikes rested solely on their ease. The Ring of Gyges has the power to obscure the obvious.

This issue has all the hallmarks of what economists and philosophers call a "moral hazard"—a situation in which greater risks are taken by individuals who are able to avoid shouldering the cost associated with these risks. It thus seems wise, if not convenient, to underscore several ethical points if we are to avoid our own "Gyges moment."

First, we might remember Marx's comment that "the windmill gives you a society with the feudal lord; the steam engine gives you one with the industrial capitalist." And precision guided munitions and drones give you a society with perpetual asymmetric wars.

The creation of technology is a value-laden enterprise. It creates the material conditions of culture and society and therefore its creation should be regarded as always already moral and political in nature. However, technology itself (the physical stuff of robotic warfare) is neither smart nor dumb, moral nor immoral. It can be used more or less precisely, but precision and efficiency are not inherently morally good. Imagine a very skilled dentist who painlessly removes the wrong tooth. Imagine a drone equipped with a precision guided munition that kills a completely innocent person, but spares the people who live in his or her neighborhood. The use of impressive technologies does not grant one impressive moral insight. Indeed, as Gyges demonstrates, the opposite can be the case.

Second, assassination and targeted killings have always been in the repertoires of military planners, but never in the history of warfare have they been so cheap and easy. The relatively low number of troop casualties for a military that has turned to drones means that there is relatively little domestic blowback against these wars. The United States and its allies have created the material conditions whereby these wars can carry on indefinitely. The non-combatant casualty rates in populations that are attacked by drones are slow and steady, but they add up. That the casualty rates are relatively low by historical standards—this is no Dresden—is undoubtedly a good thing, but it may allow the international media to overlook pesky little facts like the slow accretion of foreign casualties.

Third, the impressive expediency and accuracy in drone targeting may also allow policymakers and strategists to become lax in their moral decision-making about who exactly should be targeted. Consider the stark contrast between the ambiguous language used to define legitimate targets and the specific technical means a military uses to neutralize these targets. The terms "terrorist," "enemy combatant," and "contingent threat" are extremely vague and do very little to articulate the legitimacy of military targets. In contrast, the technical capabilities of weapon systems define and "paint" these targets with ever-greater definition. As weaponry becomes more precise, the language of warfare has become more ambiguous.

This ambiguity has, for example, altered the discourse surrounding the issue of collateral damage. There are two very different definitions of collateral damage, and these definitions affect the truth of the following statement: "Drone warfare and precision guided munitions limit collateral damage." One definition views collateral damage as the inadvertent destruction of property and persons in a given attack. In other words, collateral damage refers to "stuff we don't mean to blow up."

Another definition characterizes collateral damage as objects or individuals "that would not be lawful military targets in the circumstances ruling at the time." In other words, collateral damage refers to "the good guys." Since 1998, this is the definition that has been used. What is the difference between these definitions?

The first is a description of technical capabilities (being able to hit X while not hitting Y); the second is a normative and indeed legal judgment about who is and is not innocent (and therefore who is a legitimate target and who is not). The first is a matter of fact, the second a matter of value. There is an important difference between these statements, and they should not be confused.

Fourth, questions of combatant status should be the subject of judicial review and moral scrutiny. Instead, if these questions are asked at all, they are answered as if they were mere matters of fact, unilaterally, behind closed doors, rather than through transparent due process. That moral reasoning has become even more slippery of late, as the American government has implied that all military aged males in a strike area are legitimate targets: a "guilt by association" designation.

Finally, as the strategic repertoires of modern militaries expand to include drones and precision guided munitions, it is not at all clear that having more choices leads strategists to make better and more informed ones. In asking, "Is More Choice Better Than Less?" the philosopher Gerald Dworkin once argued that the answer is "not always." In the words of Kierkegaard: "In possibility everything is possible. Hence in possibility one can go astray in all possible ways."

Some might object that these guidelines set unrealistically high expectations on military strategists and policymakers. They would probably be right. But no one—except Gyges—said that being ethical was easy.

*John Kaag is an assistant professor of philosophy at the University of Massachusetts, Lowell.

Sarah Kreps is an assistant professor of government at Cornell University.

Distant Death: The Case for a Moratorium on Drone Strikes

by Conor Friedersdorf*

[...]

What if I told you all that an armed Predator drone is cir-cling above us right now? It isn't. So don't worry. But if an armed drone was there, would it make you feel anxious? If we could hear the buzz of its engine, would that change the tenor of our time together? Now let's imagine that this drone is hovering overhead because there's a terrorist hanging out 100 yards away from this building. We're often told how precise drone strikes are. Obama Administration officials have called them surgical. If a surgery were happening in the building next door I wouldn't be worried about getting nicked by the scalpel. Would you be worried for your safety if you were 100 yards away from drone strike? Say you're laying in bed one night, and in the house next door, a terrorist is laying in his bed.

Would you want a drone strike to take him out?

If next door is too close for comfort, do you think the U.S. military or the CIA should be allowed to carry out drone strikes on terrorists with innocent people next door?

Thankfully, the fear that drones bring to innocent people in places like Afghanistan, Pakistan, and Yemen isn't something that any of us is likely to experience first-hand—especially (if the drones know what's good for them) in the presence of this esteemed scholar from the Brookings Institution. In seriousness, I want to thank Ben Wittes for sharing the stage with me tonight. On so many subjects, we look at the world in very different ways, but I've always appreciated his commitment to participating in public discourse, and I aspire to his command of what he calls lawfare. Thank you, as well, to the organizers of this event, and to everyone who came out to watch.

Soon, I hope debates on the merits of targeted killing are taking place not only at universities, but inside the federal court system. The Obama Administration hopes to avoid that fate. Its lawyers would have us believe that targeted killing with drones is a state secret, or else a so-called political question that isn't properly decided by judges.

In Israel, a state with national-security challenges far greater than ours, the Supreme Court grappled with this same question. Do judges have any role to play in targeted killing? They didn't see it as a closed question. They saw their role as determining "the permissible and the forbidden" in combat that implicates "the most basic right of a human being—the right to life." They affirmed that "non-justiciability cannot prevent the examination of that question." I suspect James Madison would find their approach more prudent than what the Obama Administration suggests. The administration would have us believe not only that they're empowered to kill an American in secret, but that after the fact, courts should refrain from judging whether the killing violated the right to life of the target.

Does anyone else think that's a recipe for abuses?

But legal doctrine is not my area of expertise. So I'd like to begin, instead, with a moral question: Is it ever okay for the

U.S. to kill people with drones? "This is actually an easy question," Mr. Wittes once said, "since drones clearly enable more discriminating and deliberative targeting than do alternative weapon systems." I want to repeat that. He thinks that once you've decided to use force, drones could be the most moral choice, because they're more deliberative and discriminating.

That's an interesting standard.

It got me thinking: Is it ever okay for the U.S. to use biological weapons? Is *that* ever the most moral option? They're terrifying. A taboo surrounds them, and treaties prohibit their use.

And yet.

Imagine a remote al-Qaeda compound. Inside its walls are a few dozen adult bomb makers, their wives, and many scores of children. Explosives are everywhere. A drone strike or a firefight would cause the whole place to blow. But a U.S. scientist has an alternative: a biological agent that, if dispersed over the compound, would target, incapacitate and kill only the adult males. Only the militants—no one else. Would that discriminating bioweapon be the most moral option?

That's a hard question. On one hand, maybe you save a lot of innocent women and children. On the other hand, using a bioweapon would have implications that transcend any one discrete mission. Similarly, using weaponized drones has implications that go far beyond any one discrete strike. Let's think through some of them.

1) For a drone strike to be an option, the United States has to fund a drone industry to build its arsenal, negotiate leases for drone bases in various foreign countries—often non-democracies where the people do not want a drone base and would

vote against it if they were afforded rights that we think of as universal. In building this drone fleet and the infrastructure to use it, America inevitably normalizes the notion of weaponized drones all over the globe, and it seeds an industry that is certain to contribute to the weapon's proliferation in the future.

2) In thought experiments, we may be able to separate the questions, "Should force be used?" and, "If so, what is the most ethical weapon available?" But the questions are not typically asked independent of one another. A fleet of drones at the ready significantly lowers the costs of certain lethal operations. As we've seen, it also makes perpetual war possible in a way that it wasn't before. Due to drones, lethal acts occur that wouldn't have happened in a world without drones. And those acts can be carried out with more secrecy than would otherwise be possible.

3) The ability to hover for hours or even days does permit deliberation and discrimination. But hovering also imposes a cost on many thousands of innocents. Drones don't just affect targets, actual and aborted. They affect whole communities. People who live in communities where drones hover overhead report severe anxiety, terrified children, mental health problems, trouble sleeping, paranoia (and after drone strikes occur, perva- sive mistrust as people wonder if a local helped call down the Hellfire missile). Communities stop gathering in large numbers to attend prayers or public meetings. They're forced to live in what any of us might consider a dystopia, if we were forced to live there. How would you feel if every night you had to tuck your children into bed as the buzz of drones overhead made them afraid that they'd never wake up again?

As it turns out, asking if there's ever a discrete targeted kill- ing where a drone is the most ethical option tells us very little. Like land mines or bio-weapons or torture to prevent a nuclear holocaust, a drone strike might be the most ethical option in a given situation. But a blanket ban might nevertheless be an ethical imperative. Perhaps so many terrible consequences inevitably flow from building, maintaining, and using a fleet of armed drones that a ban leaves us better off.

The better question is, "Can maintaining *a drone-strike program* ever be ethical?"

To me, that is a very tough question. Since my time is limited, I want to focus on a related question that is far more urgent: Is America's actual drone-strike program ethical?

That's an easier question. It is not ethical.

What's least defensible is how we respond after killing innocents, presumably by accident. The moral thing would be to acknowledge responsibility; to apologize; to explain how it happened, and what steps are being taken to prevent the same mistake; and to compensate the victims. Our typical response is more like what you'd expect from a hit-and-run driver. We take no responsibility. We offer no explanation. If steps are taken to prevent the same mistake from recurring, they are taken in secret, and without the benefit of independent, disinterested reformers.

Worst of all, innocents with limbs blown off are left to fend for themselves; impoverished families are left to bear the costs of burying their dead and repairing their homes. Survivors, who have no idea why their loved one was killed, can't help but fear they'll be next, and the U.S. does nothing to reassure them.

We just let them live with the fear.

There are also numerous reports that the U.S. carries out so-called double-tap drone strikes, where we fire a missile at someone, then fire another at rescuers who rush to the scene or mourners who attend a funeral. Of course, it could be the case that a rescuer, or a funeral attendee, is also a terrorist. But by carrying out these strikes, we prevent rescuers from rushing to the scene even when innocents are hit.

Finally, there is a question of proportionality. Drone strikes are a response to a real threat. Terrorists are bent on attacking us. At the same time, terrorist attacks are relatively rare. Terrorist attacks perpetrated by people in Yemen, as opposed to homegrown threats like Tim McVeigh or the Tsarnaev brothers, are more rare still. Are all the people, including innocents, that we've killed in, say, Yemen really a proportionate response to the threat that we face from terrorists there?

I'd say that is far from clear.

The Obama Administration says it only takes lethal action when the target poses "an imminent threat of violent attack." It is absurd to suggest the thousands we've killed were all imminent threats. I suspect that the actual standard is hidden because it is indefensible.

If our drone program is immoral, does it at least keep us safer? The Obama Administration says so. But there is nothing resembling hard evidence to suggest that they are right. I trust you're all familiar with the argument that we are creating more terrorists than we are killing. Al-Qaeda certainly uses our drone strikes as a recruiting tool. Faisal Shahzad, who attempted to bomb Times Square, spoke in court about "the drone strikes in Somalia and Yemen and in Pakistan."

At the very least, drone strikes fuel anti-Americanism. And we have reason to worry that President Obama isn't as attuned to blowback from drone strikes as he ought to be. Presidents have a perverse incentive to focus too much on keeping us safe through the end of a four-year term, and too little on keeping us safe in the long run.

In the long run, it isn't just blowback that we ought to worry about. There's a strong case to be made that Americans are being shortsighted about drones themselves. Our military is the strongest in the world. The gap between our Air Force and the next best is huge. In the short term, our near monopoly on drones has given us an even bigger advantage. But these are naturally asymmetric weapons. Cheap. Far easier to build and operate than a fighter jet. Relatively inconspicuous. As they spread to other states and non-state actors, they'll decrease our edge. Perhaps we should've used this window, where we're the undisputed leader on drones, to shape international norms more to our long term advantage.

Instead, we've set precedents that we'd hate to see other countries adopt. As we legitimate drone warfare, we legitimate it for everyone. Does anyone else find that scary?

This shortsightedness raises a larger question that isn't often asked in the drone debate. How competent and trustworthy is America's national-security leadership? That seems like a relevant variable. If the people in charge enjoy a deserved reputation for prudence and moral behavior in waging the War on Terrorism, we might be more inclined to permit them a tool like drones that significantly lowers the cost of killing people. On the other hand, if our national-security bureaucracy often acts imprudently, immorally, or unlawfully, we might be more inclined, as citizens, to deny them this tool, or at least to subject it to strict oversight.

What I see is a national-security state undeserving of our trust. It failed to prevent the September 11 terrorist attacks; misrepresented the threat posed by Iraq; invaded that country with insufficient planning; presided over the abuse of detainees at Abu Ghraib and Guantanamo Bay; initiated an official program of torture; broke the law with warrantless spying on Americans; lost the trove of WikiLeaks documents; then lost the trove of Snowden documents. And after all of these failures of competence and character, we're supposed to trust the CIA and the Pentagon to get good intelligence prior to drone strikes; to follow the law; to act morally in a way that neither stains our national honor nor needlessly creates enemies?

And to do it all in secret?

We're supposed to trust the CIA, with its very recent history of torture and illegally destroying evidence of torture, to run a secret killing program that adequately safeguards innocents? We're supposed to trust a government that threw many innocents and low level offenders into prison at Gitmo, telling us they were all the worst of the worst, to direct drone strikes only at the worst of the worst?

Why would we trust them to do that?

And there is so much particular to our drone strike program that should deepen our mistrust. For example: the Obama Administration's decision to treat targeted killing with drones as a state secret, except when it wanted to brag about a kill; a definition of militants that encompassed all men of military age we happened to kill; the many officials who've lied about the number of innocents killed in drone strikes; the Obama Administration's alarming notion that it is empowered to secretly order the extrajudicial drone killings of American citizens, even if they're not on any battlefield; and the killing of Anwar al-Awla-ki's 16-year-old son. In that case, a presumably innocent teenager was killed; though an American citizen, the government has offered no explanation for his death.

I'd like to read you a short passage from the book *Dirty Wars* by Jeremy Scahill, who has done on the ground reporting on drone strikes in Yemen:

> A former senior official in the Obama administration told me that after Abdulrahman's killing, the president was "surprised and upset and wanted an explanation." The former official, who worked on the targeted killing program, said that according to intelligence and Special Operations officials, the target of the strike was al-Banna, the Al Qaeda in the Arabian Peninsula propagandist. "We had no idea the kid was there. We were told al-Banna was alone," the former official told me. Once it became clear that the teenager had been killed, he added, military and intelligence officials asserted, "It was a mistake, a bad mistake."
>
> However, John Brennan, at the time President Obama's senior adviser on counterterrorism and homeland security, "suspected that the kid had been killed intentionally and ordered a review. I don't know what happened with the review."

So an American kid is killed. The president has no idea why. At best, a drone strike was ordered on faulty intelligence. At worst, the kid was killed deliberately.

Even John Brennan, Obama's chief counterterrorism officer, apparently found it plausible that there was something untoward about the killing. He reportedly conducted a review. But the whole episode remains cloaked in secrecy, as if American national security depends on our not knowing the truth about why a 16-year-old kid was killed. Is there any more clear example of self-serving secrecy? And this story has only garnered attention because an American kid was involved. How many innocent 16-year-old Pakistanis or Yemenis have we killed?

The national-security state has taken steps to make sure that we don't find out. The same people implicated in killing hundreds of innocents, whether negligently or intentionally, are the ones who decide what the public will and won't be told. Again, that's a recipe for corruption. Also objectionable is the Obama Administration's habit of treating various matters as classified, then authorizing leaks so that they can get out their story anonymously, without the degree of accountability that would come from an official putting their name behind it. If something can be discussed in an authorized leak, it can be declassified.

On the subject of transparency, Robert Chesney points out that the Obama Administration has openly explained its belief that the Authorization for Use of Military Force passed after 9/11 authorizes it to kill not just al Qaeda members, but "associated forces." (I wonder, by the way, whether members of Congress understood themselves to be approving many drone strikes in Yemen 11 years later.) Anyway, Chesney goes on to point out that "the administration has resisted public disclosure of which groups come within the scope of that understanding, and has not made clear what factors suffice to make a group an associated force."

He adds that "for that matter, it has not been particularly forthcoming on these issues with Congress." Is this permissible? An administration that isn't even transparent about who the enemy is in a war that it's waging? That seems absurd.

Since Ben Wittes and I agree that America's drone-strike policies ought to be more transparent, I won't dwell on the arguments in favor. But I do want to comment on their implications. Not only do he and I agree that our drone-strike policy isn't insufficiently transparent. Here are some excellent remarks that he wrote after reading two human rights group reports on drone strikes, and that I also believe:

> It is impossible for a modestly-moral person to read these reports without something approaching nausea. They are grisly. They involve the deaths of numerous apparently-innocent people. The deaths appear to have taken place at the hands of the United States. The reports involve some substantial new reporting on these incidents. And they thus raise serious questions about the way at least those drone strikes they cover took place: What went wrong, why, and how we can minimize the chances of such disasters in the future?

I'd suggest that, if we don't know what went wrong, or why, or how we can minimize the chances of similar disasters—and if, in general, we worry that our drone strike program isn't transparent enough, which is to say, that it is more vulnerable to abuses than it ought to be—if we believe that, it is our responsibility to call for a moratorium on drone strikes. They should stop at least until they are made as transparent as they ought to be, and until we know what goes wrong, why, and how to fix it. That's what you do when a program induces nausea.

You call for it to stop.

But many who happily concede various flaws in the drone program won't go so far as to call on the Obama Administration to halt it, pending reforms that they agree are necessary.

Why?

*Conor Friedersdorf is a staff writer at *The Atlantic,* where he focuses on politics and national affairs.

Friedersdorf, Conor. "Distant Death: The Case for a Moratorium on Drone Strikes." *The Atlantic*, November 14, 2013. http://www.theatlantic.com /politics/archive/2013/11/distant-death-the-case-for-a-moratorium-on-drone-strikes/281471/.

PART 3:

Are They Legal?

U.S. drone strikes have led to much debate among lawyers about whether the strikes comply with U.S. domestic law and international law. The precise nature of the legal controversy has at times been misunderstood. It is not primarily about "drones" or "targeted killings," but is often about the use of lethal force outside traditional battlefields.

Drones themselves do not raise particularly difficult legal issues. International law does not specifically prohibit or permit drones; rather, the law sets out the circumstances in which lethal force may or may not be used. Those rules apply to the use of force, whatever the weapon. And *targeted killings*—intentional, premeditated killings of a targeted individual—are not necessarily unlawful. The term describes a form of killing, with the legality depending on the specific circumstances in which it is carried out.

The bulk of the legal debate has been about the circumstances surrounding the use of drones and targeted killings, whether strikes comply with the rules for the use of force, and whether the United States has adopted new interpretations of the law that exceed traditional limits on when a government may kill.

The U.S. government defends the legality of its practices, and since 2010, numerous senior U.S. government officials have given public speeches in which they explained U.S. views. In the speech extracted here, then Attorney General Eric Holder summarizes the government's argument that drone strikes comply with both domestic and international law. The government contends that the Constitution gives the president the power to take action to stop imminent attacks and also that Congress authorized the strikes when it passed the 2001 Authorization for the Use of Military Force Against Terrorists (AUMF) shortly after the 9/11 attacks. The government also argues that its strikes comply with international law—the United States maintains that it is in an armed conflict with al-Qaeda and other groups, that its strikes comply with the law of armed conflict, and that the United States has the right to defend itself by launching drone strikes into other countries.

However, numerous experts, NGOs, and others have raised concerns about the legal basis for U.S. strikes. In "60 Words and a War Without End," Yemen expert and journalist Gregory D. Johnsen tells the history of the 2001 AUMF, raising concerns about whether it is now being used to authorize acts for which it was not intended. In the American Civil Liberties (ACLU) and Center for Constitutional Rights (CCR) complaint, those organizations lay out the reasons why they challenged the killing of Anwar Al-Aulaqi and his 16-year-old son, U.S. citizens killed in Yemen by the United States in 2011. The ACLU and the CCR argue that the killings violated the U.S. Constitution. Hina Shamsi, the director of the ACLU's National Security Project, argues in "Violating the Ideals He Pledged to Uphold" and in "The Legacy of 9/11: Endless War Without Oversight" that the program violates the law and that the United States "risks becoming a legal pariah." The Stimson Center report "Recommendations and Report of the Task Force on US Drone Policy" disagrees with those who argue that targeted killings violate the law, but points out that "'legality' and 'the rule of law' are not the same thing" and argues that "it would be difficult to conclude that U.S. targeted strikes are consistent with core rule of law norms." In "The Long-Term International Law Implications of Targeted Killing Practices," UN Special Rapporteur Christof Heyns and Professor Sarah Knuckey describe the international legal framework applicable to U.S. practices and outline the primary concerns from the perspective of international law. In "'Will I Be Next?' US Drone Strikes in Pakistan," Amnesty International describes some strikes that it investigated and found had likely violated international law.

As you read the articles in this section, consider the following questions:

- What roles do lawyers and what role does law play in the debate about drone strikes and targeted killings?

- To what extent does legality support (and illegality undermine) a program's perceived legitimacy? What is the relationship between what is legal and what is just, right, and necessary?

- How might U.S. legal positions influence the legal views on or use of force practices of other states in the world? How might the legal views of other states influence U.S. practices?

- Do U.S. practices accord with fundamental rule of law principles?

Attorney General Eric Holder Speaks at Northwestern University School of Law

[...]

[...] I'm grateful for the opportunity to join with you in discussing a defining issue of our time—and a most critical responsibility that we share: how we will stay true to America's founding—and enduring—promises of security, justice and liberty.

Since this country's earliest days, the American people have risen to this challenge—and all that it demands. But, as we have seen—and as President John F. Kennedy may have described best—"In the long history of the world, only a few generations have been granted the role of defending freedom in its hour of maximum danger."

Half a century has passed since those words were spoken, but our nation today confronts grave national security threats that demand our constant attention and steadfast commitment. It is clear that, once again, we have reached an "hour of danger."

We are a nation at war. And, in this war, we face a nimble and determined enemy that cannot be underestimated.

Like President Obama—and my fellow members of his national security team—I begin each day with a briefing on the latest and most urgent threats made against us in the preceding

24 hours. And, like scores of attorneys and agents at the Justice Department, I go to sleep each night thinking of how best to keep our people safe.

I know that—more than a decade after the September 11th attacks; and despite our recent national security successes, including the operation that brought to justice Osama bin Laden last year—there are people currently plotting to murder Americans, who reside in distant countries as well as within our own borders. Disrupting and preventing these plots—and using every available and appropriate tool to keep the American people safe—has been, and will remain, this Administration's top priority.

But just as surely as we are a nation at war, we also are a nation of laws and values. Even when under attack, our actions must always be grounded on the bedrock of the Constitution—and must always be consistent with statutes, court precedent, the rule of law and our founding ideals. Not only is this the right thing to do—history has shown that it is also the most effective approach we can take in combating those who seek to do us harm.

This is not just my view. My judgment is shared by senior national security officials across the government. As the President reminded us in 2009, at the National Archives where our founding documents are housed, "[w]e uphold our most cherished values not only because doing so is right, but because it strengthens our country and it keeps us safe. Time and again, our values have been our best national security asset." Our history proves this. We do not have to choose between security and liberty—and we will not.

[...]

[…] It is preferable to capture suspected terrorists where feasible—among other reasons, so that we can gather valuable intelligence from them—but we must also recognize that there are instances where our government has the clear authority—and, I would argue, the responsibility—to defend the United States through the appropriate and lawful use of lethal force.

This principle has long been established under both U.S. and international law. In response to the attacks perpetrated—and the continuing threat posed—by al Qaeda, the Taliban, and associated forces, Congress has authorized the President to use all necessary and appropriate force against those groups. Because the United States is in an armed conflict, we are authorized to take action against enemy belligerents under international law. The Constitution empowers the President to protect the nation from any imminent threat of violent attack. And international law recognizes the inherent right of national self-defense. None of this is changed by the fact that we are not in a conventional war.

Our legal authority is not limited to the battlefields in Afghanistan. Indeed, neither Congress nor our federal courts has limited the geographic scope of our ability to use force to the current conflict in Afghanistan. We are at war with a stateless enemy, prone to shifting operations from country to country. Over the last three years alone, al Qaeda and its associates have directed several attacks—fortunately, unsuccessful—against us from countries other than Afghanistan. Our government has both a responsibility and a right to protect this nation and its people from such threats.

This does not mean that we can use military force whenever or wherever we want. International legal principles, including respect for another nation's sovereignty, constrain our ability to act unilaterally. But the use of force in foreign territory would be consistent with these international legal principles if conducted, for example, with the consent of the nation involved—or after a determination that the nation is unable or unwilling to deal effectively with a threat to the United States.

Furthermore, it is entirely lawful—under both United States law and applicable law of war principles—to target specific senior operational leaders of al Qaeda and associated forces. This is not a novel concept. In fact, during World War II, the United States tracked the plane flying Admiral Isoroku Yama-moto—the commander of Japanese forces in the attack on Pearl Harbor and the Battle of Midway—and shot it down specifically because he was on board. As I explained to the Senate Judiciary Committee following the operation that killed Osama bin Laden, the same rules apply today.

Some have called such operations "assassinations." They are not, and the use of that loaded term is misplaced. Assassinations are unlawful killings. Here, for the reasons I have given, the U.S. government's use of lethal force in self-defense against a leader of al Qaeda or an associated force who presents an imminent threat of violent attack would not be unlawful—and therefore would not violate the Executive Order banning assassination or criminal statutes.

Now, it is an unfortunate but undeniable fact that some of the threats we face come from a small number of United States citizens who have decided to commit violent attacks against their own country from abroad. Based on generations-old legal principles and Supreme Court decisions handed down during World War II, as well as during this current conflict, it's clear that United States citizenship alone does not make such individuals immune from being targeted. But it does mean that the government must take into account all relevant constitutional considerations with respect to United States citizens—even those who are leading efforts to kill innocent Americans. Of these, the most relevant is the Fifth Amendment's Due Process Clause, which says that the government may not deprive a citizen of his or her life without due process of law.

The Supreme Court has made clear that the Due Process Clause does not impose one-size-fits-all requirements, but instead mandates procedural safeguards that depend on specific circumstances. In cases arising under the Due Process Clause—including in a case involving a U.S. citizen captured in the conflict against al Qaeda—the Court has applied a balancing approach, weighing the private interest that will be affected against the interest the government is trying to protect, and the burdens the government would face in providing additional process. Where national security operations are at stake, due process takes into account the realities of combat.

Here, the interests on both sides of the scale are extraordinarily weighty. An individual's interest in making sure that the government does not target him erroneously could not be more significant. Yet it is imperative for the government to counter threats posed by senior operational leaders of al Qaeda, and to protect the innocent people whose lives could be lost in their attacks.

Any decision to use lethal force against a United States citizen—even one intent on murdering Americans and who has become an operational leader of al-Qaeda in a foreign land—is among the gravest that government leaders can face. The American people can be—and deserve to be—assured that actions taken in their defense are consistent with their values and their laws. So, although I cannot discuss or confirm any particular program or operation, I believe it is important to explain these legal principles publicly.

Let me be clear: an operation using lethal force in a foreign country, targeted against a U.S. citizen who is a senior operational leader of al Qaeda or associated forces, and who is actively engaged in planning to kill Americans, would be lawful at least in the following circumstances: First, the U.S. government has determined, after a thorough and careful review, that the individual poses an imminent threat of violent attack against the United States; second, capture is not feasible; and third, the operation would be conducted in a manner consistent with applicable law of war principles.

The evaluation of whether an individual presents an "imminent threat" incorporates considerations of the relevant window of opportunity to act, the possible harm that missing the window would cause to civilians, and the likelihood of heading off future disastrous attacks against the United States. As we learned on 9/11, al Qaeda has demonstrated the ability to strike with little or no notice—and to cause devastating casualties. Its leaders are continually planning attacks against the United States, and they do not behave like a traditional military—wearing uniforms, carrying arms openly, or massing forces in preparation for an attack. Given these facts, the Constitution does not require the President to delay action until some theoretical end-stage of planning—when the precise time, place, and manner of an attack become clear. Such a requirement would create an unacceptably high risk that our efforts would fail, and that Americans would be killed.

Whether the capture of a U.S. citizen terrorist is feasible is a fact-specific, and potentially time-sensitive, question. It may depend on, among other things, whether capture can be accomplished in the window of time available to prevent an attack and without undue risk to civilians or to U.S. personnel. Given the nature of how terrorists act and where they tend to hide, it may not always be feasible to capture a United States citizen terrorist who presents an imminent threat of violent attack. In that case, our government has the clear authority to defend the United States with lethal force.

Of course, any such use of lethal force by the United States will comply with the four fundamental law of war principles governing the use of force. The principle of necessity requires that the target have definite military value. The principle of distinction requires that only lawful targets—such as combatants, civilians directly participating in hostilities, and military objectives—may be targeted intentionally. Under the principle of proportionality, the anticipated collateral damage must not be excessive in relation to the anticipated military advantage. Finally, the principle of humanity requires us to use weapons that will not inflict unnecessary suffering.

These principles do not forbid the use of stealth or technologically advanced weapons. In fact, the use of advanced weapons may help to ensure that the best intelligence is available for planning and carrying out operations, and that the risk of civilian casualties can be minimized or avoided altogether.

Some have argued that the President is required to get permission from a federal court before taking action against a United States citizen who is a senior operational leader of al Qaeda or associated forces. This is simply not accurate. "Due process" and "judicial process" are not one and the same, particularly when it comes to national security. The Constitution guarantees due process, not judicial process.

The conduct and management of national security operations are core functions of the Executive Branch, as courts have recognized throughout our history. Military and civilian officials must often make real-time decisions that balance the need to act, the existence of alternative options, the possibility of collateral damage, and other judgments—all of which depend on expertise and immediate access to information that only the Executive Branch may possess in real time. The Constitution's guarantee of due process is ironclad, and it is essential—but, as a recent court decision makes clear, it does not require judicial approval before the President may use force abroad against a senior operational leader of a foreign terrorist organization with which the United States is at war—even if that individual happens to be a U.S. citizen.

That is not to say that the Executive Branch has—or should ever have—the ability to target any such individuals without robust oversight. Which is why, in keeping with the law and our constitutional system of checks and balances, the Executive Branch regularly informs the appropriate members of Congress about our counterterrorism activities, including the legal framework, and would of course follow the same practice where lethal force is used against United States citizens.

Now, these circumstances are sufficient under the Constitution for the United States to use lethal force against a U.S. citizen abroad—but it is important to note that the legal requirements I have described may not apply in every situation—such as operations that take place on traditional battlefields.

The unfortunate reality is that our nation will likely continue to face terrorist threats that—at times—originate with our own citizens. When such individuals take up arms against this country—and join al Qaeda in plotting attacks designed to kill their fellow Americans—there may be only one realistic and appropriate response. We must take steps to stop them—in full accordance with the Constitution. In this hour of danger, we simply cannot afford to wait until deadly plans are carried out—and we will not.

This is an indicator of our times—not a departure from our laws and our values. For this Administration—and for this nation—our values are clear. We must always look to them for answers when we face difficult questions, like the ones I have discussed today. As the President reminded us at the National Archives, "our Constitution has endured through secession and civil rights, through World War and Cold War, because it provides a foundation of principles that can be applied pragmatically; it provides a compass that can help us find our way."

Our most sacred principles and values—of security, justice and liberty for all citizens—must continue to unite us, to guide us forward, and to help us build a future that honors our founding documents and advances our ongoing—uniquely American—pursuit of a safer, more just, and more perfect union. In the continuing effort to keep our people secure, this Administration will remain true to those values that inspired our nation's founding and, over the course of two centuries, have made America an example of strength and a beacon of justice for all the world. This is our pledge.

[. . .]

*Eric Holder has served as attorney general of the United States since 2009. He announced his resignation in 2014.

Holder, Eric. Speech delivered at Northwestern University School of Law, Chicago, Illinois, March 5, 2012. http://www.justice.gov/iso/opa/ag/speeches/2012/ag-speech-1203051.html.

60 Words and a War Without End: The Untold Story of the Most Dangerous Sentence in U.S. History

by Gregory D. Johnsen*

[. . .]

[Abu Anas al-]Libi knew he was a wanted man. He had been on the FBI's most wanted list for more than a decade, following an indictment in 2000 for his alleged role in al-Qaeda's attacks on U.S. embassies in Kenya and Tanzania two years earlier. Along with Libi the indictment named 20 other individuals, including Osama bin Laden and Ayman al-Zawahiri, as defendants.

"He suspected that at any moment he would be killed," his son later told *The New York Times*. Still, on [a] Saturday morning in early October, much of the danger seemed to have passed. Libi had been living in the open for nearly a year, attending prayers and settling local disputes, where his history as a fighter and knowledge of the Qur'an made him a respected arbiter. Neighbors called him simply "the shaykh," a sign of respect in the conservative circles in which Libi still moved.

He had also taken steps to address his past. Three weeks earlier, on Sept. 15, Libi had sat down with Libya's attorney general to discuss his indictment, according to one report. [. . .] But mostly he just wanted to move on with his life. He had applied for his old job at the Ministry of Oil and Gas and he couldn't stop talking about how much he was looking forward to becoming a grandfather for the first time.

A trio of cars around 6 a.m. ended all of that.

Inside the family's apartment, Libi's wife heard the commotion. From a window she looked out over the beige wall that surrounded their building and into the street where several men had surrounded her husband, who was still in the driver's seat of his black Hyundai.

"Get out," the men shouted in Arabic. "Get out." Then they smashed the window. Most of the men were masked, but she could see a few faces, she said later in Arabic interviews. They looked Libyan; they sounded Libyan. Some of them had guns; some didn't, but they all moved quickly.

By the time the rest of the family made it to the street, all that was left was a single sandal and a few drops of blood.

[. . .]

More than a dozen years after the Sept. 11 attacks, this is what America's war looks like, silent strikes and shadowy raids. The Congressional Research Service, an analytical branch of the Library of Congress, recently said that it had located at least 30 similar occurrences, although the number of covert actions is likely many times higher with drone strikes and other secret operations. The remarkable has become regular.

The White House said that the operations in both Libya and Somalia drew their authority from the Authorization for the Use of Military Force, a 12-year-old piece of legislation that was drafted in the hours after the Sept. 11 attacks. At the heart of the AUMF is a single 60-word sentence, which has formed the legal foundation for nearly every counterterrorism operation the U.S. has conducted since Sept. 11, from Guantanamo Bay and drone strikes to secret renditions and SEAL raids. Everything rests on those 60 words.

Unbound by time and unlimited by geography, the sentence has been stretched and expanded over the past decade, sprouting new meanings and interpretations as two successive administrations have each attempted to keep pace with an evolving threat while simultaneously maintaining the security of the homeland. In the process, what was initially thought to authorize force against al-Qaeda and the Taliban in Afghanistan has now been used to justify operations in several countries across multiple continents and, at least theoretically, could allow the president—any president—to strike anywhere at anytime. What was written in a few days of fear has now come to govern years of action. Culled from interviews with former and current members of Congress, as well as staffers and attorneys who served in both the Bush and the Obama administrations, this is the story of how those 60 words came to be, the lone objector to their implementation, and their continuing power in the world today. The story, like most modern ones of America at war, begins in the shadow of 9/11 with a lawyer and Word document.

Just over 24 hours after United Flight 175 flew into the south tower at 9:03 in the morning on Sept. 11, Alberto Gonzalez, the White House counsel, called one of his deputies into his office.

The U.S. still didn't know for certain who was behind the attacks or how many people had been killed. The CIA thought it might be Osama bin Laden's al-Qaeda network, and early casualty reports put the death toll at more than 5,000. Only one of those things would turn out to be true. But on that first day the only thing anyone knew for certain was that the U.S. had been attacked and that it had to respond.

Gonzales gave a key part of that task to Timothy Flanigan, a graying, slightly paunchy 48-year-old lawyer with a background in corporate law.

Gonzales wanted his deputy to draft the congressional resolution that would authorize the president to go after those responsible. [...]

After a quick search online, Flanigan located the last time Congress had given the president permission to act: the 1991 Authorization for the Use of Military Force against Iraq. Then, according to an account in Kurt Eichenwald's best-selling 2012 book *500 Days*, he copied and pasted the text of that resolution into a new document.

Next Flanigan called David Addington, a gruff, standoffish man in Vice President Dick Cheney's office. Addington had started his career as a lawyer in the CIA and he had a better sense of the issues at stake. So too did John Yoo, a 34-year-old law professor from Berkeley, Calif., whose innovative legal arguments in *Bush v. Gore* a year earlier had secured him a place in the Bush White House. Together the three men hammered out a first draft of the resolution, which they faxed to congressional leaders that evening.

Almost no one liked Flanigan's initial offering. Everyone was working long hours and fighter jets were still patrolling the skies over Washington, but Congress wasn't ready to give President George W. Bush a blank check to go after an ill-defined enemy no one knew anything about.

At a Democratic caucus in the basement of the Capitol building, several members complained that the wording was too broad. Republicans were similarly concerned. One part of Flanigan's draft authorized the president to "use all necessary and appropriate force" both in the United States as well as abroad. *What exactly did that mean?* officials wondered. *Could President Bush use the military domestically? What about the CIA?* No one seemed to know.

Flanigan and Yoo spent much of Thursday, Sept. 13, walking scared and sleep-deprived congressional staffers through the brief text. [...] The day before, Senate Majority Leader Tom Daschle had warned President Bush to be careful with his rhetoric, particularly his use of the word "war." And now his staff was driving home a similar point. Mostly they wanted to make sure that the resolution adhered to the War Powers Resolution language, which Congress had passed in the wake of the Vietnam War as a way of checking the president's ability to unilaterally wage war.

[...]

Nothing had been settled. The two sides were going in circles. From around the table the frustration was palpable. Finally, House Speaker Dennis Hastert's chief of staff, Scott Palmer, spoke up. "We don't have time for this," he blurted out from his seat in the back.

[...]

Palmer's outburst got the meeting moving again, and when it broke up, a White House official wandered over. "Thanks for popping off," he told Palmer. "We could have been here all night."

By late that evening the White House and Congress had something resembling a working draft. They had even found a compromise to one of the more vexing phrases, which would have given the president the authority "to deter and pre-empt any future acts of terrorism or aggression against the United States."

Congressional lawyers had pointed out that the clause would give the president unprecedented power, allowing him to strike anyone anywhere in the world at any time. One even argued that given the potential activities that could be crammed into the word "aggression," the president might never again have to seek congressional authorization to combat terrorism. He could simply target anyone he considered a threat and say he was preempting terrorism. Did Congress really want to give the president such open-ended and wide-ranging power?

Flanigan and Yoo agreed to remove the clause on the condition that they place similar language in the "whereas" section of the resolution. Convinced this was the best they could get and comforted by the fact that the whereas section carried no legal weight—it existed only to provide the context for the resolution—Daschle and the rest of the Democratic negotiators agreed to the deal.

They brought the revised draft—five whereas clauses, the 60-word body, and a War Powers section—back to the Capitol basement for the second Democratic caucus of the day. Hours earlier, a bomb threat had forced the Capitol to close for 45 minutes as security swept the building. Milling about on the grass outside the Capitol in suits and shoes designed for hallways and offices, the members tried to maintain their composure, but the long days and stress were starting to take a toll. Like the rest of the country, they wanted to hit back.

"I say bomb the hell out of them," Democratic Sen. Zell Miller of Georgia had told *The New York Times* a day earlier. "If there's collateral damage, so be it. They certainly found our civilians to be expendable."

Not everyone was so sure. Barbara Lee, a 55-year-old congresswoman with short black hair and the worn-through voice of a lifelong activist, had stayed silent during the first caucus. There had been enough people talking, and as a second-term congresswoman from the liberal California San Francisco Bay Area, she was still relatively junior. But now, as support for the resolution seemed to be gaining momentum, she decided it was time to speak up.

Lee knew what she was about to say would be unpopular. . . . [. . .] "This is still a blank check," she said when it came her turn to speak. The faces staring back at her looked somber and reflective, but Lee could sense the undercurrent of anger running through the room.

"Let's take a step back," she begged. "We don't know what the implications of our actions will be." A few heads had started to nod along with her, and as Lee sat down, several other members stood up to voice concerns about the dangers inherent in such a broad resolution.

By the end of the meeting, it was clear that this was the resolution, a single sentence and 60 words:

> That the President is authorized to use all necessary and appropriate force against those nations, organizations, or persons he determines planned, authorized, committed, or aided the terrorist attacks that occurred on September 11, 2001, or harbored such organizations or persons in order to prevent any future acts of international terrorism against the United States by such nations, organizations or persons.

That was it. [...] Congress was moving forward with the resolution. The only question that remained was how she would vote. [...]

[...]

Carl Levin, a portly 67-year-old senator from Michigan with boxy glasses perched low on his nose, addressed the floor. "This authorization for the use of force is limited to the nations, organizations, or persons involved in the terrorist attacks of Sept. 11," he said. "It is not a broad authorization for the use of military force against any nation, organization, or person who were not involved in the Sept. 11 terrorist attacks."

Later that day, Levin's Democratic colleague, Joe Biden, seconded his interpretation of what the Senate had passed to *The New York Times*. The current resolution, Biden claimed, was nothing like the 1964 Gulf of Tonkin Resolution, which had been used to justify military escalation in Vietnam for nearly seven years until it was repealed in 1971.

The Senate, Biden and senior Democrats like John Kerry suggested, had learned its lesson. No one wanted another Vietnam. That, after all, is why they had insisted that Flanigan and Yoo add the War Powers language. But in the rush to draft and pass the resolution, no one had managed to insert a sunset option—a time limit on the use of force. The legal authority Congress was giving to the president would last until Congress took it back. There was no end date, just a vague sentence and the broad authority to "use all necessary and appropriate force."

On Sept. 14, 2001, no one was thinking about how the war would eventually end, only that it needed to begin.

Just as Daschle had hoped, the voting was over in minutes. Each of the 98 senators present voted in favor of the resolution. [. . .]

On the other side of the building, in the Democratic cloakroom, Lee was still wrestling with her vote. She had already decided to pass on [attending a 9/11] memorial service. The House was scheduled to vote on the resolution on Saturday and she wanted to spend most of Friday making calls and thinking about what to do.

As everyone else was gathering to get on the bus, Lee sipped from a can of ginger ale and chatted with Elijah Cummings, a close colleague from Maryland. "Are you going?" Cummings asked.

"Well," Lee hesitated. "I think I'm going to stick around." But as she spoke, Lee could feel something inside her shift. She couldn't explain it to Cummings then, or even to herself later. She just knew she needed to go. [. . .]

[. . .]

Rev. Jane Holmes Dixon opened the service with a short reading and a prayer. The next speaker, Nathan Baxter, a third-generation priest and dean of the cathedral, held to a similar script, reading from Jeremiah 31:15: "A voice is heard in Ramah, lamenting and bitter weeping, Rachel is weeping for her children and she refuses to be comforted because they are no more."

The tall African-American priest paused briefly to look out across the darkened cathedral as he moved from Jeremiah's words to his own. "Now let us seek that assurance in prayer," he said in a slow, deliberate baritone. "That as we act we not become the evil we deplore."

That's it, Lee thought from her seat. For much of the past 24 hours, she had been looking for a reason to vote no. In her heart she knew that was the right vote, but she hadn't been able to articulate why. Baxter's words did it for her: "As we act, let us not become the evil we deplore."

She was as angry and heartbroken as anyone else. Her chief of staff had lost a cousin when Flight 93 went down in Pennsylvania. But she wanted a measured response, not a blank check for a perpetual war. Something else was bothering her as well. Several of the speakers seemed to be more focused on retaliation than remembering the dead.

This is supposed to be a memorial service, Lee thought. *Not a rush-to-war service.*

Part of the tone was deliberate. President Bush and his advisers had wanted to strike a note of defiance. In his own remarks, Bush gave voice to the attitude that would come to define his administration. "Just three days removed from these events, Americans do not yet have the distance of history," he said from the cathedral's lectern. "But our responsibility to history is already clear: To answer these attacks and rid the world of evil."

[...]

Late that afternoon, Lee received a phone call in her office. The vote that had been scheduled for Saturday had been moved up. The hours of prep time she had been counting on to get the language of her floor statement just right were gone. If she wanted to speak, she needed to get to the floor.

[...]

[In the chamber,] Lee [scribbled] her floor speech on loose notebook paper. She dashed off a quick paragraph and started on a second before hesitating and scratching out half a line. Lee wrote for a few more minutes, pausing here and there to draw a line through something in the cramped cursive she didn't like. She filled two pages with notes and then added a single line on a third sheet. She was ready.

At 5:45 on Friday afternoon, the House was called to order. One of Lee's close friends, Eleanor Holmes Norton, a petite 64-year-old member of the black caucus from the District of Columbia, spoke early in the debate.

"The language before us is limited only by the slim anchor of its Sept. 11 reference, but allows war against any and all prospective persons and entities," Norton warned. "The point is to give the president the authority to do what he has to do, not whatever he wants to do."

But for all of Norton's worries about a "slim anchor" and that the text could be stretched to go after those who had nothing to [do] with the attacks, she still said she supported the resolution to authorize the president to use "all necessary and appropriate force."

Lee came to the podium seven minutes later. "I rise today, really, with a very heavy heart," she said as emotion cracked her voice. Then, from the well of the U.S. House of Representatives, she started to cry. The mother of two boys, who had agonized and prayed over her vote, Lee jostled the microphone and tugged nervously at the lapels of her jacket as she struggled to regain control. A pair of deep breaths helped.

"However difficult this vote may be," she said, her voice steady once more, "some of us must urge the use of restraint. Our country is in a state of mourning. Some of us must say, 'Let's step back for a moment, let's just pause, just for a minute, and think through the implications of our actions today so that this does not spiral out of control.'" Lee closed her brief remarks with Baxter's line, the one that had convinced her to vote her heart. "As we act," she said. "Let us not become the evil we deplore."

[…]

Lee was on her way back to her office when the final vote was announced: 420-1. The nods of affirmation she had seen in the Capitol basement the night before had disappeared on the House floor. And Lee's "some" had become one. Out of 535 elected officials in Congress, she was the only one to vote no.

[…]

On Sept. 18, 2001, President Bush signed the joint resolution authorizing him to use "all necessary and appropriate force" into law.

One week later, on Sept. 25, John Yoo wrote Timothy Flanigan a memo. Yoo wanted to reestablish the preemption language Daschle and Congress had forced them to move to the whereas section during the negotiations, effectively stripping it of its legal weight. Yoo's memo, less than two weeks later, made an end run around Daschle's block and once again gave the idea of preemption legal cover.

"The President," Yoo wrote, "may deploy military force preemptively against terrorist organizations or the States that harbor or support them, whether or not they can be linked to the specific terrorist attack of September 11."

In the pages of dense, legal prose that followed, Yoo acknowledged that while the AUMF is limited only to enemies connected to the Sept. 11 attacks, the president actually had greater freedom of action based on his powers as commander in chief under Article II of the Constitution.

[...]

For Yoo, [Article II] meant that the president could "take whatever actions he deems appropriate" when it came to combating terrorism. He could kill whomever he wants, whenever he wants, wherever he wants. At its most basic level, John Yoo's legal analysis restated Richard Nixon's famous line that "when the president does it, that means that it is not illegal."

For years, a small but outspoken group of legal scholars and outside experts had pushed back against Yoo's idea of an unchecked executive. They argued at conferences and wrote op-eds, but they had little real power and no ability to effect change. Finally, toward the end of Bush's second term, they saw an opportunity to influence policy and help steer the next administration. On Sept. 15, 2008—almost seven years to the day that the AUMF had been passed—one of those scholars boarded an Amtrak train in New Haven, Conn., for the nearly five-and-a-half-hour trip to Washington, D.C.

The next day, Harold Koh, . . . the [dean] of . . . [Yale Law School], took his seat at the witness table in front of the Senate Judiciary Committee. [...] He was characteristically outspoken, calling the AUMF a "broadly worded law" that the Bush administration had used "to justify National Security Agency surveillance, indefinite detentions, and torture of foreign detainees."

[...]

Toward the end of his prepared remarks, Koh laid out what he saw as the key issue moving forward. "As difficult as the last seven years have been, they loom far less important in the grand scheme of things than the next eight, which will determine whether the pendulum of U.S. policy swings back from the extreme place to which it has been pushed, or stays stuck in the 'new normal' position."

Two days after Barack Obama took the oath of office on the balcony of the U.S. Capitol building, he put Koh's advice into action. In his testimony, Koh had recommended that "as soon as the new president takes office he should issue executive orders," including one to close Guantanamo Bay by a certain date.

Sitting in the Oval Office, on Jan. 22, 2009, President Obama did just that. He signed a pair of executive orders announcing his intention to close Guantanamo within a year and setting up a task force to review current cases against the detainees.

The detention facility at Guantanamo Bay is one of the best examples of the unanticipated power of the 60 words at the heart of the AUMF. Like a science experiment gone wrong, the words of that sentence have mutated and changed over the years, sprouting new meanings and interpretations that were never anticipated when Timothy Flanigan cut and pasted the text back on Sept. 12, 2001.

In June 2004, more than two years after Bush established Guantanamo, the Supreme Court decided in *Hamdi v. Rumsfeld* that since Congress had given the president the power to kill, it must also have, at least implicitly, granted the president the power to capture and detain.

Congress built on the court's expansion by endorsing another one two years later. In 2006, Congress said that military commissions had jurisdiction over al-Qaeda, the Taliban, and what had come to be called "associated forces," a broad category of enemies who had allied themselves with either al-Qaeda or the Taliban.

Eleanor Norton's "slim anchor," which held the language of the law to those responsible for the Sept. 11 attacks, had finally broken loose. The AUMF had ceased to be a scalpel. Now it was broadsword that could be used against a wide variety of groups, many of which had not even existed in 2001. The fact that the 60 words made no mention of detention authority or associated forces no longer mattered. The sentence stayed the same, only the meaning had changed.

By the end of the Bush administration, even some officials who had initially been in favor of a broad reading of the authority enshrined in the AUMF began to grow wary of building so much of U.S. counterterrorism strategy on such a shaky foundation.

"It is like a Christmas tree," John Bellinger III told me recently. "All sorts of things have been hung off of those 60 words."

[...]

Obama was supposed to change all that. He was the president of hope and change, the man who would restore America's reputation and once again restore a healthy respect for the rule of law.

The day after his inauguration, *The New York Times'* editorial page crowed that it took Obama "less than 12 hours" to order a halt to the military tribunals at Guantanamo. It turns out, the paper said, that closing Guantanamo wasn't actually "so hard." All it took was a president with the courage of his convictions, someone who was willing to do what was right.

Inside the new administration, things looked a little different. President Obama had halted the tribunals and ordered

Guantanamo Bay closed, but then the new president moved on leaving his aides and appointees to sort out the details. None of them really knew exactly what their boss wanted. And when they asked the White House for direction, their queries went unanswered.

[...]

During that time, the list of enemies had grown significantly. In addition to those responsible for the Sept. 11 attacks—al-Qaeda and the Taliban in Afghanistan—the U.S. was now effectively at war with the broader, catchall category of "associated forces." Government lawyers also claimed that the U.S. could detain—which given legal logic meant that the U.S. could also target for killing—anyone who "substantially supported" any of the three categories of enemies, although they failed to clarify exactly what constituted substantial support. The U.S. could also go after anyone who carried out an attack against a "coalition partner," as well as "any person who committed a belligerent act," which they also neglected to define. [...]

Judge Bates, a long-necked, willowy man who had been appointed to the bench by George W. Bush in the months after Sept. 11, pushed back on the government's refusal to define either "associated forces" or "substantial support." Both concepts drastically broadened the scope of the AUMF and who the U.S. could kill, and the judge wanted to know exactly what the government meant.

But, he wrote in his opinion, it had become clear to him that the government had no "definitive justification for the 'substantial support' concept in the law of war." Bates said he was open to the idea of associated forces but this had to mean more than a "terrorist organization who merely share an abstract philosophy or even a common purpose with al-Qaeda—there must be an actual association in the current conflict with al-Qaeda or the Taliban."

Bates issued his opinion on May 19, 2009. Two days later Barack Obama walked into the limestone and marble rotunda of the National Archives to address the nation. Standing beneath a pair of 1936 Barry Faulkner murals depicting the Declaration of Independence and the Constitutional Convention, Obama pledged not to repeat the mistakes of the Bush administration.

"The last eight years established an ad hoc legal approach for fighting terrorism that was neither effective nor sustainable," he said. "All too often our government made decisions based on fear rather than foresight." This, the president promised, would change on his watch.

To help him make this a reality, Obama asked Harold Koh, the Yale legal scholar, to join his administration as the legal adviser to the State Department. Koh's new position brought him into direct conflict with another lawyer on Obama's national security team [Jeh Johnson]. . . .

[...]

From the time Koh arrived in Washington in late June, the two were at odds, both institutionally and temperamentally. Aggressive and often condescendingly brusque, Koh represented the more liberal State Department, which typically sought to make U.S. action more palatable to its international allies. Johnson had a more chameleon-like quality that led him to adopt the mind-set of those he represented, which in this case was the conservative, security-first Department of Defense.

Along with several other officials, throughout the summer and fall of 2009, the two clashed on nearly every aspect of U.S. national security law, with Koh consistently staking out the liberal position and Johnson the more conservative counterargument. No one ever quite came right out and said it, but everyone seemed to realize that they were fighting for the nature of Obama's presidency. How should a Democratic president combat al-Qaeda? Who could he kill and whom could he capture? Was there a difference between the two, or should he be able to kill anyone he could legally detain? And, most importantly of all: What did it mean for a democracy to be in a multigenerational war with a terrorist group?

This was Koh's attempt to push the pendulum of the Bush years back. Johnson wanted to push it back as well, just not nearly so far. Both agreed that the U.S. could go after al-Qaeda's "associated forces," but what about associates of associates? How much of a connection did the target need to have to Sept. 11 to be legal? After all, the AUMF was explicit in authorizing force only against those who were responsible for the attacks. The Sept. 11 attacks had been planned and carried out by, at most, a few dozen men, and now, in years of strikes around the world, the U.S. had killed thousands. How big should the circle of responsibility be?

The decisions made in these D.C. conference rooms often made the difference between life and death half a world away, and despite anonymous claims from government officials, both lawyers knew that innocent people were sometimes killed. Not as many as activists might claim, but still too many to maintain a clean conscience.

Besides, they were unelected officials making decisions about whom the U.S. should kill. Over the years since Sept.

11, Congress had acquiesced, mostly in silence, to the gradual expansion of the AUMF. Neither chamber had ever explicitly revisited the power they had granted the president in the hours after the attacks, or even questioned how that authorization was being interpreted and used.

That hadn't always been the case. During the height of the Vietnam War, the chairman of the Senate Foreign Relations Committee, J. William Fulbright, held a series of hard-hitting hearings in an effort to repeal the Gulf of Tonkin Resolution and end the war. [...]

[...]

Part of the reason is that the wars themselves are different. Vietnam captivated the country in a way the war against al-Qaeda hasn't, at least not since the initial bombing of Afghanistan in 2001. There is no longer a single battlefield, and no one seems to know what victory looks like. Perfect security, we are constantly told, isn't possible, but how many people does the U.S. need to kill until it is safe enough?

Maybe it shouldn't be so surprising that Congress didn't think about how the war would end when it passed the AUMF on Sept. 14, 2001, but after more than a dozen years, we are no closer to an answer.

"This is a bizarro war," Jack Goldsmith told me recently. A tenured law professor at Harvard who worked in the Office of Legal Counsel under George W. Bush, Goldsmith has written a pair of books on national security law. "What we don't see, we don't care about."

And for most of us there is little to see. With the exception of Afghanistan, this is a war that is being fought out of sight with drones and small teams of special forces operatives. A war that is largely ignored at home has come to define us abroad.

The apathy lifted slightly in early 2010 when word leaked that the U.S. was actively targeting an American citizen for killing. The White House reacted to the increased scrutiny by rolling out Koh, the most liberal and publicly vocal critic of Bush-era policies, to make the case that Obama's drone strikes were different. They were grounded in the AUMF and on solid legal footing.

Koh took to the podium at the Ritz-Carlton Hotel in Washington to address the American Society of International Law on March 25, 2010, in a conservative black suit and red tie. After a few jokes about the event being as close as most in the room would ever come to the Oscars and a red carpet, he got down to business.

Unlike the Bush administration, he said, which had relied on vague constitutional arguments about presidential power, the Obama administration had based its decisions "on legislative authority granted to the president by Congress in the 2001 AUMF." Of course, he added, "construing what is 'necessary and appropriate' under the AUMF requires some translation."

Gone was Koh the private scholar, who in 2008 had complained about the "vaguely worded" AUMF that had allowed the Bush administration to justify everything from NSA excesses to torture. Now, as a government lawyer, he rested the Obama administration's legal edifice squarely on the foundation of the AUMF and those same 60 words. Everything the Obama administration did, he reassured the ballroom of legal colleagues and friends, "including lethal operations conducted with the use of unmanned aerial vehicles," was legal and just.

[...]

Months after Koh's speech, in early 2011, Congress stirred briefly to life with some members suggesting that it might be time to start codifying the evolving interpretations of the AUMF. This, they argued, would put the U.S. on more solid legal ground. The AUMF, after all, governed both Guantanamo and drones and yet had made no mention of either. Surely, it would be better to make those authorities explicit.

Obama's top aides pushed back immediately. This was not what the administration had in mind when it talked about repealing the AUMF and ending the war. Later that year at an event at the Heritage Foundation, a conservative think tank in Washington, Jeh Johnson explained why the administration had opposed any new legislation. "I think the reason that we in this administration have concerns about efforts to do that is because at the end of the political process, what I don't want to end up with is something less than what we thought we already had by way of legal authorities through the authorities on the books and our interpretation of our authorities that are on the books."

In other words, any attempt to update the AUMF, moving it from what was written in the hours after the 9/11 attacks to something that took into account the changes of a decade of war, might limit the president's options. The Obama administration was happy to rely on a 2001 authorization to deal with a 2011 threat because its own internal interpretations gave it so much flexibility. If Congress started messing with the 60-word foundation, the administration's whole legal edifice might come tumbling down.

What was supposed to be a rather routine Senate hearing early in Obama's second term provided a glimpse into just how expansively the administration had been interpreting the sentence at the heart of the AUMF. On May 16, 2013, the Defense

Department sent a quartet of officials to the Capitol to answer questions about the AUMF and the current state of the war against al-Qaeda. In the course of their joint testimony, Michael Sheehan and Robert Taylor, who were speaking for the four, both claimed that the 2001 AUMF and its 60 words were "adequate" for the administration's needs.

[...]

Toward the end of the panel, as the chairman was preparing to dismiss the Pentagon officials, Sheehan raised his hand. "Just one clarification," he said. "Certainly the president has military personnel deployed all over the world today, in probably over 70 to 80 countries, and that authority is not always under AUMF."

Sitting behind the witnesses, waiting his turn to testify, Jack Goldsmith, the former Bush administration lawyer, was shocked. Exactly how many of the 70 to 80 countries where military personnel are deployed fall under the AUMF? he asked the next day on *Lawfare*, a legal blog he co-founded. "The phrase 'not always' suggests a high number."

"The hearing made clear that the Obama administration's long insistence that it is deeply legally restrained under the AUMF is misleading and at a minimum requires much more extensive scrutiny," Goldsmith wrote. Goldsmith's post and Sheehan's public evasions raised a key question: Twelve years after 9/11, who exactly is the U.S. at war with?

When I contacted the Pentagon to get an answer, a spokeswoman emailed back: "The list is classified and not for public release."

One week later, on May 23, 2013, President Obama walked into the auditorium at the National Defense University in southeast

Washington to deliver a major national security address. Sounding more like McCain than Sheehan, his own assistant secretary, Obama made a series of pledges.

"I intend to engage Congress about the existing Authorization to Use Military Force, or AUMF, to determine how we can continue to fight terrorism without keeping America on a perpetual wartime footing," Obama said. "The AUMF is now nearly 12 years old. The Afghan war is coming to an end. Core al-Qaeda is a shell of its former self."

Standing on a raised platform in front of the crowd, which included members of activist group Code Pink who would soon interrupt him, Obama continued. "I look forward to engaging Congress and the American people in efforts to refine, and ultimately repeal, the AUMF's mandate. And I will not sign laws designed to expand this mandate further. Our systematic effort to dismantle terrorist organizations must continue," he said. "But this war, like all wars, must end. That's what history advises. That's what our democracy demands."

But like his Guantanamo pledge five years earlier, this was more rhetoric than reality. In the more than seven months since Obama gave that speech, the White House has taken no public steps to roll back the AUMF. From the outside, the string of unfilled promises looked like a president who wants to end the war without giving up his powers to wage war. It's easy to see why.

The 12-year-old sentence gives the president both incredible power—power that has been blessed by Congress and the courts—as well as maximum flexibility. Read inventively enough, the AUMF permits a wide range of military activities, all of which might at some point be necessary. Repealing or refining those 60 words would only tie the president's hands and limit his options. It would also force him to reengage with Congress, which helped block him on Guantanamo, and to explain to the American people what the U.S. is doing and who it is fighting.

Then there is the issue of Afghanistan: the war Obama once called a "war of necessity," and the war he has made his own. If he fulfills his promise to withdraw troops from Afghanistan by the end of this year, the president will have effectively ended the war against the Taliban. And that will create its own problems.

By building its detention authority on the AUMF, the Obama administration has forced itself into a corner. Once the war is the over, the power to detain disappears. What this means is that as soon as Obama declares an end to the war in Afghanistan, there will be a series of legal challenges from individuals still in Guantanamo Bay, claiming affiliation with the Taliban and demanding their release. The old legal authorities will no longer hold. The Obama administration will either have to find a new basis for holding them—13 years after many of them were captured—or it will have to release people it has said are too dangerous to set free.

Perhaps the most interesting question about the AUMF and its 60 words is this: What does that sentence prohibit? What—more than 12 years after Congress passed it—is clearly out of bounds?

Several of the lawyers I talked to, officials from both the Bush and Obama administrations, spoke eloquently and at great length about the limits of the AUMF and being constrained by the law. And maybe that is true. But none of them were able to point to a case in which the U.S. knew of a terrorist but couldn't target him because it lacked the legal authority. Each time the president wanted to kill someone, his lawyers found the authority embedded somewhere in those 60 words.

[...]

"None of us, not one who voted for it, could have envisioned we were voting for the longest war in American history," Dick Durbin, a Senate Democrat from Illinois, told *Politico* early in 2013. "Or that we were about to give future presidents the authority to fight terrorism as far-flung as Yemen and Somalia."

One person, of course, did envision exactly this sort of open-ended, ill-defined war. But even now, more than a decade after her lonely vote, Barbara Lee still just wants the debate Congress never had in 2001.

"Let the congressional debate begin," she told me recently. If the U.S. wants to use force in places like Yemen or Somalia and "if people think it's worth it, for whatever reason, then let their member of Congress vote for it. That's the point."

[...]

Analysts disagree over whether the new incarnation of al-Qaeda—smaller and more fragmented—is weaker or stronger than it once was. But one thing is certain. It is different. The only thing that has remained the same [since 2001] is that one sentence: 60 words and a war without end.

*Gregory D. Johnsen** is the 2013–2014 BuzzFeed Michael Hastings National Security Reporting Fellow and author of *The Last Refuge: Yemen, al-Qaeda and America's War in Arabia*.

Johnsen, Gregory D. "60 Words and a War Without End: The Untold Story of the Most Dangerous Sentence in U.S. History." BuzzFeedNews, January 16, 2014. http://www.buzzfeed.com/gregorydjohnsen/60-words-and-a-war-without-end-the-untold-story-of-the-most#29cyj5x.

Al-Aulaqi v. Panetta: Complaint

*by American Civil Liberties Union and Center for
Constitutional Rights**

Complaint

(Violation of Fourth and Fifth Amendments and Bill of Attainder Clause—targeted killing)

Introduction

1. Since 2001, and routinely since 2009, the United States has carried out deliberate and premeditated killings of suspected terrorists overseas. The U.S. practice of "targeted killing" has resulted in the deaths of thousands of people, including many hundreds of civilian bystanders. While some targeted killings have been carried out in the context of the wars in Afghanistan and Iraq, many have taken place outside the context of armed conflict, in countries including Yemen, Somalia, Pakistan, Sudan, and the Philippines. These killings rely on vague legal standards, a closed executive process, and evidence never presented to the courts. This case concerns the role of Defendants Leon C. Panetta, William H. McRaven, Joseph Votel, and David H. Petraeus (collectively, "Defendants") in authorizing and directing the killing of three American citizens in Yemen

last year. The killings violated fundamental rights afforded to all U.S. citizens, including the right not to be deprived of life without due process of law.

2. In late 2009 or early 2010, Anwar Al-Aulaqi, an American citizen, was added to "kill lists" maintained by the Central Intelligence Agency ("CIA") and the Joint Special Operations Command ("JSOC"), a component of the Department of Defense ("DOD"). On September 30, 2011, unmanned CIA and JSOC drones fired missiles at Anwar Al-Aulaqi and his vehicle, killing him and at least three other people, including Samir Khan, another American citizen. Defendants authorized and directed their subordinates to carry out the strike.

3. On October 14, 2011, Defendants authorized and directed another drone strike in Yemen, this one approximately 200 miles away from the strike that had killed Anwar Al-Aulaqi and Samir Khan two weeks earlier. The October 14 strike killed at least seven people at an open-air restaurant, including two children. One of the children was 16-year-old Abdulrahman Al-Aulaqi, who was Anwar Al-Aulaqi's son and also an American citizen.

4. Defendants' killing of Anwar Al-Aulaqi was unlawful. At the time of the killing, the United States was not engaged in an armed conflict with or within Yemen. Outside the context of armed conflict, both the United States Constitution and international human rights law prohibit the use of lethal force unless, at the time it is applied, lethal force is a last resort to protect against a concrete, specific, and imminent threat of death or serious physical injury. Upon information and belief, Anwar Al-Aulaqi was not engaged in activities that presented such a threat, and the use of lethal force against him was not a last resort. Even in the context of an armed conflict, the law of war cabins the government's authority to use lethal force and

prohibits killing civilians who are not directly participating in hostilities. The concept of "direct participation" requires both a causal and temporal nexus to hostilities. Upon information and belief, Defendants directed and authorized the killing of Anwar Al-Aulaqi even though he was not then directly participating in hostilities within the meaning of the law of war.

5. Defendants' killing of Samir Khan and Abdulrahman Al-Aulaqi was also unlawful. Upon information and belief, neither Samir Khan nor Abdulrahman Al-Aulaqi was engaged in any activity that presented a concrete, specific, and imminent threat to life; nor was either of them directly participating in hostilities. The news media have reported, based on statements attributed to anonymous U.S. government officials, that Samir Khan was not the target of the September 30 strike and that Abdulrahman Al-Aulaqi was not the target of the October 14 strike. If the Defendants were targeting others, they had an obligation under the Constitution and international human rights law to take measures to prevent harm to Samir Khan, Abdulrahman Al-Aulaqi, and other bystanders. Even in the context of an armed conflict, government officials must comply with the requirements of distinction and proportionality and take all feasible measures to protect bystanders. Upon information and belief, Samir Khan and Abdulrahman Al-Aulaqi were killed because Defendants failed to take such measures.

6. Plaintiffs are the personal representatives of the estates of Anwar Al-Aulaqi, Samir Khan, and Abdulrahman Al-Aulaqi. They seek damages from Defendants for their role in authorizing and directing the killings of Plaintiffs' sons and grandson in violation of the Fourth and Fifth Amendments and the Bill of Attainder Clause.

Jurisdiction and Venue

7. This complaint is for compensatory damages resulting from the conduct of Defendants, all of them U.S. government officials, in violation of the Fourth and Fifth Amendments and the Bill of Attainder Clause.

8. This Court has jurisdiction over this case pursuant to 28 U.S.C. § 1331 (federal question) and the U.S. Constitution.

9. Venue is proper in this district pursuant to 28 U.S.C. § 1391(e)(1).

Parties

10. Plaintiff Nasser Al-Aulaqi is the father of Anwar Al-Aulaqi and the grandfather of Abdulrahman Al-Aulaqi. He is a citizen and resident of Yemen. He brings this suit as the personal representative of the estates of his son and grandson, American citizens who were killed by missile strikes authorized and directed by Defendants.

11. Plaintiff Sarah Khan, an American citizen, is the mother of Samir Khan. She brings this suit as the personal representative of the estate of her son, an American citizen who was killed by missile strikes authorized and directed by Defendants.

12. Defendant Leon C. Panetta is the Secretary of Defense, a post he has held since July 2011. As Defense Secretary, he has ultimate authority over U.S. armed forces worldwide, including over JSOC. He authorized Anwar Al-Aulaqi's continued placement on JSOC's kill list after July 2011 and authorized and directed the missile strikes that killed Anwar Al-Aulaqi, Samir Khan, and Abdulrahman Al-Aulaqi. Between February 2009 and

June 2011, Defendant Panetta was the Director of the CIA. As CIA Director, he authorized the addition of Anwar Al-Aulaqi to the CIA's kill list. He is sued in his individual capacity.

13. Defendant William H. McRaven is Commander of the U.S. Special Operations Command ("USSOCOM"), a post he has held since August 2011. As Commander of USSOCOM, Defendant McRaven has authority over JSOC, a subordinate unified command within USSOCOM. He authorized and directed the missile strikes that killed Anwar Al-Aulaqi, Samir Khan, and Abdulrahman Al-Aulaqi. Between June 2008 and June 2011, he was the Commander of JSOC. In that capacity, he authorized the addition of Anwar Al-Aulaqi to JSOC's kill list. He is sued in his individual capacity.

14. Defendant Joseph Votel is the Commander of JSOC, a post he has held since June 2011. As Commander of JSOC, he has authority over JSOC operations. He authorized and directed the missile strikes that killed Anwar Al-Aulaqi, Samir Khan, and Abdulrahman Al-Aulaqi. He is sued in his individual capacity.

15. Defendant David H. Petraeus is the Director of the CIA, a post he has held since September 2011. As CIA Director, he has ultimate authority over the CIA's operations worldwide. He authorized and directed the missile strikes that killed Anwar Al-Aulaqi, Samir Khan, and Abdulrahman Al-Aulaqi. He is sued in his individual capacity.

Factual Allegations

"Targeted Killings" by the United States

16. The first reported post-2001 targeted killing by the U.S. government outside Afghanistan occurred in Yemen in November 2002, when a CIA-operated Predator drone fired a missile at a terrorism suspect traveling in a car with other passengers. The strike killed all passengers in the vehicle, including an American citizen. The United Nations Special Rapporteur on Extrajudicial, Summary or Arbitrary Executions later stated that the strike constituted "a clear case of extrajudicial killing" and set an "alarming precedent."

17. Since 2002, the United States has continued to carry out targeted killings outside the context of armed conflict. The pace of these killings has increased dramatically since 2009. In the course of carrying out these killings, the government has killed many hundreds of civilian bystanders. In December 2009, a U.S. missile strike in the village of al-Majalah, Yemen, killed 41 people, including 21 children.

18. In April 2012, Deputy National Security Advisor John Brennan acknowledged publicly that the United States carries out targeted killings of suspected terrorists "beyond hot battlefields like Afghanistan," often using "remotely piloted aircraft" known as "drones." Both the CIA and JSOC are involved in authorizing, planning, and carrying out these killings; both the CIA and JSOC have carried out such killings in Yemen; and, according to a December 2011 report in the *Washington Post* and other news sources, the CIA and JSOC "share intelligence and coordinate attacks." Greg Miller, *Under Obama, an Emerging Global Apparatus for Drone Killing*, Wash. Post, Dec. 27, 2011.

19. Both the CIA and JSOC maintain "kill lists" setting out the names of the individuals they intend to kill. *See* Jo Becker & Scott Shane, *Secret 'Kill List' Proves a Test of Obama's Principles and Will*, N.Y. Times, May 29, 2012. Upon information and belief, the inclusion of an individual on one or both of the lists represents a standing order authorizing and directing certain government personnel to kill that individual. In a February 2011 interview with *Newsweek*, the CIA's former acting general counsel John Rizzo described the CIA's list as "basically a hit list." He stated that there are approximately 30 individuals on the list "at any given time," and that "[t]he Predator [drone] is the weapon of choice, but it could also be someone putting a bullet in your head." Tara McKelvey, *Inside the Killing Machine*, Newsweek, Feb. 13, 2011.

20. Senior government officials, including then-Director of National Intelligence Dennis Blair and Deputy National Security Advisor John Brennan, have made clear that the government's claimed authority to carry out the targeted killing of suspected terrorists, including killings executed outside the context of armed conflict, extends to American citizens. However, government officials have offered incomplete and inconsistent explanations of the legal standards that govern the placement of U.S. citizens on the kill lists. Some officials have suggested that the U.S. government targets its citizens only if they present "imminent" threats, but they have defined the term "imminent" so broadly as to negate its meaning.

Defendants' Decision to Authorize the Killing of Anwar Al-Aulaqi

21. Plaintiff Nasser Al-Aulaqi is a Yemeni citizen who moved to the United States in 1966 to study as a Fulbright scholar at

New Mexico State University. He and his wife lived in the United States until 1978, when they moved back to Yemen. In Yemen, he served as Minister of Agriculture and Fisheries and president of Sana'a University, and founded and served as president of Ibb University. He currently resides in Yemen with his wife, who is an American citizen, and their family.

22. Plaintiff Nasser Al-Aulaqi's son, Anwar, was born in 1971 in New Mexico. He moved to Yemen with his parents in 1978. In 1991, he returned to the United States to attend college at Colorado State University. He obtained his master's degree from San Diego State University and then enrolled in a Ph.D. program at George Washington University, which he attended through December 2001. While living in the United States, he married and had children, including Abdulrahman. He left the United States in 2003, first for the United Kingdom and then for Yemen.

23. In January 2010, the *Washington Post* reported that JSOC had added Anwar Al-Aulaqi to its kill list and had tried unsuccessfully to kill him in December 2009. Dana Priest, *U.S. Military Teams, Intelligence Deeply Involved in Aiding Yemen on Strikes*, Wash. Post, Jan. 27, 2010. Other media organizations reported the same information. In March 2010, the *Wall Street Journal* reported that then-CIA Director Defendant Panetta stated that Anwar Al-Aulaqi was "someone that we're looking for" and that "there isn't any question that he's one of the individuals that we're focusing on." Keith Johnson, *U.S. Seeks Cleric Backing Jihad*, Wall St. J., Mar. 26, 2010. In April 2010, multiple media organizations, including the *Washington Post*, reported that Anwar Al-Aulaqi had been added to the CIA's kill list. *See* Greg Miller, *Muslim Cleric Aulaqi Is 1st U.S. Citizen on List of Those CIA Is Allowed to Kill*, Wash. Post, Apr. 7, 2010.

24. The decision to add Anwar Al-Aulaqi to government kill lists was made after a closed executive process. Defendant Panetta participated in this process, and upon information and belief Defendant McRaven participated in this process as well. Upon information and belief, Defendants authorized and directed Anwar Al-Aulaqi's killing even though, at the time lethal force was used, Anwar Al-Aulaqi was not engaged in activities that presented a concrete, specific, and imminent threat to life, and even though there were means short of lethal force that could reasonably have been used to address any such threat. Upon information and belief, Defendants authorized and directed Anwar Al-Aulaqi's killing even though he was not then directly participating in hostilities within the meaning of the law of war.

25. In or around June 2010, the Department of Justice's Office of Legal Counsel completed a memorandum providing legal justifications for the killing of Anwar Al-Aulaqi. Substantial portions of the memorandum were summarized in October 2011 by the *New York Times*, which reported, based on conversations with individuals who had read the document, that the memorandum "provided the justification for acting [against Anwar Al-Aulaqi] despite an executive order banning assassinations, a federal law against murder, protections in the Bill of Rights and various strictures of the international laws of war." Charlie Savage, *Secret U.S. Memo Made Legal Case to Kill a Citizen*, N.Y. Times, Oct. 8, 2011.

26. Between the time Anwar Al-Aulaqi was added to the JSOC and CIA kill lists and the time he was killed, government officials told reporters that Al-Aulaqi had "cast his lot" with terrorist groups and encouraged others to engage in terrorist activity. Later, they claimed he had played "a key role in setting the strategic direction" for "Al Qaeda in the Arabian Peninsula

(AQAP)." The government never publicly indicted Anwar Al-Aulaqi for any crime.

Nasser Al-Aulaqi's Lawsuit to Enjoin the Government from Killing His Son

27. On August 30, 2010, Nasser Al-Aulaqi filed suit in this Court as next friend of his son, Anwar, asking that the Court enter an injunction barring the President, the CIA, and DOD (including JSOC) from carrying out the targeted killing of his son unless the executive concluded that he presented a concrete, specific, and imminent threat to life, and that there were no reasonably available measures short of lethal force that could be expected to address that threat. After hearing argument on November 8, 2010, the Court dismissed the Complaint on December 7, 2010, holding that Nasser Al-Aulaqi lacked standing to assert his son's constitutional rights and that at least some of the issues raised by the Complaint were non-justiciable political questions. No appeal was taken.

Samir Khan

28. Plaintiff Sarah Khan is a U.S. citizen who has lived in the United States since 1992 with her husband and children. Her son, Samir, was born in 1985 and became a U.S. citizen in 1998.

29. Samir Khan attended elementary school in Queens, New York, and high school on Long Island, New York. After graduating from high school in 2003, he moved to North Carolina, where he attended a community college and worked part-time. He left for Yemen in October 2009.

30. Anonymous government officials have told reporters that Samir Khan was a "propagandist" for AQAP. The government never publicly indicted him for any crime.

The September 30, 2011 Killing of Anwar Al-Aulaqi and Samir Khan

31. On the morning of September 30, 2011, Anwar Al-Aulaqi and Samir Khan were in the Yemeni province of al-Jawf, some 90 miles northeast of Sana'a. Upon information and belief, Defendants Panetta, McRaven, Votel, and Petraeus authorized and directed personnel under their command to fire missiles at Anwar Al-Aulaqi and his vehicle from unmanned U.S. drones. The missiles destroyed the vehicle and killed Anwar Al-Aulaqi, Samir Khan, and at least two others. Witnesses reported that the missile strike left the vehicle a "charred husk" and "tore the [victims'] bodies to pieces." Dominic Rushe, et al., *Anwar al-Awlaki Death: US Keeps Role Under Wraps to Manage Yemen Fallout*, Guardian, Sept. 30, 2011; Sudarsan Raghavan, *Awlaqi Hit Misses al-Qaeda Bombmaker, Yemen Says*, Wash. Post, Sept. 30, 2011. According to a September 30, 2011 article in the *Washington Post* and a June 2012 book by journalist Daniel Klaidman, personnel under Defendants' command had been surveilling Anwar Al-Aulaqi for a period as long as three weeks leading up to the strike. Greg Miller, *Strike on Aulaqi Demonstrates Collaboration Between CIA and Military*, Wash. Post, Sept. 30, 2011; Daniel Klaidman, *Kill or Capture* (2012). Defendants' lengthy surveillance suggests that the use of lethal force was not a last resort and that additional measures could have been taken to protect bystanders from harm.

32. The surveillance and the strike were carried out by the CIA and JSOC. Upon information and belief, Defendant Petraeus

was personally responsible for authorizing and directing the CIA's involvement in the September 30 strike, and Defendants Panetta, McRaven, and Votel were personally responsible for authorizing and directing JSOC's involvement in it. Defendants coordinated with each other in planning the attack and carrying it out.

33. Senior government officials, including Defendant Panetta and President Barack Obama, have acknowledged the responsibility of the United States for killing Anwar Al-Aulaqi. On the same day the strike was carried out, DOD published a news article stating that "[a] U.S. airstrike . . . killed . . . Anwar [Al-Aulaqi] early this morning" and that he had been "high on the military-intelligence list of terrorist targets." Lisa Daniel, *Panetta: Awlaki Airstrike Shows U.S.-Yemeni Cooperation*, Am. Forces Press Service, Sept. 30, 2011. The following day, Defendant Panetta stated in a public speech that "it is because of th[e] teamwork between our intelligence and our military communities that we were successful in . . . taking down al-Awlaki." Three weeks later, President Obama stated on national television that "working with the Yemenis, we were able to remove [Anwar Al-Aulaqi] from the field." *Tonight Show with Jay Leno* (NBC television broadcast Oct. 25, 2011).

34. Defendants' killing of Anwar Al-Aulaqi was unlawful. Upon information and belief, Defendants authorized and directed the strike even though, at the time the strike was carried out, Anwar Al-Aulaqi was not engaged in activities that presented a concrete, specific, and imminent threat of death or serious physical injury. Upon information and belief, Defendants authorized and directed the strike even though there were means short of lethal force that could reasonably have been used to neutralize any threat that Anwar Al-Aulaqi's activities may have presented. The

killing of Anwar Al-Aulaqi was unlawful even if analyzed under the law of war because, upon information and belief, Defendants authorized and directed the strike even though Anwar Al-Aulaqi was not then directly participating in hostilities within the meaning of the law of war.

35. Defendants' killing of Samir Khan was also unlawful. Samir Khan was not engaged in any activity that presented a concrete, specific, and imminent threat of death or serious physical injury; nor was he directly participating in hostilities. If he was killed because of the government's targeting of Anwar al-Aulaqi, his killing was unlawful because Al-Aulaqi's killing was unlawful and because, upon information and belief, Defendants authorized and directed the strike without taking legally required measures to avoid harm to bystanders. Even in the context of an armed conflict, government officials must comply with the requirements of distinction and proportionality and take all feasible measures to protect bystanders. Upon information and belief, Samir Khan was killed because Defendants failed to take such measures.

The October 14, 2011 Killing of Abdulrahman Al-Aulaqi

36. Plaintiff Nasser Al-Aulaqi's grandson, Abdulrahman Al-Aulaqi, was born in Denver, Colorado, on August 26, 1995. He was raised in the United States until 2002, when he moved with his family to Yemen. At the time of his death, he was a student in his first year of high school and resided in Sana'a, Yemen, with his mother, siblings, grandmother, and grandfather.

37. On October 14, 2011, Abdulrahman was at an open-air restaurant near the town of Azzan, in the southern Yemeni province of Shabwa. Upon information and belief, Defendants Panetta,

McRaven, Votel, and Petraeus authorized and directed personnel under their command to fire missiles from unmanned U.S. drones at a person at or near the restaurant. According to media sources, the intended target was Ibraham Al-Banna, an Egyptian national, but it was later reported that he was not among those killed by the strike. *See* Gregory Johnsen, *Signature Strikes in Yemen*, Waq al-Waq, Apr. 19, 2012. The strike killed at least seven people, including Abdulrahman and one of his cousins, another minor. Abdulrahman himself was 16 years old.

38. After the strike, a senior Obama administration official described Abdulrahman to the *Los Angeles Times* as a "military-aged male." Ken Dilanian, *Grieving Awlaki Family Protests Yemen Drone Strikes*, L.A. Times, Oct. 19, 2011. Other news sources described Abdulrahman as a militant in his twenties. To correct these erroneous descriptions, Abdulrahman's family provided his birth certificate to the *Washington Post*. After the *Washington Post* published the birth certificate, U.S. officials acknowledged in anonymous statements to the press that Abdulrahman had been a minor.

39. Upon information and belief, Defendant Panetta was personally responsible for authorizing and directing the CIA's involvement in the October 14 strike, and Defendants Petraeus, McRaven, and Votel were personally responsible for authorizing and directing JSOC's involvement in the October 14 strike. Defendants coordinated with each other in planning the attack and carrying it out.

40. The killing of Abdulrahman Al-Aulaqi was unlawful. Abdulrahman was not engaged in any activity that presented a concrete, specific, and imminent threat of death or serious physical injury; nor was he directly participating in hostilities. If he was killed because the government was targeting another

individual, his killing was unlawful because, upon information and belief, Defendants authorized and directed the strike without taking legally required measures to avoid harm to him. Even in the context of an armed conflict, the government must comply with the requirements of distinction and proportionality and take all feasible measures to protect bystanders. Upon information and belief, Abdulrahman Al-Aulaqi was killed because Defendants failed to take such measures.

Causes of Action

FIRST CLAIM FOR RELIEF
FIFTH AMENDMENT: DUE PROCESS

41. Defendants' actions described herein violated the substantive and procedural due process rights of Anwar Al-Aulaqi, Samir Khan, and Abdulrahman Al-Aulaqi under the Fifth Amendment to the Constitution. Defendants Panetta, McRaven, Votel, and Petraeus violated the Fifth Amendment due process rights of Anwar al-Aulaqi, Samir Khan, and Abdulrahman Al-Aulaqi by authorizing and directing their subordinates to use lethal force against them in the circumstances described above. The deaths of Anwar al-Aulaqi, Samir Khan, and Abdulrahman Al-Aulaqi were a foreseeable result of Defendants' actions and omissions.

SECOND CLAIM FOR RELIEF
FOURTH AMENDMENT: UNREASONABLE SEIZURE

42. Defendants' actions described herein violated the rights of Anwar Al-Aulaqi, Samir Khan, and Abdulrahman Al-Aulaqi to be free from unreasonable seizures under the Fourth Amendment to the Constitution. Defendants Panetta, McRaven, Votel,

and Petraeus violated the Fourth Amendment rights of Anwar al-Aulaqi, Samir Khan, and Abdulrahman Al-Aulaqi by authorizing and directing their subordinates to use lethal force against them in the circumstances described above. The deaths of Anwar al-Aulaqi, Samir Khan, and Abdulrahman Al-Aulaqi were a foreseeable result of Defendants' actions and omissions.

THIRD CLAIM FOR RELIEF
BILL OF ATTAINDER

43. Defendants' actions described herein with respect to Anwar Al-Aulaqi violated the Constitution's Bill of Attainder Clause. Defendants' actions constituted an unconstitutional act of attainder because Defendants designated Anwar Al-Aulaqi for death without the protections of a judicial trial in the circumstances described above. The death of Anwar al-Aulaqi was a foreseeable result of Defendants' actions and omissions.

Prayer for Relief

Wherefore, Plaintiffs respectfully request that this Court enter judgment awarding them:

A. Damages in an amount to be determined at trial; and

B. Such other relief as the Court deems just and proper.

Respectfully submitted,

Arthur B. Spitzer [...]
American Civil Liberties Union of the Nation's Capital

[...]

Jameel Jaffer [...]
Hina Shamsi [...]
Nathan Freed Wessler
American Civil Liberties Union Foundation

[...]

Pardiss Kebriaei [...]
Maria C. LaHood [...]
Baher Azmy
Center for Constitutional Rights

[...]

*The **American Civil Liberties Union** is a national, nonprofit organization that aims to preserve individual rights in the United States. Its operations focus on lobbying, litigation, and education.

The **Center for Constitutional Rights** is dedicated to advancing and protecting the rights guaranteed by the United States Constitution and the Universal Declaration of Human Rights.

American Civil Liberties Union and Center for Constitutional Rights. *Al-Aulaqi v. Panetta: Complaint.* United States District Court for the District of Columbia. July 18, 2012.

Used by permission.

Violating the Ideals He Pledged to Uphold

by Hina Shamsi*

The White House is once again weighing whether to kill an American citizen overseas as part of its "targeted killing" program.

This extrajudicial killing program should make every American queasy. Based on largely secret legal standards and entirely secret evidence, our government has killed thousands of people. At least several hundred were killed far from any battlefield. Four of the dead are Americans. Astonishingly, President Obama's Justice Department has said the courts have no role in deciding whether the killing of U.S. citizens far from any battlefield is lawful.

The president, it seems, can be judge, jury, and executioner.

This is not the law. Our Constitution and international law strictly limit extrajudicial killing, for good reason. In areas of actual armed conflict, killing can be lawful because of battlefield requirements. Outside that context, an extrajudicial killing is legal only as a last resort, and only in response to a truly imminent threat. This makes sense: If a threat is imminent, there is no time for judicial review. In every other context, the Constitution requires the government to prove its case to a court before it kills. After all, allegations aren't evidence—the difference between the two is due process.

The program's defenders, however, argue that the president must be able to take lethal action against targets "who pose a continuing and imminent threat" and who are too risky to capture, as the president explained last May. But if, as reported, the Justice Department has the time to build a case against a suspected terrorist for months, then the threat he presents is not imminent. And if the threat is not imminent, then the administration's arguments for killing, and against external judicial review, fall away.

The Obama administration has apparently "solved" this logical inconsistency by redefining imminence to mean its opposite. Under the concept of "continuing imminence," the White House says it can order the killing of an American it suspects may someday strike—even without evidence of an actual plot.

The killing program isn't only unlawful, it's unwise.

When Americans hear of a drone strike, many think of a terrorist threat neutralized. But human-rights investigators and reporters have documented numerous horrific casualties of people killed due to mistaken identity or being at the wrong place at the wrong time.

Deaths like these have made the killing program toxic throughout most of the world and have turned potential allies into enemies. The blowback is so severe that retired Army Gen. Stanley McChrystal, who commanded U.S. and coalition forces in Afghanistan, has repeatedly called for restraint. "[T]here is a perception of helpless people in an area being shot at like thunderbolts from the sky by an entity that is acting as though they have omniscience and omnipotence," McChrystal said recently.

Perception isn't the only problem. We would do well to remember the 67-year-old grandmother killed by a drone while picking vegetables in her garden in Pakistan. Or the 16-year-old American boy blown up while eating dinner outdoors in Yemen. Or the 10-year-old Yemeni child who died in a CIA strike—only a few weeks after the president announced that drone missiles would not be fired unless there was a "near certainty" that no civilians would be killed.

There are some powers people should never concede to their government. That's why the Founders included due process in our Bill of Rights. Extraordinary powers consolidated in one office inevitably will be abused. That's true no matter who's behind the desk.

By asserting the right to kill based on his authority alone, President Obama violates the constitutional principles he swore to uphold and undermines the security we all seek. He also paves the way for a President Christie, Clinton, or Cruz to decide who lives and who dies.

*Hina Shamsi is director of the American Civil Liberties Union's National Security Project.

Shamsi, Hina. "Violating the Ideals He Pledged to Uphold." Philly.com, March 2, 2014. http://articles.philly.com/2014-03-02/news/47863605 _1_terrorist-threat-killing-continuing-and-imminent-threat.

The Legacy of 9/11: Endless War Without Oversight

by Hina Shamsi*

This 'everywhere and forever' war on terror that rides rough-shod over the rule of law only empowers America's enemies

Almost ten years after 9/11, in May of this year, a majority of the US House of Representatives voted to give President Obama—and all future presidents—more war authority than Congress gave to President Bush two days after the 9/11 attacks: a president would no longer have to show a connection to 9/11, or even any specific threat to America, before using military force anywhere in the world that a terrorism suspect may be found, including within the United States.

The House vote sought to place the nation on a permanent war footing at a time when responsible policy-making called for the opposite. Osama bin Laden had been killed days before the vote. As Defense Secretary Leon Panetta would soon confirm, we were "within reach of strategically defeating al-Qaida". The Obama administration had threatened to veto the bill, telling the House that the executive branch already had all the war powers it needed. And America is exhausted by the high cost in blood and treasure of two wars begun with the stated goal of combating terrorism. Yet, instead of pausing to consider whether the time had come to ratchet down the nation's war against terrorism, the House voted to expand it. If the House bill is approved by the full Congress (so far, the Senate has not gone along with the House), it would be the single largest handover of unchecked war power to the executive branch in American history.

Why would so many in the House be so willing to give such vast and undefined war powers to the executive?

The answer lies in the unrelenting drumbeat by some of our political leaders to force America into a military response to *any* act or even threat of terrorism anywhere in the world, including far from any actual battlefield. But it is not only some in Congress who have embraced a worldwide war against terrorism. Since 9/11, both the Bush and Obama administrations have contended that the United States is engaged in a global armed conflict against loosely defined terrorist entities and undefined "associated forces". The most concrete policies that have followed are the indefinite military detention and lethal targeting of civilians far from any conventional theatre of war.

Guantánamo Bay, which from its inception was a laboratory for unlawful military interrogation, detention and trials, remains an enduring symbol of indefinite military detention. And President Obama's pledge to close Guantánamo on his second day in office has been undermined by his own subsequent announcement of a policy enshrining at Guantánamo the principle of indefinite military detention without charge or trial.

Indefinite detention is unnecessary: federal "material support" statutes allow the government to secure convictions without having to show that any specific act of terrorism has taken place, or is being planned, or even that a defendant intended to further terrorism. If the government does not have evidence that a person meets even these minimal standards, it is hard to imagine any possible justification for indefinitely detaining that person.

But the real danger of the Guantánamo indefinite detention principle is that its underlying rationale has no definable limits. Military detention may be legitimate for those captured on an actual battlefield, as our supreme court recognised in Hamdi v Rumsfeld. But in the context of a war against terrorism without specified enemies and geographic or temporal limitations, it is simply not possible, let alone lawful, for us to detain indefinitely everyone who we suppose may, at some point, present a danger.

Targeted killing poses an even graver threat to human rights and the international rule of law because the government claims the unchecked authority to impose an extrajudicial death sentence on people located far from any battlefield. In an actual war, the government's use of lethal force may be lawful, of course, but outside that context, the intentional killing of a civilian without prior judicial process is illegal, except in the narrowest and most extraordinary circumstances—as a last resort to prevent concrete, specific and imminent threats that are likely to cause death or serious physical injury.

Under the targeted killing programme begun by the Bush administration and vastly expanded by the Obama administration, the government now compiles secret "kill lists" of people who remain on those lists for months at a time—and so, by definition, cannot always pose "imminent" threats. And it has refused to disclose the legal criteria it uses to make its targeted killing decisions. There is no way for the American public or the world to know whether the targeted killing programme is lawful, let alone whether the people our government kills truly present an imminent threat to our nation. We do know, though, that in the decade since 9/11, the government has repeatedly labelled people as terrorists—including at Guantánamo—only for us to find out later, or for a court to find, that the government's evidence was exaggerated, wrong, or nonexistent.

In the last ten years, America has become an international legal outlier in invoking the right to use lethal force and indefinite detention against suspected terrorists outside battle zones. If we further entrench the militarisation of our counter-terrorism efforts, our nation risks becoming a legal pariah, to the detriment of those efforts. Abiding by their own international and domestic law obligations, key allies have rightly refused to extradite suspected terrorists to the United States for military detention or military prosecution, requiring assurances that prosecution will take place only in our criminal justice system.

In the name of national security, our leaders are also undermining our more enduring security: the international legal framework that protects our long-term interests. Political leaders who insist that the laws of war permit our executive to treat as a battlefield any location where a terrorism suspect is found are giving a green light to other nations—including those with less respect for international legal institutions—to do the same.

For Congress and our executive branch to commit us to an "everywhere and forever" war undermines values that define us in our own eyes and in the eyes of the world, and it sends the dangerous message that we are willing to give terrorists what they seek—the status of military warriors, not common criminals. Such a global war approach to counter-terrorism does not make us safer. It is not too late to chart a different course, but the American people, and our political leaders, now need to show the courage, and the will, to do so.

*Hina Shamsi is director of the American Civil Liberties Union's National Security Project.

Shamsi, Hina. "The Legacy of 9/11: Endless War Without Oversight." theguardian. com, September 7, 2011. http://www.theguardian.com/commentisfree/ cifamerica/2011/sep/07/us-constitution-and-civil-liberties-congress.

Recommendations and Report of the Task Force on US Drone Policy

(excerpt)

by Stimson Center*

[…]

Dispelling Misconceptions

[…]

UAVs Do Not "Cause" Disproportionately High Civilian Casualties.

Lethal UAV strikes frequently have been criticized for their alleged tendency to cause excessive civilian casualties. This criticism has little basis in fact. Contrary to popular belief, UAV technologies, in fact, enable greater precision in targeting than most other common means of warfare.

UAVs are a platform for tactical air-to-surface missiles, such as Hellfire II missiles, which themselves are very accurate munitions for tactical strikes, whether they are launched from manned or unmanned platforms. In contrast to manned aircraft, however, UAVs enable "persistent surveillance": they can spend hours, days, weeks or even months monitoring a potential

target. Equipped with imaging technologies that enable operators, who may be thousands of miles away, to see details as fine
as individual faces, modern UAV technologies allow their operators to distinguish between civilians and combatants far more
effectively than most other weapons systems—including, most
especially, manned aircraft.

No weapons system is perfect, and targeting decisions—
whether for UAV strikes or for any other weapons delivery
system—are only as good as the intelligence on which they are
based. We do not doubt that some US UAV strikes have killed
innocent civilians. There is no reason to believe UAVs cause
more civilian casualties than other weapons delivery systems.[1]
The frequency and number of civilian casualties resulting from
US drone strikes also appear to have dropped sharply in recent
years, as UAV technologies have improved and targeting rules
have been tightened.[2]

UAVs Do Not Turn Killing into "a Video-Game."

There is also little reason to view UAVs as uniquely creating
a "PlayStation mentality" about war. As noted earlier, there is
nothing new about discomfort with innovations in long-distance
weapons. UAVs permit killing from a safe distance—but so do
cruise missiles and snipers' guns. And ironically, the men and
women who remotely operate lethal UAVs have a far more "up
close and personal" view of the damage they inflict than the
pilots of manned aircraft, who speed past their targets in seconds from far above. In fact, some evidence suggests that UAV
operators are particularly vulnerable to post-traumatic stress:
they may watch their targets for weeks or even months, seeing
them go about the routines of daily life, before one day watching on-screen as they are obliterated.[3]

[...]

Legal and Ethical Issues Connected to Targeted Lethal UAV Strikes

LAW VERSUS THE RULE OF LAW

From a US government perspective, the United States is in an ongoing armed conflict with al-Qaida and its "associated forces."

As a domestic law matter, the use of lethal force against al-Qaida was authorized by the 2001 Authorization for the Use of Military Force (AUMF) passed by Congress a few days after the 9/11 attacks. The AUMF placed no geographic or temporal limitations on the use of force; it states only that the president may use "all necessary and appropriate force against those nations, organizations or persons he determines planned, authorized, committed or aided the terrorist attacks that occurred on Sept. 11, 2001."[4] The Obama administration has interpreted this broadly, arguing that the AUMF should be read to authorize the use of force against not only al-Qaida and the Taliban, but against any organizations or persons it views as "associated forces" of al-Qaida, even if those "associated" groups or individuals had no connection to the 9/11 attacks and pose no direct threat to the United States.[5]

As an international law matter, the existence of an armed conflict between the United States and al-Qaida triggers the applicability of the law of armed conflict, which permits the United States to target al-Qaida operatives as enemy combatants. The law of armed conflict permits status-based targeting: that is, al-Qaida combatants are targetable because of who they are, not because of their activities. By extension, members of organizations that fight alongside al-Qaida are also targetable as co-belligerents. And unlike ordinary domestic law or international human rights law, the law of armed conflict does not require the United States to provide due process to enemy combatants before targeting them, and it does not require the United States to compensate enemy combatants or their families for injuries, deaths or property damage.

Beyond the law of armed conflict, international law also recognizes that states have the right to use armed force outside their own borders when doing so is necessary to prevent an imminent attack.[6] US officials therefore have argued that cross-border targeted strikes against terror suspects are permitted both under the law of armed conflict and under the international law of self-defense.

These are plausible interpretations of existing US and international law, and we disagree with those critics who have declared that US targeted killings are "illegal." But "legality" and "the rule of law" are not the same thing. Changing technologies and events have made it increasingly difficult to apply the law of armed conflict and the international law relating to the use of force in a consistent and principled manner, leading to divergence between "the law" and the core *rule of law* principles that traditionally have animated US policy.

The law of armed conflict and the international legal rules governing the use of force by states arose in an era far removed from our own. When the Geneva Conventions of 1949 were drafted, for instance, it was assumed that most conflicts would be between states with uniformed, hierarchically organized militaries, and that the temporal and geographic boundaries of armed conflicts would be clear.

The paradigmatic armed conflict was presumed to have a clear beginning (a declaration of war) and a clear end (the surrender of one party, or a peace treaty); it was also presumed the armed conflict to be confined geographically to specific, identifiable states and territories. What's more, the law of armed conflict presumes that it is a relatively straightforward matter to identify "combatants" and distinguish them from "civilians," who are not targetable unless they participate directly in hostilities. The assumption is that it is also a straightforward matter to define "direct participation in hostilities."

The notion of "imminent attack" at the heart of international law rules relating to the use of force in state self-defense was similarly construed narrowly: traditionally, "imminent" was understood to mean "instant, overwhelming, and leaving no choice of means, and no moment for deliberation."[7]

But the rise of transnational non-state terrorist organizations confounds these preexisting legal categories. The armed conflict with al-Qaida and its associated forces can, by definition, have no set geographical boundaries, because al-Qaida and its associates are not territorially based and move easily across state borders. The conflict also has no temporal boundaries— not simply because we do not know the precise date on which the conflict will end, but because there is no obvious means of determining the "end" of an armed conflict with an inchoate, non-hierarchical network.

In a conflict so sporadic and protean—a conflict with enemies who wear no uniforms, operate in secret and may not use traditional "weapons"—the process of determining where and when the law of armed conflict applies, who should be considered a combatant and what counts as "hostilities" inevitably is fraught with difficulty. While our military and intelligence communities have grown increasingly adept, both at identifying and confirming the identities of al-Qaida affiliates and at precise and careful targeting, the criteria used to determine who might be considered targetable remain unknown to the public.

As it becomes increasingly difficult to articulate a consistent or principled definition of "combatant" or "hostilities," it also becomes similarly difficult to determine the circumstances in which a civilian becomes targetable because he is "participating directly in hostilities." In addition, it is unclear what standards should be used for determining what organizations might constitute "associated forces" or "co-belligerents" that "fight alongside" al-Qaida.[8] Finally, it is difficult to understand how the US government determines the "imminence" of unknown types of future attacks being planned by unknown individuals.

Reliance on intelligence and other targeting information provided by a host nation government adds an extra layer of uncertainty. In such contexts—when it is already so difficult to articulate clear criteria for determining what law applies, and to whom—we face the additional challenge of ensuring that we are not being drawn into a civil war, or being used to target the domestic political enemies of the host state leadership.

While the legal norms governing armed conflicts and the use of force look clear on paper, the changing nature of modern conflicts and security threats has rendered them almost incoherent in practice. Basic categories such as "battlefield," "combatant" and "hostilities" no longer have a clear or stable meaning. And when this happens, the rule of law is threatened.[9]

A great deal of ink has been spilled in efforts to define "the rule of law." For present purposes, it is probably sufficient to use the definition adopted by the US Army:

"Rule of law is a principle of governance in which all persons, institutions and entities, public and private, including the state itself, are accountable to laws that are publicly promulgated, equally enforced and independently adjudicated, and which are consistent with international human rights principles."[10]

The Army's *Rule of Law Handbook* adds that the rule of law further requires that

- Individuals are secure in their persons and property;

- The state is itself bound by law and does not act arbitrarily;

- The law can be readily determined and is stable enough to allow individuals to plan their affairs;

- Individuals have meaningful access to an effective and impartial legal system; and

- The state protects basic human rights and fundamental freedoms.[11]

The United States was founded upon rule of law principles,[12] and historically has sought to ensure that its own actions, international law and the actions of foreign states are consistent with these principles. Today, however, despite the undoubted good faith of US decision-makers, it would be difficult to conclude that US targeted strikes are consistent with core rule of law norms.

Consider US targeted strikes from the perspective of individuals in—for instance—Pakistan or Yemen. From the perspective of a Yemeni villager or a Pakistani living in the Federally Administered Tribal Areas (FATA), life is far from secure. Death can come from the sky at any moment, and the instability and incoherence of existing legal categories means that there is no way for an individual to be certain whether he is considered targetable by the United States. (Would attending a meeting or community gathering also attended by an al-Qaida member make him targetable? Would renting a building or selling a vehicle to a member of an "associated" force render him targetable? What counts as an "associated force?" Would accepting financial or medical aid from a terrorist group make him a target? Would extending hospitality to a relative who is affiliated with a terrorist group lead the United States to consider him a target?)

From the perspective of those living in regions that have been affected by US UAV strikes, this uncertainty makes planning impossible, and makes US strikes appear arbitrary. What's more, individuals in states such as Pakistan or Yemen have no ability to seek clarification of the law or their status from an effective or impartial legal system, no ability to argue that they have been mistakenly or inappropriately targeted or that the intelligence that led to their inclusion on a "kill list" was flawed or fabricated, and no ability to seek redress for injury. Their national laws and courts can offer no assistance in the face of foreign power, and far from protecting their fundamental rights and freedoms, their own states may in fact be deceiving them about their knowledge of and cooperation with US strikes. Meanwhile, geography and finances make it impossible to access US courts, and a variety of legal barriers—such as the state secrets privilege, the political question doctrine, and issues of standing, ripeness and mootness—in any case would prevent meaningful access to justice.[13]

INTERNATIONAL PRECEDENTS

As noted earlier, we believe that the US officials involved in targeted strike decisions are acting in good faith and with appropriate care. Nonetheless, we must consider how US targeted strikes appear to those outside the US executive branch—and particularly to those who live in other parts of the world.

From the perspective of many around the world, the United States currently appears to claim, in effect, the legal right to kill any person it determines is a member of al-Qaida or its associated forces, in any state on Earth, at any time, based on secret criteria and secret evidence, evaluated in a secret process by unknown and largely anonymous individuals—with no public disclosure of which organizations are considered "associated forces" (or how combatant status is determined, how the United States defines "participation in hostilities"), no means for anyone outside that secret process to raise questions about the criteria or validity of the evidence, and no means for anyone outside that process to identify or remedy mistakes or abuses. As we have noted, these rule of law concerns have led to significant international criticism of US targeted strikes.[14] But US practices also set a dangerous precedent that may be seized upon by other states—not all of which are likely to behave as scrupulously as US officials.[15] Imagine, for instance, if Russia began to use UAV strikes to kill individuals opposed to its annexation of Crimea and its growing influence in Eastern Ukraine. Even if the United States strongly believed those targeted by Russian were all nonviolent political activists lawfully expressing their opinions, Russia could easily take a page out of the United States' book and assert that the targeted individuals were members of anti-Russian terrorist groups with which Russia is in an armed conflict. Pressed for evidence, Russia could simply repeat the words used by US officials defending US targeted killings, asserting that it could not provide any evidence without disclosing sources and methods and creating a risk that terrorists would go underground. In such circumstances, how could the United States credibly condemn Russian targeted killings?

As noted earlier, US targeted strikes using lethal UAV technologies create strategic risks, including those associated with the erosion of norms of sovereignty and the possibility that other states will echo US arguments and engage in potentially destabilizing targeted strikes of their own. From the perspective of international rule of law and human rights, the same risks apply: is the United States inadvertently handing abusive foreign regimes a playbook for murdering those it considers politically inconvenient, under the guise of combating terrorism?

DEMOCRATIC ACCOUNTABILITY

Increased US reliance on lethal UAVs in cross-border targeted strikes also poses challenges to democracy and the American system of checks and balances. While we understand the administration's reasons for considering additional transparency difficult, the effect of the lack of transparency is that the United States has been fighting what amounts to a covert, multi-year killing program. But without additional information about the locations and frequency of UAV targeted strikes; without information about the numbers and identities of those killed and injured; without information even about the budgetary implications of covert targeted strikes: how can the citizenry evaluate US targeted strikes?

UAV strikes also raise questions about the continued efficacy of traditional congressional oversight mechanisms. Because UAV strikes do not require placing US troops into combat situations— and because such strikes may be sporadic—the administration has asserted that it is not required to notify the full Congress of targeted strikes or seek congressional authorization.[16] At the moment, the Obama administration continues to rely on the 2001 Authorization for Use of Military Force as the primary domestic legal basis for US targeted strikes outside of "hot" battlefields. But as noted earlier, the administration's interpretation of the AUMF is extraordinarily broad, and even many former executive branch officials question whether Congress intended to authorize such an unbounded conflict when the AUMF was passed in 2001.[17]

NOTES

(Notes have been renumbered.)

1. Brooks, Rosa. "The Constitutional and Counterterrorism Implications of Targeted Killing." Statement before US Congress. Senate. 113th Cong., 1s sess. April 23, 2013. Accessed June 2, 2014. http://www.judiciary.senate .gov/imo/media/doc/04-23-13BrooksTestimony.pdf; see also Saletan, William. "In Defense of Drones." Slate, February 19, 2013. Accessed October 6, 2014. http://www.slate.com/articles/health_and_science/ human_nature/2013/02/drones_war_and_civilian_casualties_how_ unmanned_aircraft_reduce_collateral.html.

2. In Pakistan, the number of civilian casualties has decreased in relation to the number of strikes over time. In 2009, the year when the most strikes occurred in Pakistan, there were around 100 civilian casualties for 100 strikes. However, this proportion of casualties to strikes has decreased over time. In 2011, there were 52-62 civilian casualties for 75 strikes, in 2012 there were around 4-5 civilian casualties for 50 strikes, and in 2013 there were zero civilian casualties for 27 drone strikes. (The Bureau of Investigative Journalism. "Pakistan Drone Statistics Visualized." Get the data: Drone wars. Last modified July 2, 2012. Accessed June 2, 2014. http://www.thebureauinvestigates.com/2012/07/02/ resources-and-graphs/.) See note 21, above, for further information regarding sources of BIJ data and its strike classification methodology.

3. Bumiller, Elisabeth. "Air Force Drone Operators Report High Levels of Stress." New York Times, December 18, 2011. Accessed June 2, 2014. http://www.nytimes.com/2011/12/19/world/asia/air-forcedrone- operators-show-high-levels-of-stress.html.

4. The Authorization for Use for Military Force, passed by Congress shortly after the 9/11 attacks, allows the President of the United States to use "all necessary and appropriate force against those nations, organizations or persons he determines planned, authorized, committed or aided the terrorist attacks that occurred on Sept. 11, 2001. Discussion has been raised about whether the original confines are AUMF are appropriate

to counter current threats—contributing to concerns of mission creep from the authorization. According to Robert Chesney, Jack Goldsmith, Matthew Waxman, and Benjamin Wittes, "This situation—which one of us has described as the emergence of 'extra-AUMF'—threats poses a significant problem in so far as counterterrorism policy rests on the AUMF for its legal justification." See: A Statutory Framework for Next-Generation Terrorist Threats. Stanford: Hoover Institution, 2013. Accessed June 2, 2014. http://media.hoover.org/sites/default/files/documents/Statutory-Framework-for-Next-Generation-Terrorist-Threats. pdf; Authorization for Use of Military Force. Public Law 107–40. 107th Cong., 1s sess. September 18, 2011.

5. According to speeches and congressional testimony by Administration officials, the Administration defines an "associated force" as "an organized, armed group that has entered the fight alongside al-Qa'ida or the Taliban and [is] a co-belligerent with al-Qa'ida or the Taliban in hostilities against the United States or its coalition partners." See, e.g., Preston, Stephen W. "The Framework Under U.S. Law for Current Military Operations." Statement before US Congress. Senate. 113th Cong., 2d sess. May 21, 2014. Accessed October 1, 2014. http://www.foreign.senate.gov/imo/media/doc/Preston_Testimony.pdf. Preston asserts that the concept of "associated forces" is not "open-ended": "A group that simply embraces al-Qa'ida's ideology is not an 'associated force,' nor is every group or individual that commits terrorist acts." It is unclear, however, how the Administration understands the phrase "entered the fight alongside [AQ or the Taliban]," or how it understands the phrase "hostilities against the United States or its coalition partners." Depending on how these key phrases are understood, the term "associated forces" could be given either a narrow or broad meaning. See generally Brooks, Rosa. "The Law of Armed Conflict, the Use of Military Force, and the 2001 Authorization for Use of Military Force." Statement before US Congress. Senate. 113th Cong., 1s sess. May 16, 2013. Accessed June 2, 2014. http://www.armed-services.senate.gov/imo/media/doc/Brooks_05-16-13.pdf; See, e.g, Chesney, Robert, Jack Goldsmith, Matthew C. Waxman, and Benjamin Wittes. A Statutory Framework for Next-Generation Terrorist Threats. Stanford: Hoover Institution, 2013. Accessed June 4, 2014. http://media.hoover.org/sites/default/files/documents/Statutory-Framework-for-Next-Generation-Terrorist-Threats.pdf; Miller, Greg, and Karen DeYoung. "Administration Debates Stretching 9/11 Law to Go After New al-Qaeda Offshoots." The Washington Post, March 6, 2013. Accessed June 2, 2014. http://www.washingtonpost.com/world/national-security

/administrationdebates-stretching-911-law-to-go-after-new-al-qaeda-offshoots/2013/03/06/fd2574a0-85e5-11e2-9d71f0feafdd1394_print.html.

6. According to Ashley Deeks, professor of law at the University of Virginia: "More than a century of state practice suggests that it is lawful for State X, which has suffered an armed attack by an insurgent or terrorist group, to use force in State Y against that group if State Y is unwilling or unable to suppress the threat. Yet there has been virtually no discussion, either by states or scholars, of what that standard means. What factors must the United States consider when evaluating Pakistan's willingness or ability to suppress the threats to US (as well as NATO and Afghan) forces? Must the United States ask Pakistan to take measures itself before the United States lawfully may act? How much time must the United States give Pakistan to respond? What if Pakistan proposes to respond to the threat in a way that the United States believes may not be adequate?" See: Deeks, Ashley. "'Unwilling or Unable': Toward an Normative Framework for Extra-Territorial Self-Defense." Virginian Journal of International Law, August 19, 2011. Accessed June 2, 2014. http://papers.ssrn.com/sol3/Delivery.cfm/SSRN_ID2032747_code984441.pdf?abstractid=1971326&mirid=1.

7. See the Caroline Incident. Arend, Anthony Clark. "International Law and the Preemptive Use of Military Force." The Center for Strategic and International Studies (CSIS), 2003. Accessed June 2, 2014. http://www.cfr.org/content/publications/attachments/highlight/03spring_arend.pdf.

8. In general, US policy says that those with links to the terrorist attacks on 9/11 or a co-belligerent that has entered the fight alongside al-Qaeda are targetable. CIA Director John Brennan stated in 2013 that those in al-Qaeda and associated forces who play an operational effort and are overseeing activities are targetable. President Obama added in his speech at the National Defense University in May 2013 that the United States "only targets al-Qaeda and associated forces…who pose a continuing and imminent threat to the American people…[and] does not take strikes to punish individuals." See: Johnson, Jeh. National Security Law, Lawyers and Lawyering in the Obama Administration. Remarks presented at Yale Law School, New Haven, CT, February 22, 2012. Accessed June 3, 2014. http://www.cfr.org/defense-and-security/jeh-johnsons-speech-national-security-law-lawyers-lawyering-obama-administration/p27448; US Congress. Senate. Open Hearing on the Nomination of John O. Brennan to be

Director of the Central Intelligence Agency. 113th Cong., 1st sess., February 7, 2013. 125; Obama, Barack. "Remarks by the President at the National Defense University." Address at the National Defense University, Washington, D.C., May 23, 2013, 4. Accessed November 15, 2013. http://www.whitehouse.gov/the-press-office/2013/05/23/remarks-president-national-defense-university.

9. As noted earlier in this report, the United States stands increasingly alone in its interpretation of international law on many of these issues. The US legal theories underlying targeted strikes outside "hot" battlefields have been questioned by most European states, several UN rapporteurs, and courts Pakistan and elsewhere. See: European Parliament. Joint Motion for a Resolution-On the Use of Armed Drones. 2014. Accessed June 2, 2014. http://www.reprieve.org.uk/media/downloads/2014_01_27_PUB_European_Parliament_resolution_on_use_of_drones.pdf.

10. US Army. Field Manual (3-07): Stability Operations. October 2008. Accessed June 2, 2014. http://usacac.army.mil/cac2/repository/FM307/FM3-07.pdf.

11. The Judge Advocate General's Legal Center and School. US Army. Rule of Law Handbook: A Practitioner's Guide for Judge Advocates. 2011. Accessed June 12, 2014. http://www.loc.gov/rr/frd/Military_Law/pdf/rule-of-law_2011.pdf.

12. Consider the Declaration of Independence's statement of "unalienable rights," and the list of grievances against George III.

13. Vladeck, Stephen I. The New National Security Canon. Washington, DC: American University, 2012. Accessed June 4, 2014. http://papers.ssrn.com/sol3/papers.cfm?abstract_id=2133024.

14. European Parliament. Joint Motion for a Resolution-On the Use of Armed Drones. 2014. Accessed June 2, 2014. http://www.reprieve.org.uk/media/downloads/2014_01_27_PUB_European_Parliament_resolution_on_use_of_drones.pdf.

15. Concern has already been raised with China's potential use of lethal UAVs against an alleged drug kingpin in 2013. (See generally: Bergen, Peter, and Jennifer Rowland. "Nine Facts About Armed Drones." CNN, May 13, 2014. Accessed June 2, 2014. http://www.cnn.com/2014/05/13/opinion/bergen-nine-factsspread-of-armed-drones/index.html.) More generally, we have seen numerous examples of US counterterrorism policies being cited as precedent by foreign regimes as excuses for repression. For example, Russia has justified continued repression of

Chechens in the Caucasus as part of the larger "war on terror" begun by the United States after 9/11.

16. See, e.g., Admin claim that no congressional notification was required for Libya. See: Koh, Harold. "Authorization For Use of Military Force after Iraq and Afghanistan." Statement before US Congress. Senate. Authorization for Use of Military Force after Iraq and Afghanistan. 113th Cong., 2d sess., May 21, 2014. Accessed June 5, 2014. http://www.foreign .senate.gov/imo/media/doc/Koh_Testimony.pdf.

17. Chesney, Robert, Jack Goldsmith, Matthew C. Waxman, and Benjamin Wittes. A Statutory Framework for Next-Generation Terrorist Threats. Stanford: Hoover Institution, 2013. Accessed June 4, 2014. http://media. hoover.org/sites/default/files/documents/Statutory-Framework-for-Next-Generation-Terrorist-Threats.pdf; Miller, Greg, and Karen DeYoung. "Administration Debates Stretching 9/11 Law to Go After New al-Qaeda Offshoots." The Washington Post, March 6, 2013. Accessed June 3, 2014. http://www. washingtonpost.com/world/national-security/ administration-debates-stretching-911-law-to-go-afternew-al-qaeda-offshoots/2013/03/06/fd2574a0-85e5-11e2-9d71-f0feafdd1394_print .html.

*The **Stimson Center** is a nonprofit and nonpartisan think tank that finds pragmatic solutions to global security challenges.

The Long-Term International Law Implications of Targeted Killing Practices

*by Christof Heyns and Sarah Knuckey**

One of the most crucial and enduring questions about "targeted killings" is: How will the currently expanding practices of singling out individuals in advance and eliminating them in other countries without accountability impact the established international legal system?

International law, since at least World War II, has developed various mechanisms to limit killing in general, including targeted killings. These take the form of vigorous protections for the right to life under human rights law; safeguards against the interstate use of force while permitting states to protect themselves where necessary; and aiming to strike a balance between the principles of humanity and military necessity during armed conflict through international humanitarian law (IHL).[1]

Targeted killings are not a new practice—governments have long sought to prevail over their enemies by engaging in premeditated killings of individual suspects.[2] What is new now is the rapid development and proliferation,[3] and increasing deployment,[4] of technologies which permit such killings to be carried out with greater ease and with little immediate risk to one side's citizens, together with concerted efforts by some to offer general legal justifications for current targeted killings practices, and, in some cases, to attempt to redefine existing legal frameworks to expand the circumstances in which such killings may be carried out "lawfully."[5]

A small number of states with the necessary capabilities—particularly the United States—clearly find targeted killing attractive today. As unmanned aerial technologies becomes more widely available, many other states may feel the same pull towards the advantages of drone attacks in the future. Some 76 countries now have unmanned aerial systems,[6] it has recently been reported that the Pentagon has approved the export of drones from U.S. manufacturers to 66 countries,[7] and reports suggest that an increasing number of countries are developing their own armed drones.[8]

Current targeted killings practices and the attempts to legally justify those strikes present a challenge to the systematic protection of the right to life under international law. We are now witnessing a significant effort by some states to insulate their "targeted" uses of deadly force from international scrutiny and to redefine international law in order to serve narrow and short-term interests. This presents a serious risk of leaving everyone less secure, particularly if other states around the world, as they acquire the new technology, claim for themselves the same expanded rights to target their enemies without meaningful transparency or accountability.

The challenge is to ensure that strong protections of the right to life under international law survive the practices of a few states, technological developments, and outlier attempts to redefine core legal standards.

For the past decade, successive U.N. Special Rapporteurs on extrajudicial, summary, or arbitrary executions have reported on and sought accountability and transparency for targeted killings of various forms, including those in the context of the so-called "War on Terror." Since the creation of the U.N. mandate thirty years ago in 1982, the U.N. Special Rapporteur on extrajudicial executions has been the primary international actor with the mandate to investigate, prevent, and promote accountability for all unlawful killings under international human rights and IHL.[9] The mandate exists to ensure respect for every individual's right not to be arbitrarily deprived of his or her life, to document and promote redress for violations, and to clarify the applicable international law. The mandate addresses a wide range of killings, including politically motivated killings by state agents, excessive use of force by law enforcement officials, custodial deaths, lack of due diligence by states in dealing with killings by private individuals, and violations of IHL during armed conflict by both government and non-state actors.[10]

Over the years, successive mandate holders have addressed targeted killings carried out through drone strikes and kill/capture raids, and have built up a detailed record of individual cases and analysis of the applicable international law. In 2003, for example, then U.N. Special Rapporteur, Asma Jahangir, concluded that a 2002 U.S. strike in Yemen was a "clear" extrajudicial execution.[11] Since then, numerous official U.N. communications have been exchanged with the U.S. government about targeted killings, seeking clarification about incidents as well as the U.S. government's views on the applicable law.[12] Country mission reports on Afghanistan and the United States have documented targeted killings, raised concerns about the legality of particular strikes, and called for accountability.[13] In 2010, then U.N. Special Rapporteur Professor, Philip Alston, reported in detail to the U.N. Human Rights Council on the legal frameworks and rules relevant to targeted killings,[14] as well as to the U.N. General

Assembly on accountability failures and of potentially "grave damage" to the "legal framework that the international community has so painstakingly constructed in order to protect the right to life."[15] The U.N. Special Rapporteurs on extrajudicial executions and on counter-terrorism have also asked the U.S. government for factual and legal clarification after the killing of Osama bin Laden.[16] In October 2012, the Special Rapporteurs announced that they would report to the United Nations in 2013 on the legal and factual issues around targeted killings, and an initiative will be launched to investigate strikes.[17] The U.S. has signaled that it is considering cooperating with this investigative work, a step that would go a significant way towards restoring international accountability.[18]

The applicable basic principles of international law relevant to the taking of life are clear and tested by time. International law does not wholesale prohibit targeted killings. Rather, rules have developed to impose principled limits on all uses of lethal force, and to ensure that the limits are respected through meaningful transparency and accountability. (Indeed, in some circumstances, "targeted" killings are precisely what international law prescribes.) However, as evidenced by both government practices and legal pronouncements, some states appear to want to offer only general legal justifications for highly contentious practices, to invent new law, or to stretch existing law beyond long-accepted understandings.

This issue will remain on the international agenda for the foreseeable future, and it is important to consider the outlines of the terrain. What rules bind states and should continue to guide action in the future?

It is undisputed that the right to life is part of international customary law,[19] and as such it imposes legal duties on all states, irrespective of their ratification of specific treaties. Some see the right to life as "the supreme right," and it has been described as a norm of *jus cogens*.[20]

Operations in the territory of other countries could potentially violate state sovereignty, and they may be considered acts of aggression in violation of the UN Charter absent consent or legitimate self-defense.[21] While self-defense has been advanced as a justification for targeted killings,[22] it is far from clear that its established legal confines have been satisfied in actual current practice. Self-defense (and the use of force on another state's territory) is justified in response to an "armed attack" that meets the required threshold, and there must be a direct link between the "armed attack" and the subsequent use of force in self-defense. As a general rule, self-defense may only justify force in response to attacks that have already occurred.[23] It is difficult to see in most cases how targeted killings carried out in 2012 can be justified as a self-defense response to the September 11, 2001 terrorist attacks in the United States. As targeted killings take place in more and more countries and against more groups with, at best, tenuous links to those responsible for the September 11 attacks, this difficulty only increases.

What about new threats? While states may engage in self-defense against truly "imminent" attacks, there is little available evidence to suggest that all of those individuals targeted by drone attacks would meet this requirement. The premeditated nature of targeted killings means that, in many cases, claims of imminence ring hollow. The reported presence for long periods of time of the names of those on "kill lists," for example, undermines claims of such an imminent threat. More permissive standards of "pre-emptive strikes," without a clear basis in the U.N. Charter, are being advanced in support of what would normally be regarded as acts of aggression. Indeed, it appears that the U.S. is attempting to redefine "imminence."[24] As noted above, if one government is allowed to use force whenever it is of the opinion that there is some perceived danger that may be realized at some point in the future, with no transparency or accountability, there is no basis on which to hold others back from doing the same.

Moreover, it is clear that even where consent or a self-defense justification for inter-state force is present, it does not obviate the need for further inquiry into whether the demands of IHL or international human rights law have been met in respect of the particular use of force. The question of the legality of extra-territorial use of force should not be confused with the question of the legality of the use of lethal force against a particular target. These are two *separate* inquiries. Questions of *jus ad bellum* and *jus in bello* should not be conflated. The "self-defense" test pertains to whether the use of inter-state force is or is not a violation of state sovereignty, and to when a state may use force extra-territorially. It does not answer the question of whether the specific type, level, timing, or scope of force used is lawful vis-à-vis the individual targeted person. The legality of this use of force depends on whether it complies with either human rights law or IHL.[25]

Where there is no armed conflict, international human rights law applies. Human rights law affords a high level of protection to the right to life: the use of force must be strictly *necessary* and *proportionate*. Lethal force may only intentionally be used where necessary to counter an imminent threat to life.[26] Unless the requirements of an armed conflict are met, international human rights law applies strictly—and it is far from clear on publicly available evidence that all of the targeted individuals posed an imminent threat to life, and that lethal force was in fact necessary.[27] It is also important to note that the obligation under human rights law to respect the right to life binds not only the state employing lethal force against an individual, but also, where lethal force is used extraterritorially, the state on whose territory any attack takes place.[28]

In the exceptional situation of armed conflict, the *lex specialis* rules of IHL also apply, and any killings must satisfy the foundational principles of proportionality, distinction, necessity, and humanity.[29] With respect to the question of whether an armed conflict exists, it is unhelpful to talk about a "hot" or a "cold" battlefield—either the killing is carried out in an armed conflict or it is not. The test for determining whether an armed conflict exists is an objective one, and it is not determined according to the mere subjective will or pronouncements of the parties involved.[30] In addition, and importantly, the targeted individual must be a lawful target: in the context of non-international armed conflict, the key legal test is that they must directly participate in hostilities.[31]

It is not at all clear that the targeted killings carried out by the U.S. are taking place against individuals directly participating in a recognized armed conflict, and in accordance with the specific rules of IHL. Although U.S. officials have relied on the existence of an armed conflict against al Qaeda and the ill-defined "associated forces" category as the basis for the legality of targeted killings, the U.S. government has presented little to no evidence to indicate that all strikes have in fact taken place against direct participants in hostilities or—if that category is used—against individuals who have a continuous combat function in an armed group which is a party to a recognized armed conflict. Strikes have also taken place in circumstances where it is far from evident that sufficient precautions in attack were taken or that the principles of proportionality and distinction were adequately observed.[32]

The Bureau of Investigative Journalism, which tracks drone strikes around the world, has reported that, in Pakistan, drone strikes have killed some 472–885 civilians, including 176 children, out of a total of 2,593–3,387 persons killed.[33] The Bureau also reports the use of secondary drone strikes on apparent "first responders" shortly after a first strike.[34] Significant civilian casualty reports raise serious questions about whether the principles of distinction and proportionality have been met. Similarly, concerns have been raised about adequate precautions and distinction following contentious revelations by anonymous government sources to the New York Times that adult males were generally counted as "combatants" if they were killed in a strike zone.[35] The so-called "signature strikes," in which targets are chosen based on patterns of behavior, are also troubling.[36] And, if civilian "rescuers" are intentionally being targeted in drone attacks in a situation of armed conflict, there is no doubt about the law: those strikes are war crimes.

The use of the term "targeted killing" can be misleading in the context of some strikes, since it creates the impression that little violence occurs and only the "target" is affected. It is true that a specific drone strike target may be identified with precision, and that immediate collateral damage in a particular case may be reduced. But because drones effectively eliminate the personal risk to the soldiers of the state using it, they enable this form of targeted killing to be used more often, with attendant risks to civilians. Furthermore, and as documented in first-hand testimony of witnesses and victims in a recent report by law clinics at Stanford and New York Universities (co-authored by

Sarah Knuckey), there is evidence indicating that targeted killings and drone strike practices have negative impacts on civilian mental health, educational and economic opportunities, and community institutions.[37]

The requirements of transparency and accountability with respect to the use of force apply under international human rights law as well as under IHL. The "first line of defense" against violations of the right to life is at the level of the national legal system. But if violations are not properly addressed domestically, the position of the state in question becomes a matter of legitimate international concern. This is the kind of accountability that the U.N. Human Rights Council deals with on a regular basis—for example, currently with respect to Syria, and previously with respect to Sri Lanka. Accountability for violations of the right to life is not a matter of choice or policy; it is a duty to be observed under both domestic and international law in all cases.

Consistent with the demands made by successive U.N. Special Rapporteur mandate holders over the last decade, the U.S. public and the international community urgently need clarity from the governments concerned on the general question about the legal basis upon which they carry out targeted killings, and also transparency about the facts that make a full assessment of legality and accountability possible. Key questions include: Who has been killed? What was the factual basis for targeting them? Were there civilian casualties and what procedures are in place to ensure compliance with international law? Only on this basis can the questions of legality be determined, and can redress be provided where necessary. Continuing failures to provide such basic information undermines democratic accountability, meaningful public debate about crucial policies, and ultimately the supervisory role of international law. Occasional "leaks" and anonymously sourced official accounts provided to journalists have provided some further details about U.S. practices, but have also raised concerns about the targeted killing program's compliance with international law. And they are no substitute for official statements and formal cooperation with existing domestic and international accountability mechanisms.

Current U.S. practices, together with vague legal justifications or those purporting to expand the circumstances in which states may kill their own or other states' citizens, threaten to undermine crucial international legal protections and the system of international accountability established after World War II. Other states have also thus far failed to hold the U.S. to account, or to adequately respond to U.S. practices or its novel legal interpretations. Individuals and states have always faced security threats. The existing legal frameworks were developed to balance legitimate security concerns with respect for territorial integrity, state sovereignty, the rule of law, due process, and individual rights.[38] Current targeted killing practices risk weakening the rule of law and disrupting settled restraints on the use of force. They could also set dangerous precedents for the future.

The international regulatory framework is often slow in responding to developments, including technological ones, and its response to the use of armed drones is no exception. The rapid proliferation of drones calls for a concerted international response. It is clear how difficult it can be to regulate new technologies once they are already developed and in use. In a number of important areas, however, the international community still has an opportunity to act in advance of new developments. We currently face many new issues—such as the domestic proliferation of police surveillance drones, which, without strong regulation, will pose serious risks to privacy and may undermine, for example, the exercise of protest rights.[39] The potential deployment of police drones equipped with less-lethal or lethal weapons also lies on the horizon.[40] The prospect of domestic police drones needs urgent attention from civil society and governments. Furthermore, the development of lethal autonomous weapons systems is on the horizon.[41] Weapons may in the future be programmed to autonomously locate, select, and "decide" who should be targeted for lethal attacks. The international community needs to confront squarely the dangers posed by these technologies before they are already in use.

Let us fast forward ten, or perhaps just five, years. Should there be an international legal order that permits governments around the world to operate "secret" and unaccountable programs to eliminate their enemies wherever they are with few binding limits and no meaningful international scrutiny? Some officials no doubt hope that they can successfully expand the scope of lawful killings through sheer force of repetition of practice and claims of "legality." This cannot and should not be accepted. The international community should act to uphold and restore the integrity on the international rule of law, and the protections guaranteed by human rights and international humanitarian law.

NOTES

1. Many efforts have also been directed at banning or regulating specific weapons. For an overview of the major disarmament treaties, see Bonnie Docherty, *Ending Civilian Suffering: The Purpose, Provisions, and Promise of Humanitarian Disarmament Law*, AUSTL. REV. OF INT'L & EUR. L. (forthcoming 2013).

2. See Special Rapporteur on extrajudicial, summary or arbitrary executions, *Rep. of the Special Rapporteur on extrajudicial, summary or arbitrary executions, Addendum: Study on Targeted Killings*, Human Rights Council, ¶ 11, U.N. Doc. A/HRC/14/24/Add.6 (May 28, 2010) (by Philip Alston)

[hereinafter *Rep. of the Special Rapporteur: Study on Targeted Killings*] (referring to previous targeted killings, and describing the general practice of states to deny such killings, and of other states to condemn them).

3. *See generally* P.W. Singer, Wired for War: The Robotics Revolution and Conflict in the Twenty-First Century (2009) (describing the development of drone technology for military purposes); U.S. Gov't Accountability Office, GAO-12-536, Nonproliferation: Agencies Could Improve Information Sharing and End-Use Monitoring on Unmanned Aerial Vehicle Exports 9 (July 2012) (describing the "rapid growth globally in UAV [unmanned aerial vehicle] acquisition, development, and military applications."). New and smaller, faster, and more sophisticated drone technologies are now regularly reported as being developed.

4. Drone strikes, generally, have drastically increased, although the proportion of these that would qualify as targeted killings in the various theaters of use is, on publicly available information, unclear. Under President Bush, the U.S. carried out an estimated 52 drone strikes in Pakistan. Under President Obama, there have been some 301 reported strikes. In addition, there have been at least 40 reported strikes in Yemen, and since 2011, there have been some strikes in Somalia. *See Covert War on Terror—The Data*, BUREAU OF INVESTIGATIVE JOURNALISM, http://www.thebureauinvestigates.com/category/projects/drone-data/ (last visited Dec. 07, 2012) [hereinafter *Covert War on Terror—The Data*]. The number of drone strikes overall appears to be the highest in Afghanistan, where a reported 333 strikes took place in 2012 alone. *See* Noah Shachtman, *Military Stats Reveal Epicenter of U.S. Drone War*, Wired (Sept. 11, 2012), http://www.wired.com/dangerroom/2012/11/drones-afghan-air-war/. It was recently reported that since 2008, almost 1,200 drone strikes took place (by the U.S. and the U.K.) in Afghanistan, Iraq, and Libya. *See* Chris Woods & Alice K. Ross, *Revealed: U.S. and Britain Launched 1,200 Drone Strikes in Recent Wars*, BUREAU OF INVESTIGATIVE JOURNALISM (Dec. 4, 2012), http://www.thebureauinvestigates.com/2012/12/04/revealed-us-and-britain-launched-1200-drone-strikes-in-recent-wars/. U.S. Special Operations kill/capture raids in Afghanistan have also reportedly increased under President Obama. *See* Jonathan Masters, *Targeted Killings: Backgrounder*, COUNCIL ON FOREIGN REL. (Apr. 30, 2012), www.cfr.org/counterterrorism/targeted-killings/p9627.1

5. It is important not to overly-focus on the technologies themselves. Targeted killings, whether carried out by drone or sniper, raise essentially the same legal issues and are constrained by the same legal frameworks. However, it is also important to recognize that drones are presently

perceived by those who deploy them to offer new opportunities and unique advantages for expanded surveillance and targeting, and that in this sense they appear to be facilitating the expanding practice, policy, and legal frontiers of targeted killings.

6. U.S. Gov't Accountability Office, *supra* note 5, at 15 (providing information that since 2005, the number of countries that have acquired a UAV system jumped from 42 to at least 76).

7. Actual sales will need approval by the U.S. State Dep't and Cong. *See* Doug Palmer & Jim Wolf, *Pentagon OK with Selling U.S. Drones to 66 Countries*, NBCNews.com (Sept. 6, 2012), http://usnews.nbcnews.com/_news/2012/09/06/13695931-pentagon-ok-with-selling-usU.S.-drones-to-66-countries?lite.

8. *See, e.g., Sukhoi to Build Strike, Recon Unmanned Planes*, RIA Novosti (Nov. 13, 2012 10:58 AM), http://en.ria.ru/military_news/20121113/177420795.html (describing armed UAV developments in Russia); Staff Writers, *Latest China Military Hardware Displayed at Airshow*, Space Travel (Nov. 13, 2012),http://www.space-travel.com/reports/Latest_China_military_hardware_displayed_at_airshow_999.html (describing armed UAV developments in China); Jon Boone, *Pakistan Developing Combat Drones*, Guardian (Nov. 13, 2012), http://www.guardian.co.uk/world/2012/nov/13/drones-pakistan (reporting efforts by Pakistan to develop its own armed UAV).

9. *See, e.g.,* Comm'n on Human Rights Res. 1982/29, ¶ 2 (Mar. 11, 1982); Econ. & Soc. Council Res. 1982/35, ¶ 2 (May 7, 1982); Special Rapporteur on extrajudicial, summary or arbitrary executions, *Rep. of the Special Rapporteur on extrajudicial, summary or arbitrary executions*, Econ. & Soc. Council, U.N. Doc. E/CN.4/1983/16 (Jan. 31, 1983) (by S. Amos Wako); Special Rapporteur on extrajudicial, summary or arbitrary executions, *Summary or Arbitrary Executions: Rep. by the Special Rapporteur*, Econ. & Soc. Council, U.N. Doc. E/CN.4/1992/30 (Jan. 31, 1992) (by S. Amos Wako); Special Rapporteur on extrajudicial, summary or arbitrary executions, *Rep. of the Special Rapporteur on extrajudicial, summary or arbitrary executions*, Human Rights Council, U.N. Doc. A/HRC/Res/8/3 (Jun. 18, 2008); Special Rapporteur on extrajudicial, summary or arbitrary executions, *Rep. of the Special Rapporteur on extrajudicial, summary or arbitrary executions*, Human Rights Council, U.N. Doc. A/HRC/Res/17/5 (Jul. 6, 2011).

10. For details on each of the primary forms of extrajudicial executions addressed by the mandate, as well as the relevant international law,

see Philip Alston & Sarah Knuckey, INTERNATIONAL LAW AND POLICY OF EXTRAJUDICIAL EXECUTIONS (forthcoming 2013). *See also* Special Rapporteur on extrajudicial, summary or arbitrary executions, *Rep. of the Special Rapporteur on extrajudicial, summary or arbitrary executions*, Comm'n on Human Rights, ¶ 5–12, U.N. Doc. E/CN.4/2005/7 (Dec. 22, 2004) (by Philip Alston).

11. *See* Special Rapporteur on extrajudicial, summary or arbitrary executions, *Rep. of the Special Rapporteur on extrajudicial, summary or arbitrary executions*, Comm'n on Human Rights, ¶ 39, U.N. Doc. E/CN.4/2003/3 (Jan. 13, 2003) (by Asma Jahangir).

12. *See, e.g.*, Special Rapporteur on extrajudicial, summary or arbitrary executions, *Rep. of the Special Rapporteur on extrajudicial, summary or arbitrary executions, Addendum: Summary of Cases Transmitted to Government and Replies Received*, Human Rights Council, 342–61, U.N. Doc. A/HRC/4/20/Add.1 (Mar. 12, 2007) (by Philip Alston). In response to the Special Rapporteur's work on this issue, the U.S. initially adopted the novel and untenable position that the U.N. Human Rights Council and the Special Rapporteur have no mandate to address killings which took place (or which the U.S. said took place) in an armed conflict. See Special Rapporteur on extrajudicial, summary or arbitrary executions, *Rep. of the Special Rapporteur on extrajudicial, summary or arbitrary executions, Addendum: Summary of Cases Transmitted to Government and Replies Received*, Comm'n on Human Rights, 264–65, E/CN.4/2006/53/Add.1 (Mar. 27, 2006) (by Philip Alston) (allegation letter sent to the U.S. government about the killing by drone strike of Haitham al-Yemeni in May 2005). *See also id.*, at 125–36 (concerning alleged targeted killings by Israel); Special Rapporteur on extrajudicial, summary or arbitrary executions, *Rep. of the Special Rapporteur on extrajudicial, summary or arbitrary executions, Addendum: Observations on Communications Transmitted to Governments and Replies Received*, Human Rights Council, ¶ 82, U.N. Doc. A/HRC/20/22/Add.4 (June 18, 2012) (by Christof Heyns) (concerning killing of Osama bin Laden); *id.*, ¶ 85 (concerning alleged use of drones in targeted killing by U.S. government in Yemen); Special Rapporteur on extrajudicial, summary or arbitrary executions, *Rep. of the Special Rapporteur on extrajudicial, summary or arbitrary executions, Addendum: Summary of Information, Including Cases, Transmitted to Governments and Replies Received*, Human Rights Council, 394, U.N. Doc. A/HRC/17/28/Add.1 (May 27, 2011) (by Christof Heyns) (concerning alleged targeted killing of Anwar Al-Awlaki by the U.S. government); Special Rapporteur on extrajudicial, summary or arbitrary executions,

Rep. of the Special Rapporteur on extrajudicial, summary or arbitrary executions, Addendum: Follow-Up to Country Recommendations, Human Rights Council, U.N. Doc. A/HRC/8/3/Add.3 (May 14, 2008) (by Philip Alston) (concerning alleged targeted killings by Sri Lankan forces and the Liberation Tigers of Tamil Eelam).

13. *See, e.g.*, Special Rapporteur on extrajudicial, summary or arbitrary executions, *Rep. of the Special Rapporteur on extrajudicial, summary or arbitrary executions, Addendum: Follow-Up to Country Recommendations—United States of America*, Human Rights Council, U.N. Doc. A/HRC/20/22/Add.3 (Mar. 30, 2012) (by Christof Heyns) (following up on country recommendations after visit to the U.S. in 2008); Special Rapporteur on extrajudicial, summary or arbitrary executions, *Rep. of the Special Rapporteur on extrajudicial, summary or arbitrary executions, Addendum: Mission to the United States of America*, Human Rights Council, ¶ 71–73, U.N. Doc. A/HRC/11/2/Add.5 (May 28, 2009) (by Philip Alston); *id.*, ¶ 83 (reporting on targeted killings by the U.S.); Special Rapporteur on extrajudicial, summary or arbitrary executions, *Rep. of the Special Rapporteur on extrajudicial, summary or arbitrary executions, Addendum: Mission to Afghanistan*, Human Rights Council, U.N. Doc. A/HRC/11/2/Add.4 (May 6, 2009) (by Philip Alston) (reporting on alleged targeted killings by U.S. raids in Afghanistan).

14. *See Rep. of the Special Rapporteur: Study on Targeted Killings, supra* note 4, at ¶¶ 28–36.

15. Special Rapporteur on extrajudicial, summary or arbitrary executions, *Interim Rep. of the Special Rapporteur on extrajudicial, summary or arbitrary executions*, General Assembly, ¶ 11, U.N. Doc. A/65/321 (Aug. 23, 2010) (by Philip Alston) [hereinafter *Interim Rep. of the Special Rapporteur to the General Assembly*].

16. *See* Press Release, U.N. Office of the High Commissioner for Human Rights, *Osama bin Laden: Statement by the U.N. Special Rapporteurs on Summary Executions and on Human Rights and Counter-Terrorism* (May 6, 2011), http://www.ohchr.org/en/NewsEvents/Pages/DisplayNews.aspx?NewsID=10987&LangID=E; *see also* Special Rapporteur on extrajudicial, summary or arbitrary executions, *Rep. of the Special Rapporteur on extrajudicial, summary or arbitrary executions, Addendum: Observations on Communications Transmitted to Governments and Replies Received*, Human Rights Council, ¶ 82, U.N. Doc. A/HRC/20/22/Add.4 (Jun. 18, 2012) (by Christof Heyns) (calling for factual and legal clarification surrounding the killing of Osama bin Laden).

17. *See* Owen Bowcott, *UN to Investigate Civilian Deaths from US Drone Strikes*, GUARDIAN (Oct. 25, 2012), http://www.guardian.co.uk/world/2012/oct/25/un-inquiry-us-drone-strikes?newsfeed=true.

18. *See* Julie Pecquet, *U.S. Open to Cooperating with U.N. Probe into Drone Strikes*, Hill (Nov. 12, 2012), http://thehill.com/blogs/global-affairs/terrorism/267373-obama-administration-doesnt-rule-out-un-probe-into-drone-strikes.

19. *See* Human Rights Comm., *General Comment No. 24 on Issues Relating to Reservations Made upon Ratification or Accession to the Covenant or the Optional Protocols thereto, or in Relation to Declarations under Article 41 of the Covenant*, ¶¶ 8, 10, U.N. Doc. CCPR/C/21/Rev.1/Add.6 (Nov. 4, 1994); see also MANFRED NOWAK, U.N. COVENANT ON CIVIL AND POLITICAL RIGHTS: CCPR COMMENTARY 122 (2005); Nigel S. Rodley & Matt Pollard, THE TREATMENT OF PRISONERS UNDER INTERNATIONAL LAW 247 (2009).

20. *See* Human Rights Comm., *supra* note 21, at ¶¶ 8, 10; see also U.N. Secretariat, *Compilation of General Comments and General Recommendations Adopted by Human Rights Treaty Bodies*, HRI/GEN/1/Rev.8 (May 8, 2006).

21. U.N. Charter arts. 2(4), 51; *see also* Special Rapporteur on extrajudicial, summary or arbitrary executions, *Rep. of the Special Rapporteur on extrajudicial, summary or arbitrary executions*, Human Rights Council, ¶¶ 35, 45, U.N. Doc. A/HRC/14/24 (May 20, 2010) (by Phillip Alston).

22. Various senior U.S. officials have justified targeted killings practices on the basis that they are carried out in the context of an armed conflict, and/or that they are a manifestation of the state's inherent right of self-defense. Following significant pressure from civil society calling upon the U.S. government to explain how its targeted killings practices comport with international law, over the last two years, U.S. officials have made a number of public speeches briefly explaining and seeking to legally justify current policies. *See, e.g.*, Eric Holder, Attorney General, Dep't of Justice, Address at Northwestern University School of Law (Mar. 5, 2012), http://www.justice.gov/iso/opa/ag/speeches/2012/ag-speech-1203051.html; Harold K. Koh, Legal Advisor, Dep't of State, Address at the Annual Meeting of the American Society of International Law: The Obama Administration and International Law (Mar. 25, 2010), http://www.state.gov/s/l/releases/remarks/139119.htm.

23. *See* Legal Consequences of the Construction of a Wall in the Occupied Palestinian Territory, Advisory Opinion, 2004 I.C.J. 136 (July 8);

Military and Paramilitary Activities in and Against Nicaragua (Nicar. v. U.S.), 1986 I.C.J. 14 (June 27).

24. *See* Jennifer K. Elsea, Cong. Research Serv., Legal Issues Related to the Lethal Targeting of U.S. Citizens Suspected of Terrorist Activities 14–20 (May 4, 2012), http://www.fas.org/sgp/crs/natsec/target.pdf; *see also* Human Rights First, How to Ensure that the U.S. Drone Program Does Not Undermine Human Rights: Blueprint for the Next Administration 4 (December, 2012), http://www.humanrightsfirst. org/wp-content/uploads/pdf/blueprints2012/HRF_Targeted_Killing_blueprint.pdf; Special Rapporteur on extrajudicial, summary or arbitrary executions, *Rep. of the Special Rapporteur on extrajudicial, summary or arbitrary executions*, General Assembly, ¶ 42, U.N. Doc. A/66/330 (Aug. 30, 2011) (by Christof Heyns).

25. *See Rep. of the Special Rapporteur: Study on Targeted Killings, supra* note 4, ¶ 28–36; *see also* D. Fleck, The Handbook of International Humanitarian Law 1–15 (2008); Kevin Jon Heller, One Hell of a Killing Machine: Signature Strikes and International Law, J. of Int'l Crim. Just. (forthcoming 2013) (manuscript at 3–5) (noting that this position is "widely accepted by scholars" and "explicitly endorsed" by the International Law Commission); Michael Elliot, Where Precision Is the Aim: Locating the Targeted Killing Policies of the United States and Israel within International Humanitarian Law, 47 Can. Y.B. of Int'l L. 108 (2009).

26. *See Rep. of the Special Rapporteur: Study on Targeted Killings, supra* note 4, ¶ 33.

27. The facts reported in the following story, for example, raise general questions about the necessity of lethal force: Adam Baron, *Family, Neighbors of Yemeni Killed by U.S. Drone Wonder Why He Wasn't Taken Alive*, McClatchy (Nov. 28, 2012), http://www.mcclatchydc. com/2012/11/28/175794/family-neighbors-of-yemeni-killed.html# storylink=cpy#storylink=cpy?storylink=addthis#storylink=cpy.

28. Thus, for example, to the extent that a state in fact consents to the use of force by another state on its territory, it cannot in law consent to violations by the attacking state of the right to life of those within its jurisdiction. The state on whose territory attacks take place is under a legal obligation to protect their right to life.

29. *See Rep. of the Special Rapporteur: Study on Targeted Killings, supra* note 4, ¶ 29.

30. *See id.* ¶ 46.

31. *See* Nils Melzer, Int'l Comm. of the Red Cross, Interpretive Guidance on the Notion of Direct Participation in Hostilities under International Humanitarian Law (May 2009), http://www.icrc.org/eng/assets/files/other/icrc-002-0990.pdf (outlining the civilian direct participation in hostilities, and continuous combat function tests). In this sense, the widespread use of the term "militant" in public discourse is deeply unsatisfactory. "Militant" is not a legal category, and obfuscates attempts to determine the legality of any particular targeting decision and strike.

32. Numerous examples of strikes for which evidence has been brought forward of civilian harm is available on the Bureau's website, and also in a report published by human rights clinics at Stanford and NYU; Stanford International Human Rights and Conflict Resolution Clinic and Global Justice Clinic at NYU School of Law, Living under Drones: Death, Injury, and Trauma to Civilians from U.S. Drone Practices in Pakistan, (Sept., 2012), http://livingunderdrones.org/wp-content/uploads/2012/10/Stanford-NYU-LIVING-UNDER-DRONES.pdf [hereinafter Living Under Drones]. Recently, the Times published a very detailed report of evidence of civilian harm following a U.S. strike in Pakistan on October 24, 2012. According to alleged witnesses and victims interviewed by the Times, a 67-year-old woman was killed, and a number of children injured. *See* Robin Pagnamenta, *My Dead Mother Wasn't an Enemy of America. She was Just an Old Lady*, Times (London) (Nov. 20, 2012), http://www.thetimes.co.uk/tto/news/world/asia/article3605267.ece.

33. *See Covert War on Terror—The Data, supra* note 6. The Bureau's numbers are primarily based on its compilation and aggregation of media reports of strikes and deaths. This raises important issues about the accuracy of the numbers reported by the Bureau, given the constraints of on-the-ground media reporting in Northwest Pakistan, combined with non- transparent U.S. practices. *See* Living Under Drones, *supra* note 34, at 29–54. Nevertheless, a number of studies have found that, of the current drone strike aggregators, the Bureau's data is the most transparent and contains the most accurate reflection of available media reporting. *See id.* at 53–54; *see also* Columbia Law School Human Rights Clinic, Counting Drone Strike Deaths (Oct. 2012), http://web.law.columbia.edu/sites/default/files/microsites/human-rights-institute/COLUMBIACountingDronesFinalNotEmbargo.pdf.

34. *See* Chris Woods, *Get the Data: Obama's Terror Drones*, Bureau of Investigative Journalism (Feb. 4, 2012), http://www.thebureauinvestigates

.com/2012/02/04/get-the-data-obamas-terror-drones/; Scott Shane, *U.S. Said to Target Rescuers at Drone Strike Sites*, N.Y. Times (Feb. 5, 2012), http://www.nytimes.com/2012/02/06/world/asia/U.S.-drone-strikes-are-said-to-target-rescuers.html; Chris Woods, CIA *"Revives Attacks on Rescuers" in Pakistan*, BUREAU OF INVESTIGATIVE JOURNALISM (June 4, 2012), http://www.thebureauinvestigates.com/2012/06/04/ciarevives-attacks-on-rescuers-in-pakistan/.

35. *See* Jo Becker & Scott Shane, *Secret "Kill List" Proves a Test of Obama's Principles and Will*, N.Y. TIMES, (May 29, 2012), http://www.nytimes.com/2012/05/29/world/obamas-leadership-in-war-on-al-qaeda.html?pagewanted=all.

36. For a detailed analysis of the legal concerns raised by signature strikes, *see* Kevin Jon Heller, *supra* note 27.

37. *See* LIVING UNDER DRONES, *supra* note 34, at 73–101.

38. *See generally* ASSESSING DAMAGE, URGING ACTION: REPORT OF THE EMINENT JURISTS PANEL ON TERRORISM, COUNTER-TERRORISM AND HUMAN RIGHTS, INTERNATIONAL COMMISSION OF JURISTS (2009), http://www.ifj.org/assets/docs/028/207/3e83f1c-fbfc2cf.pdf.

39. *See* JAY STANLEY & CATHERINE CRUMP, AM. CIV. LIBERTIES UNION, PROTECTING PRIVACY FROM AERIAL SURVEILLANCE: RECOMMENDATIONS FOR GOVERNMENT USE OF DRONE AIRCRAFT (Dec. 15, 2011), https://www.aclu.org/files/assets/protectingprivacyfromaerialsurveillance.pdf (describing U.S. domestic drone surveillance, and privacy implications); Asher Moses, *Privacy Watchdog Urges Debate on Aerial Drones*, Brisbane Times.Com (Sept. 12, 2012), http://www.brisbanetimes.com.au/technology/technology-news/privacy-watchdog-urges-debate-on-aerial-drones-20120912-25ri4.html (discussing privacy implications of drones in Australia); Nikolaj Nielsen, EU *Components Used in Belarus Spy Drones, NGO Says*, EU Observer (Sept. 10, 2012, 9:03 PM), http://euobserver.com/foreign/117489 (citing to concerns expressed by Belarus civil society that the government may use drones to impinge on the rights of protesters); Noel Sharkey & Sarah Knuckey, *Occupy Wall Street's "Occucopter"—Who's Watching Whom?*, Guardian (Dec. 21, 2011), http://www.guardian.co.uk/commentisfree/cifamerica/2011/dec/21/occupy-wall-street-occucopter-tim-pool (discussing citizen and police drones); Citizen and Police Drones, Panel at *Left Forum Conference* (Pace University, New York, March, 2012) (panel organized and moderated by Sarah Knuckey, addressing legal and policy issues in the use of domestic surveillance drones).

40. *See Groups Concerned Over Arming of Domestic Drones*, CBS (May 23, 2012 1:18 PM), http://washington.cbslocal.com/2012/05/23/groups-concerned-over-arming-of-domestic-drones/ (reporting that Chief Deputy Randy McDaniel, Montgomery County Sheriff's Office, Texas, stated that "his department is considering using rubber bullets and tear gas in its drone."). *But see* Jonathan Kaminsky, *Seattle Police Plan for Helicopter Drones Hits Severe Turbulence*, REUTERS (Nov. 27, 2012), http://www.reuters.com/article/2012/11/27/us-usa-drones-seattle-idUSBRE8AQ10R20121127, McDaniel recently said he no longer wanted to equip his drones with weapons. *See* Jason Gilbert, *Shocker Drone: Hackers Attack Shocking Material to Drone Helicopter, Chase People, Stun Them*, HUFFINGTON POST (Aug. 30, 6:07 PM), http://www.huffingtonpost.com/2012/08/30/shockerdrone-hackers-attach-stun-gun-drone-helicopter_n_1843999.html (describing the arming of the $299 Parrot AR Drone with a stun gun). Recently, the International Association of Chiefs of Police proposed guidelines for the use of police drones. *See* RECOMMENDED GUIDELINES FOR THE USE OF UNMANNED AIRCRAFT, AVIATION COMM. OF THE INT'L ASSOC. OF CHIEFS OF POLICE (Aug. 2012), http://www.theiacp.org/portals/0/pdfs/IACP_UAGuidelines.pdf.

41. *See* INT'L COMM. OF THE RED CROSS, REPORT ON INTERNATIONAL HUMANITARIAN LAW AND THE CHALLENGES OF CONTEMPORARY ARMED CONFLICTS 39–40 (2011) (noting that the deployment of lethal autonomous robotics would represent a "paradigm shift and major qualitative change in the conduct of hostilities," and that "current norms do not sufficiently regulate some of the challenges posed and might need to be elaborated."); *Interim Rep. of the Special Rapporteur to the General Assembly, supra* note 17 (outlining legal concerns around the development of autonomy); Sarah Knuckey, *International Law and Lethal Autonomous Robotics*, International Drone Summit, co-hosted by the Center for Constitutional Rights, Reprieve, and CodePink, (Washington, D.C., Apr. 2012) (noting the need to address ethical and legal concerns around autonomy before the technology is deployed); *see also* HUMAN RIGHTS WATCH & HARVARD LAW SCHOOL INTERNATIONAL HUMAN RIGHTS CLINIC, LOSING HUMANITY: THE CASE AGAINST KILLER ROBOTS (November 2012), http://www.hrw.org/reports/2012/11/19/losing-humanity-0. In his 2013 report to the Human Rights Council, Christof Heyns will deal with the human rights and humanitarian law impacts of lethal robotic technologies.

*Christof Heyns** is U.N. Special Rapporteur on extrajudicial, summary or arbitrary executions and professor of human rights law and co-director,

Institute for International and Comparative Law in Africa, Faculty of Law, University of Pretoria.

Sarah Knuckey is an international lawyer and associate clinical professor of law at Columbia Law School, where she directs the Human Rights Clinic and co-directs the Human Rights Institute. She is also a special advisor to the UN Special Rapporteur on extrajudicial executions.

"Will I Be Next?" US Drone Strikes in Pakistan

by Amnesty International*

1. Introduction

[...]

The use of pilotless aircraft,[1] commonly referred to as drones, for surveillance and so-called targeted killings by the USA has fast become one of the most controversial human rights issues in the world. In no place is this more apparent than in Pakistan.

The circumstances of civilian deaths from drone strikes in northwest Pakistan are disputed. The USA, which refuses to release detailed information about individual strikes, claims that its drone operations are based on reliable intelligence, are extremely accurate, and that the vast majority of people killed in such strikes are members of armed groups such as the Taliban and al-Qa'ida. Critics claim that drone strikes are much less discriminating, have resulted in hundreds of civilian deaths, some of which may amount to extrajudicial executions or war crimes, and foster animosity that increases recruitment into the very groups the USA seeks to eliminate.

According to NGO and Pakistan government sources the USA has launched some 330 to 374 drone strikes in Pakistan between 2004 and September 2013. Amnesty International is not in a position to endorse these figures but according to these sources, between 400 and 900 civilians have been killed in these attacks and at least 600 people seriously injured.[2]

Focus of This Report

This report is not a comprehensive survey of US drone strikes in Pakistan; it is a qualitative assessment based on detailed field research into nine of the 45 reported strikes that occurred in Pakistan's North Waziristan tribal agency between January 2012 and August 2013 [. . .] and a survey of publicly available information on all reported drone strikes in Pakistan over the same period.

An area bordering Afghanistan, North Waziristan is one of the seven tribal agencies that make up the Federally Administered Tribal Areas (Tribal Areas), a loosely-governed territory in northwest Pakistan that has been the focus of all US drone strikes in the country. Research was also carried out on the general impact of the US drone program on life in North Waziristan, as well as attacks by Pakistani forces and armed groups. The report highlights incidents in which men, women and children appear to have been unlawfully killed or injured. By examining these attacks in detail, Amnesty International seeks to shed light on a secretive program of surveillance and killings occurring in one of the most dangerous, neglected and inaccessible regions of the world.

Arbitrary Deprivation of Life

Because the US government refuses to provide even basic information on particular strikes, including the reasons for carrying them out, Amnesty International is unable to reach firm conclusions about the context in which the US drone attacks . . . took place, and therefore their status under international law. However, based on its review of incidents over the last two years, Amnesty International is seriously concerned that these and other strikes have resulted in unlawful killings that may constitute extrajudicial executions or war crimes.

[...]

Armed groups operating in North Waziristan have been responsible for unlawful killings and other abuses constituting war crimes and other crimes under international law in Pakistan, Afghanistan and elsewhere. Pakistan has a very poor record of bringing these perpetrators to justice in fair trials without recourse to the death penalty. Since the creation of Pakistan, North Waziristan and the rest of the Tribal Areas have been neglected and under-developed, and their residents do not enjoy key human rights protections under Pakistani and international law.

Obligation to Investigate

All states have a duty to take robust action to protect the life and physical integrity of people within their jurisdiction, and to bring to justice perpetrators of crimes under international law. But in doing so, these governments must respect their obligations under international human rights law and, in the exceptional situations where it applies, under international humanitarian law (also known as the laws of war).

Amnesty International calls on the USA to comply with its obligations under international law to ensure thorough, impartial, and independent investigations are conducted into the killings documented in this report. The USA should make public information it has about all drone strikes carried out in Pakistan. The US authorities should investigate all reports of civilian casualties from drone strikes. Where there is sufficient admissible evidence that individuals may be responsible for an unlawful killing or other serious human rights violation, the authorities must ensure they are brought to justice in fair trials without recourse to the death penalty. Victims of violations must be provided with compensation and meaningful access to full reparation including restitution, rehabilitation, satisfaction and guarantees of non-repetition.

Amnesty International is also extremely concerned about the failure of the Pakistani authorities to protect and enforce the rights of victims of drone strikes. Pakistan stands accused of a range of human rights failings: from the possible complicity of some organs or officials of the Pakistan state in unlawful killings resulting from the US drones program, to the failure to protect people in the Tribal Areas from unlawful drone strikes or to adequately assist victims of such strikes. Pakistan has a duty to independently and impartially investigate all drone strikes in the country and ensure access to justice and reparation for victims of violations.

Apart from Pakistan, other states, including Australia, Germany and the UK, appear to be providing intelligence and other assistance to the USA in carrying out drone strikes.[...] In tackling threats from armed groups in the Tribal Areas, Pakistan, the USA and other states providing assistance must act in full conformity with their obligations under international human rights law and, where applicable, international humanitarian law. Secrecy, technology and an elastic interpretation of law and policy may have given the USA unrivalled access to one of the most remote and lawless parts of the world. But immediate security concerns, whether real or perceived, must not and cannot be addressed by trampling on the rights of people living in Pakistan's tribal areas.

[…]

3. Lives Torn Apart—Case Studies

[…]

3.1 MAMANA BIBI, GHUNDI KALA VILLAGE, OCTOBER 2012

Mamana Bibi, aged 68, was tending her crops in Ghundi Kala village [. . .] on the afternoon of 24 October 2012, when she was killed instantly by two Hellfire missiles fired from a drone aircraft. "She was standing in our family fields gathering okra to cook that evening," recalled Zubair Rehman, one of Mamana Bibi's grandsons, who was about 119ft away also working in the fields at the time. Mamana Bibi's three granddaughters: Nabeela (aged eight), Asma (aged seven) and Naeema (aged five) were also in the field, around 115 and 92ft away from their grandmother to the north and south respectively. Around 92ft to the south, another of Mamana Bibi's grandsons, 15-year-old Rehman Saeed, was walking home from school with his friend, Shahidullah, also aged 15.

Accustomed to seeing drones overhead, Mamana Bibi and her grandchildren continued their daily routine. "The drone planes were flying over our village all day and night, flying in pairs sometimes three together. We had grown used to them flying over our village all the time," Zubair Rehman continued. "I was watering our animals and my brother was harvesting maize crop," said Nabeela.

Then, before her family's eyes, Mamana Bibi was blown into pieces by at least two Hellfire missiles fired concurrently from a US drone aircraft.

"There was a very bad smell and the area was full of smoke and dust. I couldn't breathe properly for several minutes," said Zubair. "The explosion was very close to us. It was very strong, it took me into the air and pushed me onto the ground," added Nabeela. She later ventured to where her grandmother had been picking vegetables earlier in the day. "I saw her shoes. We found her mutilated body a short time afterwards," recalled Nabeela. "It had been thrown quite a long distance away by the blast and it was in pieces. We collected as many different parts from the field and wrapped them in a cloth."

Asma and Nabeela both sustained shrapnel injuries to their arms and shoulders. Shahidullah received shrapnel injuries to his lower back while Rehman Saeed sustained a minor shrapnel injury to his foot. But three-year-old Safdar, who had been standing on the roof of their home, fell 10ft to the ground, fracturing several bones in his chest and shoulders. Because he did not receive immediate specialist medical care, he continues to suffer complications from the injury.

Zubair too required specialist medical care after a piece of shrapnel lodged in his leg. According to his father Rafeequl Rehman, Zubair underwent surgery several times in Agency Headquarters Hospital Miran Shah. "But the doctors didn't succeed in removing the piece of shrapnel from his leg," he said. "They were saying that his leg will be removed or he will die." Distraught at the loss of his mother and the prospect that his eldest son may be crippled by the attack, Rafeequl took Zubair to Ali Medical Center in Islamabad but could not afford the medical fees. "The doctor asked for a lot of money," he explained. "So we decided to take him to Khattak Medical Center in Peshawar and, after selling some land, we could afford the operation for him." Doctors at the hospital successfully removed the shrapnel and Zubair is now making a full physical recovery.

Second Strike

A few minutes after the first strike a second volley of drone missiles was fired, hitting a vacant area of the field around 9ft from where Mamana Bibi was killed. Mamana Bibi's grandsons Kaleemul and Samadur Rehman were there, having rushed to the scene when the first volley struck. Kaleemul Rehman recalled: "I was sitting at my home drinking tea [when] suddenly I heard a sound of explosions. I ran outside and saw the rocket had left a big crater in the field and dead animals, and the area was full of smoke and dust. I could not see my grandmother anywhere."

As the two boys surveyed the area, they discovered their grandmother had been blown to pieces. Fearing further attacks, the two tried to flee the area when the second volley of missiles was fired. Kaleemul was hit by shrapnel, breaking his left leg and suffering a large, deep gash to that thigh. "This time I felt something hit my leg and the wave of the blast knocked me unconscious," Kaleemul said. "Later I regained consciousness and noticed that my leg was wounded and my cousin was carrying me on his back to the main road, about 1.5 miles away." From there a car drove Kaleemul to the Agency Headquarters Hospital in Miran Shah, where surgeons operated on him, inserting metal pins into his left thigh bone.

The family home was badly damaged in the strikes, with two rooms rendered uninhabitable. In total, nine people—all of them children except Kaleemul Rehman—were injured in the drone strikes that killed Mamana Bibi.

On the day Mamana Bibi was killed, her son Rafeequl Rehman—father of Zubair, Nabeela, Asma and Safdar—was in a market in Miran Shah. He was buying gifts for the family in anticipation of the Muslim holy day of Eid ul Adha the next day "After finishing my evening prayers in Miran Shah, I returned to my village and on the way I saw that villagers had gathered near our home," he said. At first nobody would tell Rafeequl what had happened that afternoon. Then some village children approached him and said his house had been hit by a drone attack and his children were wounded. "I was shocked and rushed to my home and saw a big gathering of people. I rushed passed them and saw my mother's dead body wrapped in a cloth—her body was in pieces." For a brief moment that felt like an eternity, Rafeequl thought the rest of his family had also been killed in the strike. But one of his brothers finally confirmed that all of their children had survived.

"I'm still in shock over my grandmother's killing," said Zubair. "We used to gather in her room at night and she'd tell us stories. Sometimes we'd massage her feet because they were sore from working all day." Asma added: "I miss my grandmother, she used to give us pocket money and took us with her wherever she went."

The matriarch of her household, Mamana Bibi belonged to a family of educators. Her husband Haji Wreshman Jan is a respected, retired headmaster and three of her sons are teachers in local schools. "We are ordinary people working in the education field." said Rafeequl. "All of my brothers work in the schools; four as teachers, the fifth as a school assistant. My father is a renowned principal. They even named a school after him."

Mistaken Identity?

Pakistani intelligence sources told Amnesty International that a local Taliban fighter had used a satellite phone on a road close to where Mamana Bibi was killed about 10 minutes before the strike, and then drove away.[40] They were not aware of the reason for Mamana Bibi's killing but said they assumed it was related to the Taliban fighter's proximity to her. However, if a member of the Taliban was indeed in the area, he was some distance away from Mamana Bibi. Based on detailed descriptions of the incident site by several witnesses and residents which were corroborated against satellite images of the fields and buildings where the incident occurred, the two closest roads to where Mamana Bibi was killed appear to be some 990ft to the north-west and 930ft to the southeast respectively. Witnesses also said that there was, in the words of Mamana Bibi's son Rafeequl Rehman, a "very clear blue sky."

Witnesses and family members, interviewed separately and by different research teams at different times, all denied that any militants were anywhere near Mamana Bibi at the time of the attack. Amnesty International's investigation found no evidence of military or armed group installations, hide-outs or fighters. The people physically closest to Mamana Bibi at the moment of the attack were the children who witnessed her being killed. As Rafeequl Rehman explained, "There was no [Pakistan military] operation at that time; it was completely calm and peaceful. The children were playing, some others were coming from school. The farmers were busy on their lands; everyone was busy at work."

[...]

The killing of Mamana Bibi has had a profound impact on the family. Her elderly husband Wreshman Jan is grief stricken and rarely leaves the home. "He has become mentally disturbed and cries about his dear wife," said Rafeequl Rehman. Mamana Bibi's grandchildren now live in constant fear that they too will be killed by one of the US drones that continue to hover over Ghundi Kala. "Ever since that day I am always worried," said Zubair. Refeequl Rehman observed: "My daughter [Asma] suddenly gets scared and tells me she is going to be killed. She is living in constant fear. My children are worried even to just gather outside."

Arbitrarily Deprived of Life

It is not possible for Amnesty International to fully assess the reasons behind the killing of Mamana Bibi without further information from the US authorities. If the drone attack took place as part of an armed conflict, then international humanitarian law would apply alongside international human rights law. Under international humanitarian law, not all civilian deaths that occur as a result of armed attacks are unlawful. [. . .] But even if the killing of Mamana Bibi was part of an armed conflict, it still raises serious concerns. For example, if she was killed after being mistaken for a Taliban fighter engaged in hostilities at the time of the strike, then it does not appear that the necessary precautions were taken—particularly given the touted capabilities of drones, which enable their operators to survey a target for a considerable period of time before launching an attack. The fact that an elderly woman who clearly was not directly participating in hostilities was killed, suggests some kind of catastrophic failure: she was misidentified as the intended target; the target was selected based on faulty intelligence and the attack was not cancelled after it became apparent that the target was a civilian; or drone operators deliberately targeted and killed Mamana Bibi.

Mamana Bibi's family said up to three drones were hovering above their home for some hours before and at least several minutes after her killing. This suggests that drone operators had sufficient time to observe Mamana Bibi and her grandchildren before making the decision to kill her.

If the attack took place outside an actual situation of armed conflict, then only international human rights law would apply to this case, rather than the more permissive rules of international humanitarian law. The law enforcement standards that uphold the right to life prohibit the use of intentional lethal force except when strictly unavoidable to protect life.

Amnesty International's evidence indicates that Mamana Bibi was unlawfully killed. Depending on the applicable international legal framework [. . .] , this attack may have constituted a violation of international humanitarian law, an arbitrary deprivation of life, and possibly an extrajudicial execution. For the Rehman family, the tragedy of Mamana Bibi's death and the trauma it has caused for everyone has been compounded by the lack of redress. They received no remedy from the US authorities, which has not even acknowledged that a US drone killed Mamana Bibi and injured her grandchildren. Nor have they received compensation or any other remedy from the Pakistani authorities, despite having sent a formal request following a meeting with the Political Agent for North Waziristan Siraj Ahmed Khan, the most senior representative of Pakistan's civil authorities in the tribal agency.[41]

Amnesty International calls for a prompt, thorough, independent and impartial investigation of the drone strikes that killed Mamana Bibi on 24 October 2012. As part of this, the US authorities must fully disclose all information regarding her killing, including details of the legal and factual justification for carrying out the attacks. US officials must also disclose details of any investigation into anyone involved in planning, ordering, and carrying out this attack. Where there is sufficient admissible evidence that an individual may be responsible for an unlawful killing or other serious violation of international humanitarian law or human rights law, the authorities must ensure they are brought to justice in fair trials without recourse to the death penalty.

For Mamana Bibi's family, no steps could be sufficient solace for the grief they feel. But there will be no sense of closure until those responsible for her killing are brought to justice. As Rafeequl Rehman told Amnesty International, "If I get some money, I will get a lawyer and fight for my right to get justice from the world. I am waiting for my justice."

[...]

NOTES

1. Various terms are used for these aircraft, including "remotely piloted aircraft" (RPAs), "unmanned aerial vehicles" (UAVs) and, more colloquially, "drones." In this report, AI uses the term "drones."

2. Reference to figures provided by the Government of Pakistan in Statement of the Special Rapporteur Following Meetings in Pakistan, Office of the High Commissioner for Human Rights, 14 March 2013 http://www.ohchr.org/EN/NewsEvents/Pages/DisplayNews .aspx?NewsID=13146&LangID=E (Accessed 13 September 2013). Figures for NGOs based on publicly available data compiled by The Bureau of Investigative Journalism, The New America Foundation, and The Long War Journal.

[...]

40. Amnesty International interviews in 2013. Names withheld on request.

41. Letters dated 7 November 2012 and 8 March 2013. See also section 5.4. As a semi-autonomous region, North Waziristan and the rest of the Tribal Areas are administered by Political Agents operating on behalf of the President under the supervision of the Governor of Khyber Pakhtunkhwa province. Relations between local communities and the Political Agent are based on contact between community elders and representatives of the Political Agent.

*Amnesty International is a global nongovernmental organization that campaigns to end grave abuses of human rights.

Amnesty International. *Will I Be Next? US Drone Strikes in Pakistan*. London: Amnesty International Publications, 2013, 7–9, 18–23.

Used by permission.

PART 4:

Transparency and Accountability: Efforts and Obstacles

The transparency around and accountability for U.S. strikes abroad has been one of the most debated and criticized aspects of the program.

In 2013, and after months of intensive criticism of the U.S. drone strike program, Pres. Barack Obama defended U.S. practice in an important speech at the National Defense University. In explaining his view that strikes are effective and lawful, the president also stressed the oversight in place to mitigate abuse or harm and the steps he had taken to promote transparency.

In a statement before the Senate Committee on Armed Services, the U.S. Department of Defense (DOD) argued that strikes are carried out pursuant to a rigorous internal review process, with congressional oversight, and that transparency has been improved. The DOD also explained why the public release of certain information is important, but why other information must remain confidential for security reasons.

Nevertheless, many diverse actors have critiqued the lack of transparency and accountability around U.S. policy, legal interpretations, and practice. Many of these concerns are laid out in the "Joint Letter from NGOs and Human Rights Groups to President Obama." The government has refused to release detailed explanations of why its strikes are legal and has almost never specifically responded to allegations about civilian casualties or provided information explaining the basis for attacks in any detail, as Sarah Knuckey explains in "This Debate Has Been Redacted." These transparency gaps continue, even as senior officials repeatedly promise more transparency. Many reasons have been offered for why more transparency is important. These include that transparency can deter official wrongdoing, enable independent review and oversight, facilitate informed public discussion, is necessary for democratic accountability, allow false negative information to be countered, and can improve confidence in U.S. actions.

Some commentators have also raised concerns that the way the United States carries out strikes abroad is harmful to U.S. democracy at home. Peter W. Singer, in "Do Drones Undermine Democracy?," argues that drones have removed the "last political barriers to war" because they reduce the direct human impact of war on Americans and that they have enabled a "short-circuiting" of democratic decision-making processes.

Attempts by alleged victims to get answers from U.S. officials have not been successful. One such attempt is described in "Family of Grandmother Killed in US Drone Strike Arrive for Congress Visit." In that piece, journalist Ryan Devereaux describes how a Pakistani schoolteacher and his two children visited Washington, D.C., in an attempt to learn why their 67-year-old mother/grandmother was killed by an alleged drone strike. In "Letter to Obama and [Yemeni President] Hadi," Faisal bin Ali Jaber, a Yemeni engineer, asks for an explanation for why two of his relatives were killed in a U.S. drone strike and contends that the silence of the U.S. and Yemeni governments "only makes matters worse." This section ends with an op-ed by Nasser al-Awlaki, a former Yemeni government minister and university president, whose son and 16-year-old grandson—both American citizens—were killed in U.S. strikes. In "The Drone That Killed My Grandson," he argues that the U.S. government owes him an explanation for the killing.

As you read the articles in this section, consider the following questions:

- Why is transparency important? Consider its relevance to victims, the work of NGOs, the prevention of abuse, informed democratic debate, congressional oversight, accountability, and truth.

- How much transparency should there be and about what? In what ways might certain kinds of transparency be harmful?

- Does it seem possible now for alleged victims of U.S. strikes to obtain answers and accountability through U.S. domestic or international mechanisms? If not, why? What steps might promote accountability in the future?

Remarks by the President at the National Defense University

by Barack Obama*

[...]

For over two centuries, the United States has been bound together by founding documents that defined who we are as Americans, and served as our compass through every type of change. Matters of war and peace are no different. Americans are deeply ambivalent about war, but having fought for our independence, we know a price must be paid for freedom. From the Civil War to our struggle against fascism, on through the long twilight struggle of the Cold War, battlefields have changed and technology has evolved. But our commitment to constitutional principles has weathered every war, and every war has come to an end.

With the collapse of the Berlin Wall, a new dawn of democracy took hold abroad, and a decade of peace and prosperity arrived here at home. And for a moment, it seemed the 21st century would be a tranquil time. And then, on September 11, 2001, we were shaken out of complacency. Thousands were taken from us, as clouds of fire and metal and ash descended upon a sun-filled morning. This was a different kind of war. No armies came to our shores, and our military was not the principal target. Instead, a group of terrorists came to kill as many civilians as they could.

And so our nation went to war. We have now been at war for well over a decade. [...]

[W]e strengthened our defenses—hardening targets, tightening transportation security, giving law enforcement new tools to prevent terror. Most of these changes were sound. Some caused inconvenience. But some, like expanded surveillance, raised difficult questions about the balance that we strike between our interests in security and our values of privacy. And in some cases, I believe we compromised our basic values—by using torture to interrogate our enemies, and detaining individuals in a way that ran counter to the rule of law.

So after I took office, we stepped up the war against al Qaeda but we also sought to change its course. [...]

Today, Osama bin Laden is dead, and so are most of his top lieutenants. There have been no large-scale attacks on the United States, and our homeland is more secure. Fewer of our troops are in harm's way, and over the next 19 months they will continue to come home. Our alliances are strong, and so is our standing in the world. In sum, we are safer because of our efforts.

Now, make no mistake, our nation is still threatened by terrorists. From Benghazi to Boston, we have been tragically reminded of that truth. But we have to recognize that the threat has shifted and evolved from the one that came to our shores on 9/11. With a decade of experience now to draw from, this is the moment to ask ourselves hard questions—about the nature of today's threats and how we should confront them.

And these questions matter to every American.

For over the last decade, our nation has spent well over a trillion dollars on war, helping to explode our deficits and constraining our ability to nation-build here at home. Our servicemembers and their families have sacrificed far more on our behalf. Nearly 7,000 Americans have made the ultimate sacrifice. Many more have left a part of themselves on the battlefield, or brought the shadows of battle back home. From our use of drones to the detention of terrorist suspects, the decisions that we are making now will define the type of nation—and world—that we leave to our children.

So America is at a crossroads. We must define the nature and scope of this struggle, or else it will define us. We have to be mindful of James Madison's warning that "No nation could preserve its freedom in the midst of continual warfare." Neither I, nor any President, can promise the total defeat of terror. We will never erase the evil that lies in the hearts of some human beings, nor stamp out every danger to our open society. But what we can do—what we must do—is dismantle networks that pose a direct danger to us, and make it less likely for new groups to gain a foothold, all the while maintaining the freedoms and ideals that we defend. And to define that strategy, we have to make decisions based not on fear, but on hard-earned wisdom. That begins with understanding the current threat that we face.

Today, the core of al Qaeda in Afghanistan and Pakistan is on the path to defeat. Their remaining operatives spend more time thinking about their own safety than plotting against us. They did not direct the attacks in Benghazi or Boston. They've not carried out a successful attack on our homeland since 9/11.

Instead, what we've seen is the emergence of various al Qaeda affiliates. From Yemen to Iraq, from Somalia to North Africa, the threat today is more diffuse, with Al Qaeda's affiliates in the Arabian Peninsula—AQAP—the most active in plotting against our homeland. And while none of AQAP's efforts approach the scale of 9/11, they have continued to plot acts of terror, like the attempt to blow up an airplane on Christmas Day in 2009.

Unrest in the Arab world has also allowed extremists to gain a foothold in countries like Libya and Syria. But here, too, there are differences from 9/11. In some cases, we continue to confront state-sponsored networks like Hezbollah that engage in acts of terror to achieve political goals. Other of these groups are simply collections of local militias or extremists interested in seizing territory. And while we are vigilant for signs that these groups may pose a transnational threat, most are focused on operating in the countries and regions where they are based. And that means we'll face more localized threats like what we saw in Benghazi, or the BP oil facility in Algeria, in which local operatives—perhaps in loose affiliation with regional networks—launch periodic attacks against Western diplomats, companies, and other soft targets, or resort to kidnapping and other criminal enterprises to fund their operations.

And finally, we face a real threat from radicalized individuals here in the United States. Whether it's a shooter at a Sikh Temple in Wisconsin, a plane flying into a building in Texas, or the extremists who killed 168 people at the Federal Building in Oklahoma City, America has confronted many forms of violent extremism in our history. Deranged or alienated individuals—often U.S. citizens or legal residents—can do enormous damage, particularly when inspired by larger notions of violent jihad. And that pull towards extremism appears to have led to the shooting at Fort Hood and the bombing of the Boston Marathon.

So that's the current threat—lethal yet less capable al Qaeda affiliates; threats to diplomatic facilities and businesses abroad; homegrown extremists. This is the future of terrorism. We have to take these threats seriously, and do all that we can to confront them. But as we shape our response, we have to recognize that the scale of this threat closely resembles the types of attacks we faced before 9/11.

In the 1980s, we lost Americans to terrorism at our Embassy in Beirut; at our Marine Barracks in Lebanon; on a cruise ship at sea; at a disco in Berlin; and on a Pan Am flight—Flight 103—over Lockerbie. In the 1990s, we lost Americans to terrorism at the World Trade Center; at our military facilities in Saudi Arabia; and at our Embassy in Kenya. These attacks were all brutal; they were all deadly; and we learned that left unchecked, these threats can grow. But if dealt with smartly and proportionally, these threats need not rise to the level that we saw on the eve of 9/11.

Moreover, we have to recognize that these threats don't arise in a vacuum. Most, though not all, of the terrorism we faced is fueled by a common ideology—a belief by some extremists that Islam is in conflict with the United States and the West, and that violence against Western targets, including civilians, is justified in pursuit of a larger cause. Of course, this ideology is based on a lie, for the United States is not at war with Islam. And this ideology is rejected by the vast majority of Muslims, who are the most frequent victims of terrorist attacks.

Nevertheless, this ideology persists, and in an age when ideas and images can travel the globe in an instant, our response to terrorism can't depend on military or law enforcement alone. We need all elements of national power to win a battle of wills, a battle of ideas. So what I want to discuss here today is the components of such a comprehensive counterterrorism strategy.

First, we must finish the work of defeating al Qaeda and its associated forces.

In Afghanistan, we will complete our transition to Afghan responsibility for that country's security. Our troops will come home. Our combat mission will come to an end. And we will work with the Afghan government to train security forces, and sustain a counterterrorism force, which ensures that al Qaeda can never again establish a safe haven to launch attacks against us or our allies.

Beyond Afghanistan, we must define our effort not as a boundless "global war on terror," but rather as a series of persistent, targeted efforts to dismantle specific networks of violent extremists that threaten America. In many cases, this will involve partnerships with other countries. Already, thousands of Pakistani soldiers have lost their lives fighting extremists. In Yemen, we are supporting security forces that have reclaimed territory from AQAP. In Somalia, we helped a coalition of African nations push al-Shabaab out of its strongholds. In Mali, we're providing military aid to French-led intervention to push back al Qaeda in the Maghreb, and help the people of Mali reclaim their future.

Much of our best counterterrorism cooperation results in the gathering and sharing of intelligence, the arrest and prosecution of terrorists. And that's how a Somali terrorist apprehended off the coast of Yemen is now in a prison in New York. That's how we worked with European allies to disrupt plots from Denmark to Germany to the United Kingdom. That's how intelligence collected with Saudi Arabia helped us stop a cargo plane from being blown up over the Atlantic. These partnerships work.

But despite our strong preference for the detention and prosecution of terrorists, sometimes this approach is foreclosed. Al Qaeda and its affiliates try to gain foothold in some of the most distant and unforgiving places on Earth. They take refuge in remote tribal regions. They hide in caves and walled compounds. They train in empty deserts and rugged mountains.

In some of these places—such as parts of Somalia and Yemen—the state only has the most tenuous reach into the territory. In other cases, the state lacks the capacity or will to take action. And it's also not possible for America to simply deploy a team of Special Forces to capture every terrorist. Even when such an approach may be possible, there are places where it would pose profound risks to our troops and local civilians—where a terrorist compound cannot be breached without triggering a firefight with surrounding tribal communities, for example, that pose no threat to us; times when putting U.S. boots on the ground may trigger a major international crisis.

To put it another way, our operation in Pakistan against Osama bin Laden cannot be the norm. The risks in that case were immense. The likelihood of capture, although that was our preference, was remote given the certainty that our folks would confront resistance. The fact that we did not find ourselves confronted with civilian casualties, or embroiled in an extended firefight, was a testament to the meticulous planning and professionalism of our Special Forces, but it also depended on some luck. And it was supported by massive infrastructure in Afghanistan.

And even then, the cost to our relationship with Pakistan—and the backlash among the Pakistani public over encroachment on their territory—was so severe that we are just now beginning to rebuild this important partnership.

So it is in this context that the United States has taken lethal, targeted action against al Qaeda and its associated forces, including with remotely piloted aircraft commonly referred to as drones.

As was true in previous armed conflicts, this new technology raises profound questions—about who is targeted, and why; about civilian casualties, and the risk of creating new enemies; about the legality of such strikes under U.S. and international law; about accountability and morality. So let me address these questions.

To begin with, our actions are effective. Don't take my word for it. In the intelligence gathered at bin Laden's compound, we found that he wrote, "We could lose the reserves to enemy's air strikes. We cannot fight air strikes with explosives." Other communications from al Qaeda operatives confirm this as well. Dozens of highly skilled al Qaeda commanders, trainers, bomb makers and operatives have been taken off the battlefield. Plots have been disrupted that would have targeted international aviation, U.S. transit systems, European cities and our troops in Afghanistan. Simply put, these strikes have saved lives.

Moreover, America's actions are legal. We were attacked on 9/11. Within a week, Congress overwhelmingly authorized the use of force. Under domestic law, and international law, the United States is at war with al Qaeda, the Taliban, and their associated forces. We are at war with an organization that right now would kill as many Americans as they could if we did not stop them first. So this is a just war—a war waged proportionally, in last resort, and in self-defense.

And yet, as our fight enters a new phase, America's legitimate claim of self-defense cannot be the end of the discussion. To say a military tactic is legal, or even effective, is not to say it is wise or moral in every instance. For the same human progress that gives us the technology to strike half a world away also demands the discipline to constrain that power—or risk abusing it. And that's why, over the last four years, my administration has worked vigorously to establish a framework that governs our use of force against terrorists—insisting upon clear guidelines, oversight and accountability that is now codified in Presidential Policy Guidance that I signed yesterday.

In the Afghan war theater, we must—and will—continue to support our troops until the transition is complete at the end of 2014. And that means we will continue to take strikes against high value al Qaeda targets, but also against forces that are massing to support attacks on coalition forces. But by the end of 2014, we will no longer have the same need for force protection, and the progress we've made against core al Qaeda will reduce the need for unmanned strikes.

Beyond the Afghan theater, we only target al Qaeda and its associated forces. And even then, the use of drones is heavily constrained. America does not take strikes when we have the ability to capture individual terrorists; our preference is always to detain, interrogate, and prosecute. America cannot take strikes wherever we choose; our actions are bound by consultations with partners, and respect for state sovereignty.

America does not take strikes to punish individuals; we act against terrorists who pose a continuing and imminent threat to the American people, and when there are no other governments capable of effectively addressing the threat. And before any strike is taken, there must be near-certainty that no civilians will be killed or injured—the highest standard we can set.

Now, this last point is critical, because much of the criticism about drone strikes—both here at home and abroad—understandably centers on reports of civilian casualties. There's a wide gap between U.S. assessments of such casualties and nongovernmental reports. Nevertheless, it is a hard fact that U.S. strikes have resulted in civilian casualties, a risk that exists in every war. And for the families of those civilians, no words or legal construct can justify their loss. For me, and those in my chain of command, those deaths will haunt us as long as we live, just as we are haunted by the civilian casualties that have occurred throughout conventional fighting in Afghanistan and Iraq.

But as Commander-in-Chief, I must weigh these heartbreaking tragedies against the alternatives. To do nothing in the face of terrorist networks would invite far more civilian casualties—not just in our cities at home and our facilities abroad, but also in the very places like Sana'a and Kabul and Mogadishu where terrorists seek a foothold. Remember that the terrorists we are after target civilians, and the death toll from their acts of terrorism against Muslims dwarfs any estimate of civilian casualties from drone strikes. So doing nothing is not an option.

Where foreign governments cannot or will not effectively stop terrorism in their territory, the primary alternative to targeted lethal action would be the use of conventional military options. As I've already said, even small special operations carry enormous risks. Conventional airpower or missiles are far less precise than drones, and are likely to cause more civilian casualties and more local outrage. And invasions of these territories lead us to be viewed as occupying armies, unleash a torrent of unintended consequences, are difficult to contain, result in large numbers of civilian casualties and ultimately empower those who thrive on violent conflict.

So it is false to assert that putting boots on the ground is less likely to result in civilian deaths or less likely to create enemies in the Muslim world. The results would be more U.S. deaths, more Black Hawks down, more confrontations with local populations, and an inevitable mission creep in support of such raids that could easily escalate into new wars.

Yes, the conflict with al Qaeda, like all armed conflict, invites tragedy. But by narrowly targeting our action against those who want to kill us and not the people they hide among, we are choosing the course of action least likely to result in the loss of innocent life.

Our efforts must be measured against the history of putting American troops in distant lands among hostile populations. In Vietnam, hundreds of thousands of civilians died in a war where the boundaries of battle were blurred. In Iraq and Afghanistan, despite the extraordinary courage and discipline of our troops, thousands of civilians have been killed. So neither conventional military action nor waiting for attacks to occur offers moral safe harbor, and neither does a sole reliance on law enforcement in territories that have no functioning police or security services—and indeed, have no functioning law.

Now, this is not to say that the risks are not real. Any U.S. military action in foreign lands risks creating more enemies and impacts public opinion overseas. Moreover, our laws constrain the power of the President even during wartime, and I have taken an oath to defend the Constitution of the United States. The very precision of drone strikes and the necessary secrecy often involved in such actions can end up shielding our government from the public scrutiny that a troop deployment invites. It can also lead a President and his team to view drone strikes as a cure-all for terrorism.

And for this reason, I've insisted on strong oversight of all lethal action. After I took office, my administration began briefing all strikes outside of Iraq and Afghanistan to the appropriate committees of Congress. Let me repeat that: Not only did Congress authorize the use of force, it is briefed on every strike that America takes. Every strike. That includes the one instance when we targeted an American citizen—Anwar Awlaki, the chief of external operations for AQAP.

This week, I authorized the declassification of this action, and the deaths of three other Americans in drone strikes, to facilitate transparency and debate on this issue and to dismiss some of the more outlandish claims that have been made. For the record, I do not believe it would be constitutional for the government to target and kill any U.S. citizen—with a drone, or with a shotgun—without due process, nor should any President deploy armed drones over U.S. soil.

But when a U.S. citizen goes abroad to wage war against America and is actively plotting to kill U.S. citizens, and when neither the United States, nor our partners are in a position to capture him before he carries out a plot, his citizenship should no more serve as a shield than a sniper shooting down on an innocent crowd should be protected from a SWAT team.

That's who Anwar Awlaki was—he was continuously trying to kill people. He helped oversee the 2010 plot to detonate explosive devices on two U.S.-bound cargo planes. He was involved in planning to blow up an airliner in 2009. When Farouk Abdulmutallab—the Christmas Day bomber—went to Yemen in 2009, Awlaki hosted him, approved his suicide operation, helped him tape a martyrdom video to be shown after the attack, and his last instructions were to blow up the airplane when it was over American soil. I would have detained and prosecuted Awlaki if we captured him before he carried out a plot, but we couldn't. And as President, I would have been derelict in my duty had I not authorized the strike that took him out.

Of course, the targeting of any American raises constitutional issues that are not present in other strikes—which is why my administration submitted information about Awlaki to the Department of Justice months before Awlaki was killed, and briefed the Congress before this strike as well. But the high threshold that we've set for taking lethal action applies to all potential terrorist targets, regardless of whether or not they are American citizens. This threshold respects the inherent dignity of every human life. Alongside the decision to put our men and women in uniform in harm's way, the decision to use force against individuals or groups—even against a sworn enemy of the United States—is the hardest thing I do as President. But these decisions must be made, given my responsibility to protect the American people.

Going forward, I've asked my administration to review proposals to extend oversight of lethal actions outside of warzones that go beyond our reporting to Congress. Each option has virtues in theory, but poses difficulties in practice. For example, the establishment of a special court to evaluate and authorize lethal action has the benefit of bringing a third branch of government into the process, but raises serious constitutional issues about presidential and judicial authority. Another idea that's been suggested—the establishment of an independent oversight board in the executive branch—avoids those problems, but may introduce a layer of bureaucracy into national security decision-making, without inspiring additional public confidence in the process. But despite these challenges, I look forward to actively engaging Congress to explore these and other options for increased oversight.

I believe, however, that the use of force must be seen as part of a larger discussion we need to have about a comprehensive counterterrorism strategy—because for all the focus on the use of force, force alone cannot make us safe. We cannot use force everywhere that a radical ideology takes root; and in the absence of a strategy that reduces the wellspring of extremism, a perpetual war—through drones or Special Forces or troop deployments—will prove self-defeating, and alter our country in troubling ways.

So the next element of our strategy involves addressing the underlying grievances and conflicts that feed extremism—from North Africa to South Asia. As we've learned this past decade, this is a vast and complex undertaking. We must be humble in our expectation that we can quickly resolve deep-rooted problems like poverty and sectarian hatred. Moreover, no two countries are alike, and some will undergo chaotic change before things get better. But our security and our values demand that we make the effort.

This means patiently supporting transitions to democracy in places like Egypt and Tunisia and Libya—because the peaceful realization of individual aspirations will serve as a rebuke to violent extremists. We must strengthen the opposition in Syria, while isolating extremist elements—because the end of a tyrant must not give way to the tyranny of terrorism. We are actively working to promote peace between Israelis and Palestinians—because it is right and because such a peace could help reshape attitudes in the region. And we must help countries modernize economies, upgrade education, and encourage entrepreneurship—because American leadership has always been elevated by our ability to connect with people's hopes, and not simply their fears.

And success on all these fronts requires sustained engage-ment, but it will also require resources. I know that foreign aid is one of the least popular expenditures that there is. That's true for Democrats and Republicans—I've seen the polling—even though it amounts to less than one percent of the federal budget. In fact, a lot of folks think it's 25 percent, if you ask people on the streets. Less than one percent—still wildly unpopular. But foreign assistance cannot be viewed as charity. It is fundamen-tal to our national security. And it's fundamental to any sensible long-term strategy to battle extremism.

Moreover, foreign assistance is a tiny fraction of what we spend fighting wars that our assistance might ultimately pre-vent. For what we spent in a month in Iraq at the height of the war, we could be training security forces in Libya, maintaining peace agreements between Israel and its neighbors, feeding the hungry in Yemen, building schools in Pakistan, and creat-ing reservoirs of goodwill that marginalize extremists. That has to be part of our strategy.

[...]

Targeted action against terrorists, effective partnerships, diplomatic engagement and assistance—through such a com-prehensive strategy we can significantly reduce the chances of large-scale attacks on the homeland and mitigate threats to Americans overseas. But as we guard against dangers from abroad, we cannot neglect the daunting challenge of terrorism from within our borders.

As I said earlier, this threat is not new. But technology and the Internet increase its frequency and in some cases its lethal-ity. Today, a person can consume hateful propaganda, commit themselves to a violent agenda, and learn how to kill without leaving their home. To address this threat, two years ago my administration did a comprehensive review and engaged with law enforcement.

And the best way to prevent violent extremism inspired by violent jihadists is to work with the Muslim American community—which has consistently rejected terrorism—to identify signs of radicalization and partner with law enforcement when an individual is drifting towards violence. And these partnerships can only work when we recognize that Muslims are a fundamental part of the American family. In fact, the success of American Muslims and our determination to guard against any encroachments on their civil liberties is the ultimate rebuke to those who say that we're at war with Islam.

Thwarting homegrown plots presents particular challenges in part because of our proud commitment to civil liberties for all who call America home. That's why, in the years to come, we will have to keep working hard to strike the appropriate balance between our need for security and preserving those freedoms that make us who we are. That means reviewing the authorities of law enforcement, so we can intercept new types of communication, but also build in privacy protections to prevent abuse.

[...]

Now, all these issues remind us that the choices we make about war can impact—in sometimes unintended ways—the openness and freedom on which our way of life depends. And that is why I intend to engage Congress about the existing Authorization to Use Military Force, or AUMF, to determine how we can continue to fight terrorism without keeping America on a perpetual wartime footing.

The AUMF is now nearly 12 years old. The Afghan war is coming to an end. Core al Qaeda is a shell of its former self.

Groups like AQAP must be dealt with, but in the years to come, not every collection of thugs that labels themselves al Qaeda will pose a credible threat to the United States. Unless we discipline our thinking, our definitions, our actions, we may be drawn into more wars we don't need to fight, or continue to grant Presidents unbound powers more suited for traditional armed conflicts between nation states.

So I look forward to engaging Congress and the American people in efforts to refine, and ultimately repeal, the AUMF's mandate. And I will not sign laws designed to expand this mandate further. Our systematic effort to dismantle terrorist organizations must continue. But this war, like all wars, must end. That's what history advises. That's what our democracy demands.

[...]

(Applause.)

[...]

AUDIENCE MEMBER: [...]—[C]can you take the drones out of the hands of the CIA? Can you stop the signature strikes killing people on the basis of suspicious activities?

THE PRESIDENT: We're addressing that, ma'am.

AUDIENCE MEMBER:—thousands of Muslims that got killed—will you compensate the innocent families—that will make us safer here at home. I love my country. I love (inaudible)—

THE PRESIDENT: I think that—and I'm going off script, as you might expect here. (Laughter and applause.) The voice of that woman is worth paying attention to. (Applause.) Obviously, I do not agree with much of what she said, and obviously she wasn't listening to me in much of what I said. But these are tough issues, and the suggestion that we can gloss over them is wrong.

[...]

So, America, we've faced down dangers far greater than al Qaeda. By staying true to the values of our founding, and by using our constitutional compass, we have overcome slavery and Civil War and fascism and communism. [...]

[...]

Our victory against terrorism won't be measured in a surrender ceremony at a battleship, or a statue being pulled to the ground. Victory will be measured in parents taking their kids to school; immigrants coming to our shores; fans taking in a ballgame; a veteran starting a business; a bustling city street; a citizen shouting her concerns at a President.

The quiet determination; that strength of character and bond of fellowship; that refutation of fear—that is both our sword and our shield. And long after the current messengers of hate have faded from the world's memory, alongside the brutal despots, and deranged madmen, and ruthless demagogues who litter history—the flag of the United States will still wave from small-town cemeteries to national monuments, to distant outposts abroad. And that flag will still stand for freedom.

[...]

Obama, Barack. "Remarks by the President at the National Defense University." National Defense University, Fort McNair Washington, D.C., May 21, 2013. http://www.whitehouse.gov/the-press-office/2013/05/23/remarks-president-national-defense-university.

Department of Defense Joint Statement on Law of Armed Conflict, the Use of Military Force and the 2001 Authorization for Use of Military Force

DEPARTMENT OF DEFENSE JOINT STATEMENT FOR THE RECORD ON LAW OF ARMED CONFLICT, THE USE OF MILITARY FORCE AND THE 2001 AUTHORIZATION FOR USE OF MILITARY FORCE

BEFORE THE SENATE COMMITTEE ON ARMED SERVICES

MAY 16, 2013

[. . .]

III. Management and Oversight of Military Operations

Before military force is used against members of al Qaeda, the Taliban, and associated forces, there is a robust review process, which includes rigorous safeguards to protect innocent civilians. Throughout the military chain of command, senior commanders, advised by trained and experienced staffs—including intelligence officers, operations officers, and judge advocates—review operations for compliance with applicable U.S. domestic and international law, including the law of armed conflict, and for consistency with the policies and orders of superiors in the military chain of command.

For operations outside Afghanistan, this review continues up the chain of command, through the 4-star combatant commander, to the Secretary of Defense. Before the Secretary makes a decision, the proposal is reviewed by senior military and civilian advisors, including the Chairman of the Joint Chiefs of Staff and the General Counsel of the Department of Defense. Department officials also receive input from senior officials in other departments and agencies from across our national security team. Military orders implementing a final decision are then transmitted down that chain of command to the relevant forces that carry out such operations.

Some have expressed concern that the process for managing military operations, no matter how rigorous, is largely confined to the Executive Branch. This fact reflects related practical and legal considerations. As a practical matter, officials in the military chain of command must often make real-time decisions that balance the need to act, the existence of alternative options, the possibility of collateral damage, and other factors—all of which depend on expertise and immediate access to information that only the Executive Branch may possess in real time.

As a legal matter, Article II of the Constitution makes the President the Commander-in-Chief of the armed forces. The President is therefore responsible for directing military operations in the prosecution of armed conflict. By U.S. law, the military chain of command runs from the President to the Secretary of Defense and then to combatant commanders. The current process appropriately reflects the President's role in the chain of command; alternatives that some have suggested would present significant constitutional issues.

Congress also plays a critical role in ensuring appropriate oversight of this process. The Department and the Joint Staff regularly brief members and staff of this committee and the House Armed Services Committee on military operations against al Qaeda, the Taliban, and associated forces, both on the prosecution of the conflict generally and specifically on each significant counterterrorism operation conducted outside Afghanistan.

We have also made significant efforts to increase transparency regarding whom the U.S. military targets in the current conflict against al Qaeda, the Taliban, and associated forces and the procedures by which individual targeting decisions are made. Last year, for example, we declassified information about the U.S. military's counterterrorism activities in Yemen and Somalia in a June 2012 War Powers report to Congress. This type of transparency helps preserve public confidence, dispel misconceptions that the U.S. military targets low-level terrorists who pose no threat to the United States, and address questions raised by our allies and partners abroad. On the other hand, the public release of certain information, such as the intelligence by which current or past targets were identified, could enable the enemy to avoid or manipulate our application of military force. Ultimately, we must maintain a delicate balance between transparency and protecting information from public disclosure for security reasons.

[. . .]

U.S. Congress. Senate. Committee on Armed Services. *Department of Defense Joint Statement for the Record on Law of Armed Conflict, the Use of Military Force and the 2001 Authorization for Use of Military Force before the Senate Committee on Armed Services.* 113th Cong. Sess. 1. May 16, 2013. http://www.lawfareblog.com/wp-content/uploads/2013/05/Taylor-Sheehan-Nagata-Gross_05-16-13.pdf.

Joint Letter from NGOs and Human Rights Groups to President Obama on Drone Program

December 4, 2013
The Honorable Barack Obama
President of the United States
White House
1600 Pennsylvania Ave., N.W.
Washington, D.C. 20500

Re: Shared Concerns Regarding U.S. Drone Strikes and Targeted Killings

Dear President Obama,

Six months ago, the undersigned human rights and civil rights groups wrote to you to express concern about U.S. targeted killing operations, in particular outside the internationally recognized armed conflict in Afghanistan. In that letter, attached hereto, we call on your administration to: publicly disclose key targeted killing standards and criteria; ensure that U.S. lethal force operations comply with international law; enable meaningful congressional oversight and judicial review; and effectively investigate, track and respond to allegations of unlawful strikes and civilian harm.

Since then, a number of new developments have reinforced our concerns and raised new questions. We write to urge a response to these issues.

We welcome your statements at the National Defense University (NDU) in May 2013 indicating your intent to restrict the use of lethal force and recognizing the United States' obligation to comply with international law. We also welcome your acknowledgement of the importance of greater transparency and oversight. However, your speech left many important questions unanswered, and since then the U.S. government has not publicly disclosed any further information about its targeted killing operations.

For example, the full Presidential Policy Guidance, which you summarized in your speech, remains classified. In U.S. court cases, the government continues to refuse even to acknowledge which agencies carry out lethal strikes, let alone provide basic information about the number and identities of the people these strikes have killed. The one exception is your administration's acknowledgment of the killings of four U.S. citizens—a citizenship-based distinction that does nothing to assuage concerns about the use of lethal force against citizens of other countries, or the legal basis for any of the killings. The result is that the public remains in the dark about how exactly U.S. policy governing targeted killings is operating, under which legal authorities, and who exactly are its victims.

Commitment to the rule of law requires that your administration disclose publicly the legal criteria governing each of its lethal targeting operations. In addition, your administration should disclose the full Presidential Policy Guidance as well as when and where any of these policies have been implemented. We also urge you to disclose which, if any, of the policy guidelines your administration believes are legally binding. Your administration also should disclose the identities of the individuals killed and the criteria it uses to classify these individuals as "civilian," "militant" or "combatant."

We are also particularly concerned about three specific aspects of the targeted killing policy announced in your NDU speech. The first is the standard for who may be targeted. You stated: "we act against terrorists who pose a continuing and imminent threat to the American people, and when there are no other governments capable of effectively addressing the threat." Administration officials have in the past defined an "imminent threat" in ways that emphasize the opportunity to attack a target rather than the immediacy of the threat posed. Justifying the use of lethal force against a "continuing" threat seems to similarly endorse the use of lethal force in response to fear of an unspecified adverse action at an undefined point in the future. These interpretations of imminence are inconsistent with international law.

Second, you said that "America does not take strikes when we have the ability to capture individual terrorists," without explaining how feasibility of capture is defined and determined. Your administration should elucidate this criterion, as well as explain why capture was not feasible in each instance. We urge your administration to affirm that, outside of actual armed conflict, lethal force may only be used when strictly unavoidable to protect against an imminent threat to life.

Third, you said that beyond the Afghan war theater, "before any strike is taken, there must be near-certainty that no civilians will be killed or injured—the highest standard we can set." This point follows previous statements from administration officials that U.S. drone strikes have resulted in few, if any, civilian casualties. News media and recently-released reports from Human Rights Watch and Amnesty International, however, suggest U.S. drone strikes have killed and injured people your administration would likely consider civilians, and resulted in unlawful killings.

Your administration should commit to investigating these and other credible reports of potentially unlawful deaths and civilian harm, and to releasing the results of those investigations to the public. As CIA Director John Brennan has said, the United States "need[s] to acknowledge publicly" any mistaken killings and should "make public the overall numbers of civilian deaths resulting from U.S. strikes targeting al-Qa'ida."

Director Brennan has also said that the government makes condolence payments to families of those killed "if appropriate." However, the government has not provided any information about condolence payments that may have been made. Furthermore, Amnesty International and Human Rights Watch found no evidence of payments made by the United States in either Pakistan or Yemen.

Many of our concerns are shared by two United Nations Special Rapporteurs. In new reports, the two U.N. experts strongly criticize the lack of transparency surrounding these operations. They call on states carrying out these strikes to reveal the number of individuals killed and to investigate all credible allegations of potentially unlawful deaths and injuries.

We appreciate your attention to our concerns and urge the administration to take the steps we have outlined, both here and in our previous letter.

Sincerely,

American Civil Liberties Union
Amnesty International
Center for Human Rights & Global Justice, NYU School of Law
Center for Civilians in Conflict
Center for Constitutional Rights
Global Justice Clinic, NYU School of Law
Human Rights First
Human Rights Watch
Open Society Foundations

Earnest, Thomas. "Joint Letter from NGOs and Human Rights Groups to President Obama on Drone Program," Just Security. December 5, 2013. http://justsecurity .org/4128/joint-letter-ngos-human-rights-groups-concerns-drone-program/.

This Debate Has Been Redacted

by Sarah Knuckey*

A new report details the awful civilian casualties inflicted by American drones, but the arguments over the weapons' use have begun to feel grimly familiar.

We are at an impasse in the debate over America's use of drones and so-called "targeted killings." It is an impasse that the U.S. government can, and should, resolve.

The debate has come to follow a depressingly predictable pattern. Initial reports about a drone strike quote anonymous officials claiming that a number of militants were targeted. Journalists and human rights investigators then get word that local residents say civilians were killed. More detailed investigations are carried out. Witness testimony and other evidence, such as photos or videos of the victims and fragments of the missile, are gathered. Then, long reports are published alleging that the strikes killed or injured innocent men, women or children. Supporters of current U.S. practices critique these reports of civilian casualties, questioning their biases, evidence, or methods. In response, drone program critics dispute the relevance or validity of those reviews.

Officially, the U.S. government does not respond, or simply states that all strikes are investigated and comply with the law. Anonymous officials provide additional details to a select group of journalists. Those outside the government pore over these fragments of information, attempting to extract some nugget of truth. People on all sides of the debate often demand more transparency, although they are often seeking different kinds of information for very different reasons.

At this point, it almost feels scripted.

And, so, on Thursday, Human Rights Watch (HRW) released the most detailed account yet of one of the most controversial drone strikes of President Barack Obama's time in office: a widely reported December 2013 strike on a Yemeni wedding convoy that killed at least 12 and injured 15 more. The report concluded that while the United States may have intended to target suspected members of al Qaeda in the Arabian Peninsula (AQAP), the evidence suggests that "some, if not all of those killed and wounded were civilians."

HRW's findings demand an official response from the U.S. government—and not just the platitudes officials and spokespersons have parroted for the past year. The government needs to explain this strike and respond to the evidence of civilian deaths.

HRW presents evidence of civilian harm caused by this strike, but its legal and policy conclusions are delicately couched. The group ultimately does not say definitely whether the strike violated applicable law or policy, instead stating that the strike "may have" violated the laws of war, and that it "raises serious questions" about whether policies were followed. And HRW acknowledges at various points that more information is needed to make firm conclusions.

With this careful language, HRW's latest report also brings to the fore the fundamental problem in attempting to assess U.S. strikes. There is an asymmetry of information that is virtually insurmountable: key information remains in the sole possession of the U.S. government.

The laws of war state that, in cases of doubt, individuals should be presumed civilian. But in U.S. public discussion, those killed in drone strikes de facto begin as militants. Injured victims and family members must provide evidence of their own civilian status. If the criticisms of NGOs are to have any impact in the U.S. debate, those groups must gather significant amounts of testimony, as well as additional corroborative evidence.

But how does one definitively *prove* civilian status? Or *prove* that no members of al-Qaeda were near the strike at the time it occurred, thereby countering the argument that the civilian harm was lawful and proportionate? And how can outside actors know if any nearby al-Qaeda operatives constituted high-value targets? How can outside actors assess whether the U.S. took reasonable precautions prior to the attack?

Alleged victims or NGOs can provide evidence documenting civilian deaths, but it may be possible that some other, publicly unknown information could indicate that a strike was legal or justifiable. Many cases are simply irresolvable without detailed information from Washington.

And so the American public and the international community are left concerned and ultimately guessing, repeatedly asking the same questions about the specific legal, policy, and factual basis for strikes.

The reported impact of civilian casualties in America's drone war extend beyond the immediate deaths, with significant consequences for individual Yemenis and U.S. efforts to win over their hearts and minds.

HRW's report includes gruesome details, often absent from media accounts of strikes, on the wounds allegedly suffered by survivors. One man lost an eye, another his genitals. The report also highlights the broader, secondary impacts on family members. One of those allegedly killed left behind a blind father, a wife, and seven children, including a newborn. The groom in the convoy is quoted as saying that his wedding "became a funeral." A local sheikh who says he witnessed the strike says that the United States "turned many kids into orphans, many wives into widows." Other relatives and tribesman are said to have denounced the United States and Yemen, temporarily blocked a main road in protest, and demanded an international investigation.

Yet the U.S. government refuses to meaningfully engage on the issues surrounding strikes like the one on the wedding convoy and refuses to explain its legal interpretations, specific policies, or conduct. In October 2013, HRW and Amnesty International released major reports detailing evidence of civilian deaths resulting from U.S. strikes, alleging that certain strikes between 2009 and 2013 violated international law and U.S. policy. The government responded to those reports by stating that it had not violated the law and claiming that it carefully examines whether any strike caused civilian deaths. No specific evidence refuting the reports was offered.

Government officials also referred to a May 2013 speech in which Obama publicly addressed drone strikes and released a summarized version of new policies governing targeted killings, which promulgated new restrictions on such strikes. The president stated that a strike would not be launched unless there was a "near-certainty" that no civilians would be hurt or killed and only where a target posed a "continuing and imminent threat" and could not be feasibly captured. Shortly thereafter, Secretary of State John Kerry stated, "We do not fire when we know there are children or collateral [damage]. . . . We just don't."

U.S. officials have repeatedly leaned on these kinds of assurances. They did so once more on Thursday in responding to HRW's new report. A Pentagon spokesman refused to comment on specifics, referring the Associated Press to Yemeni government statements that the targets were members of AQAP. The National Security Council's spokeswoman, Caitlin Hayden, provided the *Washington Post* and *Al Jazeera* the same response she has offered journalists many times in the past: She would not comment on specifics, said the United States takes extraordinary care in its use of drones, and emphasized that civilian casualty claims are thoroughly investigated. The State Department seems to have not responded at all.

Meanwhile, anonymous U.S. officials "leaked" to the AP that two government investigations "concluded that only members of al-Qaida were killed" in the strike. How do they know this? What investigations were undertaken?

In the past, officials have stated that they "harness" their "relevant intelligence capabilities," gathering information from a "myriad" of sources. But it is has never been clear what kinds of investigations the government actually conducts. Indeed, the author of this latest HRW report, Letta Tayler, the organization's senior terrorism and counterterrorism researcher, told me that she found no evidence that the United States had interviewed alleged witnesses of the wedding strike. And, on Thursday, Cori Crider, a lawyer at the NGO Reprieve, which investigates and has conducted advocacy against U.S. targeted killings practices, stated that the group wrote directly to the National Security Council about the strike "offering to connect them to witnesses and were ignored." In addition, two senior Yemeni officials told HRW that their sources said civilians were among the dead. But we still don't know what steps the United States took to determine that all those killed were al Qaeda.

U.S. lawmakers who had apparently watched a video of the wedding strike told the AP that the video "showed three trucks in the convoy were hit, all carrying armed men." But it is widely known that carrying guns in this region of Yemen is common and hardly indicative on its own of militancy. Surely, U.S. investigations and congressional oversight are based on far more than simply reviewing video in the aftermath of a strike, especially in a case like this. But we don't know, because the government won't explain investigation outcomes or processes.

After Obama's May 2013 speech, criticism of U.S. drone strikes significantly abated. Many critics of the administration were apparently satisfied that the targeting rules were restrictive and that real reform on improved transparency was near. But Thursday's careful, detailed HRW report indicates that much, much more needs to be done to assure the public of the legality, ethics, and strategic effectiveness of the U.S. targeted killing program—and to ensure accountability. The U.S. government should take the first necessary step to resolve the impasse over drone strikes by sharing information—by explaining, on the record, its investigations into the wedding convoy strike and releasing at the very least redacted versions of the results of its investigations. It should do the same for past strikes in which civilian casualties have been credibly alleged, and for future ones.

***Sarah Knuckey** is an international lawyer and associate clinical professor of law at Columbia Law School, where she directs the Human Rights Clinic and co-directs the Human Rights Institute. She is also a special advisor to the UN Special Rapporteur on extrajudicial executions.

Knuckey, Sarah. "This Debate Has Been Redacted." *Foreign Policy*, February 20, 2014. http://www.foreignpolicy.com/articles/2014/02/20/this_debate_has_been_redacted.

Do Drones Undermine Democracy?

by Peter W. Singer*

In democracies like ours, there have always been deep bonds between the public and its wars. Citizens have historically participated in decisions to take military action, through their elected representatives, helping to ensure broad support for wars and a willingness to share the costs, both human and economic, of enduring them.

In America, our Constitution explicitly divided the president's role as commander-in-chief in war from Congress's role in declaring war. Yet these links and this division of labor are now under siege as a result of a technology that our founding fathers never could have imagined.

Just 10 years ago, the idea of using armed robots in war was the stuff of Hollywood fantasy. Today, the United States military has more than 7,000 unmanned aerial systems, popularly called drones. There are 12,000 more on the ground. Last year, they carried out hundreds of strikes—both covert and overt—in six countries, transforming the way our democracy deliberates and engages in what we used to think of as war.

We don't have a draft anymore; less than 0.5 percent of Americans over 18 serve in the active-duty military. We do not declare war anymore; the last time Congress actually did so was in 1942—against Bulgaria, Hungary and Romania. We don't buy war bonds or pay war taxes anymore. During World War II, 85 million Americans purchased war bonds that brought the government $185 billion; in the last decade, we bought none and instead gave the richest 5 percent of Americans a tax break.

And now we possess a technology that removes the last political barriers to war. The strongest appeal of unmanned systems is that we don't have to send someone's son or daughter into harm's way. But when politicians can avoid the political consequences of the condolence letter—and the impact that military casualties have on voters and on the news media—they no longer treat the previously weighty matters of war and peace the same way.

For the first 200 years of American democracy, engaging in combat and bearing risk—both personal and political—went hand in hand. In the age of drones, that is no longer the case.

Today's unmanned systems are only the beginning. The original Predator, which went into service in 1995, lacked even GPS and was initially unarmed; newer models can take off and land on their own, and carry smart sensors that can detect a disruption in the dirt a mile below the plane and trace footprints back to an enemy hide-out.

There is not a single new manned combat aircraft under research and development at any major Western aerospace company, and the Air Force is training more operators of unmanned aerial systems than fighter and bomber pilots combined. In 2011, unmanned systems carried out strikes from Afghanistan to Yemen. The most notable of these continuing operations is the not-so-covert war in Pakistan, where the United States has carried out more than 300 drone strikes since 2004.

Yet this operation has never been debated in Congress; more than seven years after it began, there has not even been a single vote for or against it. This campaign is not carried out by the Air Force; it is being conducted by the C.I.A. This shift affects everything from the strategy that guides it to the individuals who oversee it (civilian political appointees) and the lawyers who advise them (civilians rather than military officers).

It also affects how we and our politicians view such operations. President Obama's decision to send a small, brave Navy Seal team into Pakistan for 40 minutes was described by one of his advisers as "the gutsiest call of any president in recent history." Yet few even talk about the decision to carry out more than 300 drone strikes in the very same country.

I do not condemn these strikes; I support most of them. What troubles me, though, is how a new technology is short-circuiting the decision-making process for what used to be the most important choice a democracy could make. Something that would have previously been viewed as a war is simply not being treated like a war.

The change is not limited to covert action. Last spring, America launched airstrikes on Libya as part of a NATO operation to prevent Col. Muammar el-Qaddafi's government from massacring civilians. In late March, the White House announced that the American military was handing over combat operations to its European partners and would thereafter play only a supporting role.

The distinction was crucial. The operation's goals quickly evolved from a limited humanitarian intervention into an air war supporting local insurgents' efforts at regime change. But it had limited public support and no Congressional approval.

When the administration was asked to explain why continuing military action would not be a violation of the War Powers

Resolution—a Vietnam-era law that requires notifying Congress of military operations within 48 hours and getting its authorization after 60 days—the White House argued that American operations did not "involve the presence of U.S. ground troops, U.S. casualties or a serious threat thereof." But they did involve something we used to think of as war: blowing up stuff, lots of it.

Starting on April 23, American unmanned systems were deployed over Libya. For the next six months, they carried out at least 146 strikes on their own. They also identified and pinpointed the targets for most of NATO's manned strike jets. This unmanned operation lasted well past the 60-day deadline of the War Powers Resolution, extending to the very last airstrike that hit Colonel Qaddafi's convoy on Oct. 20 and led to his death.

Choosing to make the operation unmanned proved critical to initiating it without Congressional authorization and continuing it with minimal public support. On June 21, when NATO's air war was lagging, an American Navy helicopter was shot down by pro-Qaddafi forces. This previously would have been a disaster, with the risk of an American aircrew being captured or even killed. But the downed helicopter was an unmanned Fire Scout, and the story didn't even make the newspapers the next day.

Congress has not disappeared from all decisions about war, just the ones that matter. The same week that American drones were carrying out their 145th unauthorized airstrike in Libya, the president notified Congress that he had deployed 100 Special Operations troops to a different part of Africa.

This small unit was sent to train and advise Ugandan forces battling the cultish Lord's Resistance Army and was explicitly ordered not to engage in combat. Congress applauded the president for notifying it about this small noncombat mission but did nothing about having its laws ignored in the much larger combat operation in Libya.

We must now accept that technologies that remove humans from the battlefield, from unmanned systems like the Predator to cyberweapons like the Stuxnet computer worm, are becoming the new normal in war.

And like it or not, the new standard we've established for them is that presidents need to seek approval only for operations that send people into harm's way—not for those that involve waging war by other means.

Without any actual political debate, we have set an enormous precedent, blurring the civilian and military roles in war and circumventing the Constitution's mandate for authorizing it. Freeing the executive branch to act as it chooses may be appealing to some now, but many future scenarios will be less clear-cut. And each political party will very likely have a different view, depending on who is in the White House.

Unmanned operations are not "costless," as they are too often described in the news media and government deliberations. Even worthy actions can sometimes have unintended consequences. Faisal Shahzad, the would-be Times Square bomber, was drawn into terrorism by the very Predator strikes in Pakistan meant to stop terrorism.

Similarly, C.I.A. drone strikes outside of declared war zones are setting a troubling precedent that we might not want to see followed by the close to 50 other nations that now possess the same unmanned technology—including China, Russia, Pakistan and Iran.

A deep deliberation on war was something the framers of the Constitution sought to build into our system. Yet on Tuesday, when President Obama talks about his wartime accomplishments during the State of the Union address, Congress will have to admit that its role has been reduced to the same part it plays during the president's big speech. These days, when it comes to authorizing war, Congress generally sits there silently, except for the occasional clapping. And we do the same at home.

Last year, I met with senior Pentagon officials to discuss the many tough issues emerging from our growing use of robots in war. One of them asked, "So, who then is thinking about all this stuff?"

America's founding fathers may not have been able to imagine robotic drones, but they did provide an answer. The Constitution did not leave war, no matter how it is waged, to the executive branch alone.

In a democracy, it is an issue for all of us.

*Peter W. Singer is the director of the 21st Century Defense Initiative at the Brookings Institution and author of *Wired for War: The Robotics Revolution and Conflict in the 21st Century.*

Singer, Peter W. "Do Drones Undermine Democracy?" Sunday Review. *New York Times*, January 21, 2012. http://www.nytimes.com/2012/01/22/opinion/sunday/do-drones-undermine-democracy.html?pagewanted=all&_r=0.

Family of Grandmother Killed in US Drone Strike Arrive for Congress Visit

by Ryan Devereaux*

Rafiq ur Rehman discusses his family's journey from Pakistan to Washington DC, where they will seek answers on Capitol Hill

Drawing on a pad of paper in a Washington DC hotel, Nabeela ur Rehman recalled the day her grandmother was killed. "I was running away," the nine-year told the Guardian. "I was trying to wipe away the blood."

"It was as if it was night all of the sudden."

The date was 24 October 2012, the eve of Eid al-Adha, the Muslim holy day. Nabeela's father, Rafiq ur Rehman, a school teacher living in the remote Pakistani tribal region of North Waziristan, was dropping off sweets at his sister's home when it happened.

He had hoped to make the visit a family affair but his mother urged him to go alone. Rafiq did as she wished then stopped at the local mosque for evening prayers before taking the bus home. As the vehicle came to a halt at his stop, Rehman noticed something unsettling: members of his community were preparing to bury a body at a small graveyard nearby.

"I got a little worried," Rehman said. He asked a boy what was going on. The child informed him that the mother of a man named Latif Rehman had been killed in a drone attack. The boy did not know the man he spoke to was Latif Rehman's younger brother.

"That's when I first knew," Rehman said, describing how he learned of his mother's death. The fruits Rehman had collected at the bazaar fell from his hands. "I just dropped everything. I was in a state of shock," he said. Rehman feared the worst. He knew his children were with their grandmother. "I frantically ran to my house."

Rehman arrived home to find that the charred remains of his mother had already been buried. Two of his children, Nabeela and her 12-year-old brother, Zubair, had been injured and taken to a nearby hospital, neighbors said. "At that point, I thought I had lost them as well," Rehman said.

The children survived the attack, but their recovery process was just beginning. A year later, Rehman still has no idea why his mother, Momina Bibi, a 67-year-old midwife, was blown to pieces while tending her garden. Along with Nabeela and Zubair, Rehman has traveled to Washington DC to seek answers. On Tuesday, the family will appear before members of Congress to describe their experience, marking the first time in history that US lawmakers will hear directly from the survivors of an alleged US drone strike.

On Sunday, in their first interview with US media since arriving to the country and speaking through a translator, Rehman and his children described the day Momina Bibi was killed and their efforts since then to find justice. Zubair, now 13, said the sky was clear the day his grandmother died. He had just returned home from school. Everyone had been in high spirits for the holiday, Zubair said, though above their heads aircraft were circling. Not airplanes or helicopters, Zubair said. Drones.

"I know the difference," Zubair said, explaining the different features and sounds the vehicles make. "I am certain that it was a drone." Zubair recalled a pair of "fireballs" tearing through the clear blue sky, after he stepped outside. After the explosion there was darkness, he said, and a mix of smoke and debris.

"When it first hit, it was like everyone was just going crazy. They didn't know what to make of it," Zubair said. "There was madness." A piece of shrapnel ripped into the boy's left leg, just above his kneecap. A scar approximately four inches in length remains. "I felt like I was on fire," he said. The injury would ultimately require a series of costly operations.

Nabeela, the little girl, was collecting okra when the missiles struck. "My grandma was teaching me how you can tell if the okra is ready to be picked," she said. "All of the sudden there was a big noise. Like a fire had happened.

"I was scared. I noticed that my hand was hurting, that there was something that had hit my hand and so I just started running. When I was running I noticed that there was blood coming out of my hand."

Nabeela continued running. The bleeding would not stop. She was eventually scooped up by her neighbors. "I had seen my grandmother right before it had happened but I couldn't see her after. It was just really dark but I could hear [a] scream when it had hit her."

Early media reports, citing anonymous Pakistani officials, claimed as many as four militants were killed in the attack. The strike drew the attention of an Amnesty International researcher,

Mustafa Qadri, who was investigating drone attacks in Pakistan at the time.

"We got all sorts of different stories to begin with," Qadri told the Guardian. "One was that [Bibi] was preparing a meal for some militants and that's why she was killed. Another one was that there was a militant on a motorbike, right next to her. And then there's this story of, that there was a militant in a jeep, SUV, with a satellite phone, at the exact point that she's killed, but 10 minutes earlier. He used the phone and then he drives off into the distance. And then the drones come later and they kill her. So we found that that just really did not add up."

Qadri reached out to trusted sources in North Waziristan. The family members and their neighbors were interviewed independently on multiple occasions, unaware that a human-rights group was behind the questions they were asked. Over the course of many weeks, Qadri found the family's account to be consistent. He determined it was highly unlikely that any militants were present at the time of the strike and that the missiles were likely fired by a US drone.

"It was a number of things," Qadri told the Guardian. "We got the missiles, the large fragments that the family has that we got analyzed by [an] expert who says this is very likely to be a Hellfire missile. We also had family members who saw drones physically. We also have the eyewitness of the family who said they heard the noise of missiles fired from the sky and then separate noises of missiles impacting on the ground. We have the evidence of a double sound, with each single strike."

Among the most striking evidence that the attack was carried out by a US drone, Qadri said, was the "phenomenal accuracy" of the strike. "It physically hits her," he said, referring to Momina Bibi. "She's literally hit flush and is blown to smithereens."

"It's quite awful obviously . . . but in this sort of a situation where the body is destroyed, clearly she's been targeted," Qadri added. "They meant to kill this person."

Qadri argues that US secrecy surrounding its so-called "targeted killing" program exacerbates an already complicated set of problems in Pakistan's tribal regions.

"That secrecy, the unaccountability, the lack of lawfulness to it, is the key problem," he said. "In the context of Pakistan and just in the very micro sense, I don't think drones alone is the problem. It's the way they're used and it's the way they're used in isolation, ignoring the broader factors in that region."

The State Department, in response to questions concerning the strike, directed the Guardian to the transcript of a 22 October press briefing by deputy spokesperson Marie Harf.

"There's a process that goes into how these operations are chosen, and as part of that process, we take every effort to limit these casualties," Harf said, echoing claims the president made in a counterterrorism speech in May.

The briefing fell two days before the one-year anniversary of Bibi's death. It did not address the United States' alleged responsibility for the attack. The CIA, which runs drone programs in Pakistan, declined to comment on the strike. The agency suggested the Guardian contact the White House. The White House did not respond.

Nabeela spent most of her days with her grandmother. "I really liked my grandma," she said. "I enjoyed following her and learning how to do things." Zubair said his grandmother was liked by all. "There's no one else like her. We all loved her." In the year since his mother's death, Rehman said, life has changed dramatically. "Not having her is as if a limb has been cut," he said.

For Rehman's father, a respected headmaster [at] a local school, the death of his wife has been devastating. The couple was unaccustomed to being apart, Rehman said. "After my mom's death, we haven't really seen our dad smile. It's like he doesn't have any more will for going on."

Rehman's journey to the US was the idea of his attorney, Shahzad Ahkbar, an internationally-known critic of US drone policy. In the weeks following Bibi's death, the US documentary filmmaker Robert Greenwald traveled to Pakistan to shoot for a forthcoming film on drone attacks, Unmanned: America's Drone Wars. Ahkbar introduced Greenwald to Rehman and his family.

"I could never have imagined that I would be coming to America or I'd want to come to America. I didn't know how people were," Rehman said. "But then Robert had come and they were listening to our story and then Shahzad, our lawyer, had told us that there are more people like Robert who would love to hear the truth and know the truth."

Greenwald said: "When I was in Pakistan, interviewing a whole series of people, they stayed in my mind. At the moment when I was interviewing them I had this very strong feeling that it would be very helpful if Americans could see and experience a father, a teacher, children, the loss of a mother, the loss of a grandmother. Those are universals."

He added: "On the policy side, I hope the briefing will begin the process of demanding investigation. Innocent people are being killed."

US officials say the White House does have a count of civilian drone-strike casualties. The figure, they say, is considerably lower than publicly available counts. The administration has declined to disclose its number, however, citing national security.

"Some things will never be able to be made public so we can protect, indeed, our ability to continue conducting these operations to, indeed, protect our country," Harf said last week.

Together Rehman, his attorney and the US director set out to bring the family to the US. For months they worked to secure paperwork for the children (who lacked birth certificates). Eventually Alan Grayson, a Democrat from Florida, and a number of others extended a formal invitation. A hearing was scheduled for last month, but the event was postponed when the US state department declined to issue a visa for Ahkbar.

"I ideally wanted to come with my lawyer and it was very unfortunate that he couldn't come along with me," Rehman said. Despite the setback, he continued. With Grayson's help, the family secured the Tuesday briefing in Congress.

The purpose of the briefing, Representative Grayson told the Guardian, is "simply to get people to start to think through the implications of killing hundreds of people ordered by the president, or worse, unelected and unidentifiable bureaucrats within the Department of Defense without any declaration of war."

"Under many people's view of international law, they're all illegal. All these attacks are illegal. The UN charter, as was discussed with great vehemence during the recent debate about military intervention in Syria, the UN charter sanctions the use of force only when a country is under attack, in self defense, or when it's been sanctioned by the UN security council.

"It is an abuse of the term 'self-defense' to say that our launching drone attacks in Yemen or elsewhere in the world qualifies. The fact that the technology is there doesn't change the fact that it's a use of force that ends up killing people."

Rehman described the message he hopes to convey to the American people through the briefing: "I want them to know the drones are having an impact on our lives."

"It's hitting our elders. It took my mom. It's affected my children and we haven't done anything wrong."

*Ryan Devereaux is a reporter for *Intercept*.

Devereaux, Ryan. "Family of Grandmother Killed in US Drone Strike Arrive for Congress Visit." *The Guardian*. October 27, 2013. http://www.theguardian.com/world/2013/oct/27/drones-attack-pakistan-family-rehman-congress.

Letter to Obama and Hadi on Yemeni Drones

by Faisal bin Ali Jaber*

"Our town was no battlefield. We had no warning—our local police were never asked to make any arrest. My young nephew Waleed was a policeman, before the strike cut short his life."

In August 2012 Faisal bin Ali Jabar lost his nephew and brother-in-law in a drone strike in Hadhramout, Yemen.

Jabar's brother-in-law Salem was an imam who spoke out against Al-Qaeda.

Today, the same area has been hit by drones yet again. It is also the day Obama and Yemen's President Hadi meet at the White House to discuss counter-terrorism issues.

Jabar has written a letter addressed to both Presidents, appealing for them to engage with anti-drone sentiment in Yemen.

Below is the text of Faisal's letter, sent through Reprieve:

July 31, 2013

Dear President Obama and President Hadi

My name is Faisal bin Ali Jaber. I am a Yemeni engineer from Hadramout, employed by Yemen's equivalent of the

Environmental Protection Agency. I am writing today because I read in the news that you will be meeting in the White House on Thursday, August 1, to discuss the "counter-terrorism partnership" between the US and Yemen.

My family has personally experienced this partnership. A year ago this August, a drone strike in my ancestral village killed my brother-in-law, Salem bin Ali Jaber, and my twenty-one-year-old nephew, Waleed.

President Obama, you said in a recent speech that the United States is "at war with an organisation that right now would kill as many Americans as they could if we did not stop them first." This war against al-Qa'ida, you added, "is a just war—a war waged proportionally, in last resort, and in self-defense."

President Hadi, on a trip to the United States last September, you claimed that "every operation [in Yemen], before taking place, [has] permission from the president." You also asserted that "the drone technologically is more advanced than the human brain."

Why, then, last August, did you both send drones to attack my innocent brother-in-law and nephew? Our family are not your enemy. In fact, the people you killed had strongly and publicly opposed al-Qa'ida. Salem was an imam. The Friday before his death, he gave a guest sermon in the Khashamir mosque denouncing al-Qa'ida's hateful ideology. It was not the first of these sermons, but regrettably, it was his last.

In months of grieving, my family have received no acknowledgement or apology from the U.S. or Yemen. We've struggled to square our tragedy with the words in your speeches.

How was this "self-defense"? My family worried that militants would target Salem for his sermons. We never anticipated his death would come from above, at the hands of the United States. In his death you lost a potential ally—in fact, because word of the killing spread immediately through the region, I fear you have lost thousands.

How was this "in last resort"? Our town was no battlefield. We had no warning—our local police were never asked to make any arrest. My young nephew Waleed was a policeman, before the strike cut short his life.

How was this "proportionate"? The strike devastated our community. The day before the strike, Khashamir buzzed with celebrations for my eldest son's wedding. Our wedding videos show Salem and young Waleed in a crowd of dancing revellers, joining the celebration. Traditionally, this revelry would have gone on for days—but for the attack. Afterwards, it was days before I could persuade my eldest daughter to leave the house, such was her terror of fire from the skies.

The strike left a stark lesson in its wake—not just in my village, but across Hadramout and wider Yemen. The lesson, I am afraid, is that neither the current U.S. or Yemeni administrations bother to distinguish friend from foe. In speech after speech after the attack, community leaders stood and said: if Salem was not safe, none of us are.

Your silence in the face of these injustices only makes matters worse. If the strike was a mistake, the family—like all wrongly bereaved families of this secret air war—deserve a formal apology.

To this day I wish no vengeance against the United States or Yemeni governments. But not everyone in Yemen feels the same. Every dead innocent swells the ranks of those you are fighting.

All Yemen has begun to take notice of drones—and they object. Only this month, Yemen's National Dialogue Conference, a quasi-Constitutional Convention which I understand the U.S. underwrites, almost unanimously voted to prohibit the unregulated use of drones in our country.

With respect, you cannot continue to behave as if innocent deaths like those in my family are irrelevant. If the Yemeni and American Presidents refuse to engage with overwhelming popular sentiment in Yemen, you will defeat your own counter-terrorism aims.

Thank you for your consideration. I would appreciate the courtesy of a reply.

Yours Sincerely,

Faisal bin Ali Jaber
Sana'a, Yemen

*Faisal bin Ali Jaber is a civil engineer from Yemen.

Jaber, Faisal bin Ali. "Letter to Obama and Hadi on Yemeni Drones." Middle East Monitor. August 2, 2013. https://www.middleeastmonitor.com/news/americas/6770-letter-to-obama-and-hadi-on-yemeni-drones.

The Drone That Killed My Grandson

by Nasser al-Awlaki*

SANA, Yemen—I learned that my 16-year-old grandson, Abdul-rahman—a United States citizen—had been killed by an American drone strike from news reports the morning after he died.

The missile killed him, his teenage cousin and at least five other civilians on Oct. 14, 2011, while the boys were eating dinner at an open-air restaurant in southern Yemen.

I visited the site later, once I was able to bear the pain of seeing where he sat in his final moments. Local residents told me his body was blown to pieces. They showed me the grave where they buried his remains. I stood over it, asking why my grandchild was dead.

Nearly two years later, I still have no answers. The United States government has refused to explain why Abdulrahman was killed. It was not until May of this year that the Obama administration, in a supposed effort to be more transparent, publicly acknowledged what the world already knew—that it was responsible for his death.

The attorney general, Eric H. Holder Jr., said only that Abdulrahman was not "specifically targeted," raising more questions than he answered.

My grandson was killed by his own government. The Obama administration must answer for its actions and be held accountable. On Friday, I will petition a federal court in Washington to require the government to do just that.

Abdulrahman was born in Denver. He lived in America until he was 7, then came to live with me in Yemen. He was a typical teenager—he watched "The Simpsons," listened to Snoop Dogg, read "Harry Potter" and had a Facebook page with many friends. He had a mop of curly hair, glasses like me and a wide, goofy smile.

In 2010, the Obama administration put Abdulrahman's father, my son Anwar, on C.I.A. and Pentagon "kill lists" of suspected terrorists targeted for death. A drone took his life on Sept. 30, 2011.

The government repeatedly made accusations of terrorism against Anwar—who was also an American citizen—but never charged him with a crime. No court ever reviewed the government's claims nor was any evidence of criminal wrongdoing ever presented to a court. He did not deserve to be deprived of his constitutional rights as an American citizen and killed.

Early one morning in September 2011, Abdulrahman set out from our home in Sana by himself. He went to look for his father, whom he hadn't seen for years. He left a note for his mother explaining that he missed his father and wanted to find him, and asking her to forgive him for leaving without permission.

A couple of days after Abdulrahman left, we were relieved to receive word that he was safe and with cousins in southern Yemen, where our family is from. Days later, his father was targeted and killed by American drones in a northern province, hundreds of miles away. After Anwar died, Abdulrahman called us and said he was going to return home.

That was the last time I heard his voice. He was killed just two weeks after his father.

A country that believes it does not even need to answer for killing its own is not the America I once knew. From 1966 to 1977, I fulfilled a childhood dream and studied in the United States as a Fulbright scholar, earning my doctorate and then working as a researcher and assistant professor at universities in New Mexico, Nebraska and Minnesota.

I have fond memories of those years. When I first came to the United States as a student, my host family took me camping by the ocean and on road trips to places like Yosemite, Disneyland and New York—and it was wonderful.

After returning to Yemen, I used my American education and skills to help my country, serving as Yemen's minister of agriculture and fisheries and establishing one of the country's leading institutions of higher learning, Ibb University. Abdulrahman used to tell me he wanted to follow in my footsteps and go back to America to study. I can't bear to think of those conversations now.

After Anwar was put on the government's list, but before he was killed, the American Civil Liberties Union and the Center for Constitutional Rights represented me in a lawsuit challenging the government's claim that it could kill anyone it deemed an enemy of the state.

The court dismissed the case, saying that I did not have standing to sue on my son's behalf and that the government's targeted killing program was outside the court's jurisdiction anyway.

After the deaths of Abdulrahman and Anwar, I filed another lawsuit, seeking answers and accountability. The government has argued once again that its targeted killing program is beyond the reach of the courts. I find it hard to believe that this can be legal in a constitutional democracy based on a system of checks and balances.

The government has killed a 16-year-old American boy. Shouldn't it at least have to explain why?

*Nasser al-Awlaki, the founder of Ibb University and former president of Sana University, served as Yemen's minister of agriculture and fisheries from 1988 to 1990.

al-Awlaki, Nasser. "The Drone That Killed My Grandson," op-ed. *New York Times,* July 17, 2013. http://www.nytimes.com/2013/07/18/opinion/the-drone-that-killed-my-grandson.html?module=Search&mabReward=relbias%3As&_r=0.